ARNOLD SCHOENBERG'S JOURNEY

ARNOLD SCHOENBERG'S

JOURNEY

ALLEN SHAWN

HARVARD UNIVERSITY PRESS
Cambridge, Massachusetts

First Harvard University Press paperback edition, 2003
Published by arrangement with Farrar, Straus and Giroux, LLC

Paintings and drawings by Arnold Schoenberg © 2002 Artists Rights Society
(ARS), New York/VBK, Vienna, used by permission of Belmont Music Publishers,
Los Angeles. Photograph of Igor Stravinsky © Henri Cartier-Bresson/Magnum
Photos Ltd. Photograph of Anton Webern courtesy of the Anton Webern Col-
lection, Paul Sacher Foundation, Basel. Photograph of Arnold Schoenberg ©
2002 Man Ray Trust/Artists Rights Society (ARS), New York/A.D.A.G.P.,
Paris. All other photographs of Arnold Schoenberg used by permission of the
Arnold Schoenberg Center, Vienna.

The publishers have made every effort to trace and acknowledge copyright
holders. We apologize for any omissions to this list and we welcome additions
or amendments to it for inclusion in any reprint edition.

Library of Congress Cataloging-in-Publication Data
Shawn, Allen.
    Arnold Schoenberg's journey / Allen Shawn.— 1st ed.
        p.   cm.
    Includes bibliographical references and index.
    ISBN 0-674-01101-5 (paper)
    1. Schoenberg, Arnold, 1874–1951—Criticism and interpretation.
I. Title.

ML410.S283 S43 2001
780'.92—dc21

                                            2001023807

Designed by Debbie Glasserman

FOR ANNIE AND HAROLD

For I know very well that I do not come one step closer to the true *essence of such melodies, of their life, of their continuous development, by means of this scientific approach; just as the natural sciences have knowledge about nature, about its living manifestations, reproduction, heredity, etc., but no* idea *of the true essence of nature. . . . I admit this impossibility from the very beginning, and do not conclude by means of my analysis that one should deny the* soul *of these works. And no one need believe me about that either; because whoever hears these melodies just once will forget all that I have said about them and will simply sense their soul.*

—Alban Berg in his analysis of Schoenberg's *Gurre-Lieder*

And finally I want to mention what I consider the greatest value for a possible appreciation of my music: that you say, one must listen to it in the same manner as to every other kind of music, forget the theories, the twelve-tone method, the dissonances, etc., and, I would add, if possible the author.

—Schoenberg in a letter to Roger Sessions
thanking him for his 1944 article
"Schoenberg in the United States"
in *Tempo* magazine

CONTENTS

FOREWORD

---‖---

I am neither a scholar nor a theorist. For the facts pertaining to Schoenberg's life and for the translations of his writings and of writings by others cited in this book, I am indebted to many authors, whose works I have listed under "Suggested Readings"; without their dogged efforts I would not have been able to write what I have about my subject's life. For the analytical portions of the book, which I have tried to keep to a minimum, I alone am to be blamed, as I have tried to avoid repeating what has been observed by others in order to have the pleasure of discovery and of sharing this feeling of discovery with the reader. Even these portions, however, are largely intuitive in approach, drawing more from my experiences as a composer, performer, and teacher than from previous study.

Above all I have tried to describe the music from the listener's point of view and to write in such a way that readers who cannot read music do not feel excluded. At the risk of endangering my prospects for future (or continued) employment, I'll admit at the outset that I have never been an easy student or fluent teacher of music theory, and I am therefore very much indebted to the musical discussions of many writers—among them Robert Craft, Walter Frisch, Ethan Haimo, Charles Rosen, Leonard Stein, and H. H. Stuckenschmidt—which have given me perspective on my own musical observations and, in important instances, furnished me with ideas and information.

What follows is not a biography or musical study in any conventional sense but rather a linked series of visits to points of interest in Schoenberg's life—"soundings," if you will, or informed impressions—in chronological order.

While I have made no attempt to be comprehensive in my discussion of Schoenberg's works and accomplishments—a task that would require an opus of many volumes—I *have* tried to present him whole, in the manner of an appreciative introduction, so that the reader would come away with a sense, however sketchy, of the range of his interests and activities and an idea of the way all these interests and activities reflected one mind and personality. I have left it to the reader to make many of these connections for himself, being content to simply touch on various themes, moments, incidents, or works, sometimes in detail and sometimes only fleetingly, with the hope of helping the reader encounter Schoenberg the human being, as opposed to only one or another aspect of him, be it his music, his place in the history of music, his music theories, his paintings, his ideas about Judaism, or his influence as a teacher. If I have succeeded in doing this at all, and have managed to communicate affection and pleasure as opposed to critical assessment, then I have done what I wished to do.   —January 2002

*Listen, children, hear me out. An awe for the mysterious
I'll teach you.*

—Psalm 34

Who am I, that I should believe my prayers are necessary?
—Schoenberg, *Modern Psalm*, no. 1

When I was thirteen years old my piano teacher, Frances Dillon, presented me with a set of six very short, fascinating pieces by a composer I had not yet heard of. The work was Sechs kleine Klavierstücke, op. 19, by Arnold Schoenberg. I still have the tattered, blue-covered copy of this Universal Edition music with her suggestions and remarks penciled in ("Nobody knows the trouble I've seen" for the lyrical left hand of number 3).

This attractively thin album of miniatures seemed to contain a special, intimate, and yet strangely familiar world. As in a Japanese rock garden, the pieces altered one's conventional sense of scale in a way that made each musical moment in them appear huge. In contrast to the works of Bach, Beethoven, Haydn, Mozart, Bartók, Prokofiev, and Ross Lee Finney that I was also studying, the music was not only rich in expressive markings but peppered with instructions in German such as "*fluchtig*" ("fleeting"), "*wie ein hausch*" ("like a whisper"), "*zart, aber voll*" ("sweet, but full"). These were words suggestive of an eerie, delicate poetry.

The child learning an instrument has a lover's intimate knowledge of a piece. The slowly practicing child's sense of time, slippery sense of reality, and enjoyment of repetition conspire to create out of the piece's various passages and areas so many places of rest, contemplation, and dream. The first movement of opus 19 seemed to me to conjure up scenes from a forest at night: here a breeze blows for a moment as the full moon's light glances off dark branches; here a man declares his love.

Although she generally gave lessons at her apartment, Miss Dillon occasionally came over to our house to play me recordings and listen to my attempts at composition. Only a few months before starting me on Six Little Pieces, she had introduced me to Stravinsky's *Sacre du Printemps*, which had invaded my parents' quiet living room via phonograph like a herd of wild rhinoceroses, with my teacher jumping up and down shouting, "Isn't this amazing? Isn't this fantastic?"

Miss Dillon was a believer in approaching the old from the vantage point of the new. Whether or not she believed that I should really be a composer, as I wished to be, I was never sure, but she certainly tried to feed my appetite for twentieth-century music (I worked on the Berg Sonata and the Prokofiev Second Sonata in the same year as the Schoenberg), confident that I would grow more and more interested in the works of past times as I sought to understand the origins of the modern. This turned out to be true.

Miss Dillon also had a beautiful black-and-white cat named Pita who, like many cats, loved music and who would curl up against the pedals of the piano while we played. Pita had distinct musical preferences and would occasionally leave her position if she disliked the piece one was playing. It would be very useful for the purposes of this book to be able to claim that Pita always sat quietly during my rendition of the Schoenberg. I would like to think so, but I simply don't remember.

Within a few months of starting to play Sechs kleine Klavierstücke I had written a *Klavierstück* of my own called "For Miss Dillon," which consisted of roughly twelve evocative (I thought) measures. When I performed it for some of my parents' friends I remember it created an awkward moment, after which someone said, "Very modern, dear." This concept of the "modern"—here used in an embarrassed way—was new to me. A few people, including Miss Dillon herself, seemed to particularly like the piece. My older brother made a copy of it in his own handwriting.

Two other encounters with Schoenberg occurred later, when I was fifteen. My brother and I acquired a recording of the opera *Moses und Aron*. It was not long before we were trading references to the *"unsichtbarer und unvorstellbarer Gott"* ("invisible and unimaginable God"), without, of course, having much idea what we were talking about. (These references were made alongside quotations from other operas; *"Ihr Hunde"*—"You dogs!"—from *Lulu* was another favorite.) Schoenberg also became known around the house as "Grebneohcs"—"Schoenberg" backwards—since at the time my brother and I liked to reverse words. Of course, neither of us was familiar with the concept of retrograde, let alone with Schoenberg's reverse self-portrait.

Without our having any real knowledge of Schoenberg, he became somehow associated in our minds with a tremendously rich world of expressive music and hidden, seething emotion. On a purely intuitive level, we perceived that this was a world in which what was valued was a truthful expression of inner states. (For my brother, the plays of Eugene

O'Neill and Samuel Beckett had been of consuming interest for several years.)

At music camp during the same year, an older friend and fellow budding composer played me a recording of Schoenberg's Begleitmusik zu einer Lichtspielszene (Accompaniment to a Film Scene). We sat in his tent and listened on a primitive portable phonograph. I was enchanted; again I had the sense of the strange familiarity of the moods and colors evoked and a feeling of gratitude that there was this medium of expression—music—in which such things could be said.

It was from this friend that I first heard the term *twelve-tone music* and some other terms (*hexachord* was one) associated with it. I was conscious of the fact that, whereas *Moses* and Begleitmusik were twelve-tone, Sechs kleine Klavierstücke was not, and I thought I could perceive the aural outcome of this, without being quite sure what caused the difference. The fact that none of these works was "tonal" did not pose a problem; rather it opened a doorway into another way of hearing things.

I gradually became aware that Schoenberg's music was far from universally appreciated, although he was greatly revered by many of the musicians and composers I knew. To anyone who has followed the music reviews in the *New York Times* over the past forty years, it should be clear that Schoenberg's reputation as a somehow repellent figure, associated with maddeningly complex, ugly, or calculated music has never truly been dispelled. From what one reads one gets the general impression that people just don't "like" Schoenberg and that Berg and even Webern are more enjoyable and "musical," that something went wrong with the way Schoenberg heard and thought that makes his work unapproachable to the general listener.

In my teenage years my composing took me on a path that rarely intersected with the world of Schoenberg and his followers, and in my college and graduate school days—despite the support I received from two former Schoenberg students who were my teachers, Earl Kim and Leon Kirchner—the academic legacy of Schoenberg sometimes seemed to me to be an outright threat to my sense of music and to my ability to find my own way of composing. I still loved the pieces by Schoenberg that I knew, but I had no interest in employing the twelve-tone approach in my own work; I just didn't hear and think that way, and this happened to be a time when students were often harangued by teachers (and, worse, peers) who were proponents of Schoenberg's "methods" and "theories" (although not necessarily advocates for the pieces he wrote). No less a personage than Pierre Boulez espoused the view that composers who did not descend from the "dodecaphonic" (twelve-tone) tradition started by Schoenberg were historically "useless." Even Stravinsky himself had become "a serialist" in his works written from 1951 on.

As I tried to find my own nonserialist path, I went to study with Nadia Boulanger in Paris. Paradoxically, the piece I produced that pleased me the most during this time elicited from her the derogatory comment that it was "less direct" than I was and even, unfortunately, "like Schoenberg." Although this was 1970 and the rift between the "Schoenberg" school and the old "Stravinsky" school of composers was presumably long over, one was still apparently expected to take sides.

Once I was emancipated from the academic context, I started to actually make some progress in my composing, frequently finding that I was able to draw on what I knew of twelve-tone writing for my own purposes. Eventually I ceased to see any meaningful conflict between various technical approaches to composing or even between seemingly opposite sound worlds, when compared with the dichotomy between music that was intensely satisfying and meaningful and music that was not.

In conversations with composers nowadays, of course, one finds few who don't pay at least some kind of homage to

Stravinsky *and* Schoenberg. Indeed we are descended, every last one of us, from both of them.

Now, as a teacher, I often have the pleasure of presenting music of Schoenberg's to students free of any need to take sides about the merits of his work or of his theories. I refrain from an initial discussion of Schoenberg the theorist—I want the students to become intrigued by Schoenberg's methods, if they do, because they love what they hear. I doubt very much that they will love what they hear because they have first learned of the influence of—or controversy surrounding—his musical theories. I am struck by how instantly these students gravitate to the voice speaking to them through the medium of this work, a voice that speaks of things that they fully understand, in a language that is strong, adventurous, imaginative, complex, honest, and also deeply traditional. And in fact the more the students in question are readers, or followers of painting and movies and theater, or lovers of jazz and rock, the more they are instantly taken by this powerful music. I would even go so far as to say that Schoenberg *particularly* moves, excites, and amazes young listeners, particularly those who seek, first and foremost, contact with a great imagination.

I have played Schoenberg in the local temple along with a slide show of his paintings; I have played Schoenberg's music to groups of painters; I have introduced Schoenberg's music to countless students who had never heard of him (I had one group of students lie down on the floor with their eyes closed while listening to "Farben" from the Five Pieces for Orchestra). The response to the work, unencumbered by proselytizing or prejudice, has belied the prevalent notion that Schoenberg's music is repellent or remote or that it represents a "wrong turn" taken by a master composer. The response, on the contrary, suggests that Schoenberg's art—in and of itself—moves people and speaks to them.

I in no way mean to play down the difficulties, depths, or conundrums inherent in this body of work. But I would suggest that Schoenberg's music is no more "difficult" than the work of other early-twentieth-century modernists such as Kandinsky, Eliot, Kafka, or Joyce, for whom even the general public has a feeling of affection, of receptivity, of the kind of trust that one accords great art in which there is much that one simply doesn't grasp—at first or perhaps even ever. And yet, although there are many works by Schoenberg in a more "familiar" tonal idiom—and not only from his early period—that are received by audiences with considerable warmth and that ought to pave the way toward a trust in the more "problematic" pieces (as occurs with, say, Ives), that trust is often withheld by audiences.

There are no doubt many reasons for this, but I don't believe that the fundamental reason is necessarily to be found in the language of the music itself. To be sure, it is an ornate language—it is not one that cultivates simplicity in the manner of, say, Erik Satie, or John Cage (who was a Schoenberg student, but more of that later). Are there elements of musical language so essential to the idea of music that if they are removed an insurmountable gap between composer and listener will result? Perhaps there are. But did Schoenberg's work remove these elements? Can his music be said to be harder to follow than the paintings of the cubists or, for that matter, the plays of Shakespeare?

One of the convictions that lies behind this book is that, from the very beginning, there were features in Schoenberg's work, personality, and perhaps even social position that led to his being explained and defended rather than listened to, that the works of Schoenberg have not had a fair chance to be experienced *apart* from the ideology that surrounds them. Schoenberg's voice as an artist, the voice that speaks to us through the work, has not been heard in a natural way without interference. From the time of Berg's brilliant analytical essay "Why Is Schoenberg's Music So Difficult to Understand?" to the present, this is an oeuvre that has been subjected to steady close theoretical and musicological scrutiny. In the process, the fantasy, power, songfulness, beauty, and humor of the music itself has been not so much overlooked as rendered secondary to the discussion *of* it by experts. Instead of his reputation's creating curiosity about his work, his work has been buried by (and beneath) his reputation.

For this reason, it is not entirely in a spirit of facetiousness that I have said to friends that I feel that perhaps Schoenberg's work deserves a more superficial treatment than it has hitherto received.

BRIDGE PASSAGE

1874 — 1908

Personally I had the feeling as if I had fallen into an ocean of boiling water, and not knowing how to swim or get out in another manner, I tried with my legs and arms as best I could. I did not know what saved me; why I was not drowned or cooked alive. I have perhaps only one merit: I never gave up. But how could I give up in the middle of an ocean?

ARNOLD SCHOENBERG IN 1947

Arnold Schoenberg, Los Angeles, 1940

I

ғIRST LOVES

On September 13, 1874, Arnold Schoenberg was born in Vienna into a poor Jewish family of Hungarian ancestry. His mother, Pauline, a pious Orthodox Jew, came from a family of cantors. His father, Samuel, a shoemaker, was described (by Arnold's cousin Hans Nachod) as a "free thinker . . . a dreamer, an anarchic idealist." Schoenberg was the eldest of three children. His sister, Ottilie, was born in 1876; his brother, Heinrich, in 1882.

Schoenberg took violin lessons at the age of eight, later teaching himself the cello by playing a large viola fitted with zither strings as if it were a cello. This hybrid instrument, a viola-as-cello that he held between his legs but on which he used the violin fingerings he already knew, could perhaps serve as a metaphor for Schoenberg's life in music. It was but the first instance in what would prove a permanent search for resourceful and innovative solutions to problems. As an adult he even developed a distinctive way of holding a pen because he felt that the standard way didn't give a person adequate control over his or her handwriting. The viola-as-cello idea specifically reappears in the Serenade movement of *Pierrot Lunaire*, when, in illustration of Pierrot scraping "with grotesque giant bow on his viola," it is the cello that carries the melody.

At age ten Schoenberg began composing small compositions for the instruments he knew, starting with duets composed for his violin lessons and progressing to trios and quartets he played with friends, relying on installments from an encyclopedia subscription to inform him about the rules and practices of music. He eagerly awaited the arrival of volume "S" to learn about sonata form. He also was guided by his friend and teacher Oskar Adler (1875–1955), who, in addition to instructing him in violin and viola, gave him his first notions of music theory and harmony.

His father's death on New Year's Eve 1890 brought an end to his official schooling, and he found a job as an apprentice at a bank to help support his family. In a letter to his cousin Malvina Goldschmied written during this period, the seventeen-year-old described himself as a "nonbeliever" who nonetheless recommended a close study of the Bible—a synthesis of his father's skepticism and his mother's faith. Disagreeing with his cousin's characterization of the Bible as "nonsense," he wrote that, on the contrary, one could find in it "all of the most difficult questions concerning Morals, Lawmaking, Industry, and Medical Science . . . resolved in the most simple way, often treated from a contemporary point of view." He also urged her to read his own letters to her more carefully, saying that each sentence contained something specific and that "if perhaps the surface seems smooth to you, the water is very deep, and often the smoother the surface the deeper the water." Having enclosed flowers in his previous letter, he now risked adding near the close of this one:

(I . . l . . . . D . . . !)

which she could decode as "Ich liebe Dich."

Although cousin Malvina rejected his amorous advances (she eventually married the operetta librettist Robert Bodanzky), she said in later years that even then she sensed Schoenberg's greatness, though she was not sophisticated enough to appreciate everything he had to say or, in particular, his sense of irony.

Eventually Schoenberg did purchase an inexpensive cello and learn the correct fingerings. He joined a small amateur orchestra, Polyhymnia, conducted by the composer Alexander Zemlinsky, and held his own as the cello "section." In 1901 he married Zemlinsky's sister Mathilde, a highly educated and intelligent woman who was also a fine pianist.

Of great significance to his development as a composer were two facts: that he had early firsthand experience as a chamber musician and that he was not—and never would be—a performing pianist. Even his music for extraordinarily large forces possesses a chamber music quality in its contrapuntal and soloistic treatment of each instrument. Furthermore, it could only have been written by one steeped as a performer in the chamber music tradition. Throughout his life, Schoenberg's gifts as a coach and a conductor were greatly admired.

Zemlinsky, only two years older than Schoenberg himself, gave him some lessons in composition and introduced him to the music of Wagner, as well as to the progressive artists and intellectuals who frequented the Cafe Griensteidl (also known humorously as the "Cafe Megalomania"). Primarily, though, Schoenberg taught himself, becoming an avid concertgoer and devotee of current music. A relative later recalled him during those years as "wild and energetic."

He particularly loved Wagner and later estimated that as a young person he had seen each of the Wagner operas some twenty to thirty times. But in his first compositions he drew most obviously on Brahms as a model, and it should be remembered that Brahms, who lived until 1897, composed such works as the Clarinet Quintet (1891), Clarinet Sonatas (1894), the opus 118 and 119 Piano Pieces (1892), and the Vier ernste Gesänge (1896), during the years that Schoenberg was writing his first songs and piano and chamber pieces. Brahms remained a lifelong touchstone, for the concision, asymmetry, and harmonic adventurousness of his musical language, which left an evident imprint on even twelve-tone works such as the Piano Concerto, but also for his subtle relationship to both tradition and innovation (the subject of Schoenberg's 1947 essay "Brahms the Progressive"). From Brahms Schoenberg also learned the "chamber music" way of thinking—in which each instrument in a work is a lively, soloistic participant—that characterized even his orchestral music.

Scholars note this "distinctly Brahmsian phase up to about 1897" and discern "a more chromatic, Wagnerian" one in the pieces written from 1897 to 1899. Yet nothing in Schoenberg's early music reaches the heights of the churning, tonal restlessness of *Tristan und Isolde*.

Although he was born poor, Schoenberg came of age in a milieu in which Jews were exerting a powerful intellectual influence. Arthur Schnitzler was the most widely read novelist and most frequently performed playwright in Vienna. This was also the city of, among others, the young Sigmund Freud, the architect Adolf Loos, Ludwig Wittgenstein, Martin Buber, and Oskar Kokoschka. The controversial composer Gustav Mahler became director of the Vienna State Opera in 1897.

Even while the lives of emancipated Jews were similar in most respects to those of bourgeois Catholics and even Protestants, anti-Semitism was always in the air. Schnitzler, in his book *My Youth in Vienna*, writes of his bitter memories of the tensions between Jewish and non-Jewish students when he was a medical student (a reason young Jewish men became particularly adept at fencing) and quotes from the so-called Waidhofen Manifesto of the mid-1880s barring Jews from membership in student organizations and fraternities. He quotes these lines from that document, and they are explicit: "Everyone of a Jewish mother, every human being in whose veins flows Jewish blood, is from the day of his birth without honor and void of all the refined emotions. . . . He is ethically subhuman."

Throughout Schoenberg's childhood, manifestations of this seemingly ineradicable anti-Semitism could be counted on to reemerge throughout Europe at regular intervals, a hysterical outlet for primal fears and insecurities, fed by envy (for instance, of the German Jewish banking families), paranoid fear (of the rising working class), ancient religious prejudice (dating back to Martin Luther, among others), and pure fabrication (such as the forged *Protocols of the Elders of Zion*, which surfaced at the beginning of the century in Russia and was cited as evidence that the Jews were plotting a takeover of the world). The Dreyfus case in France, which inspired Theodor Herzl's proposal for a Jewish state, occurred when Schoenberg was twenty.

Schoenberg spent his early years as a composer in Vienna and in Berlin, where he lived during three different phases of his life, from 1901 to 1903, from 1911 to 1915, and from 1926 to 1933. While in Berlin the progressive artistic climate seemed to foster social satire and political commentary, in Vienna, the city of Freud, artists tended to pursue expression that was removed from a political and social context, art turned inward to the aesthetic, spiritual, and psychological realms. Bruno Bettelheim interprets this as a cultural reaction to the decline of the Hapsburg empire, a response to the loss of Austria's six-hundred-year hegemony over Germany. Vienna began to flourish intellectually at the very moment of the dissolution of the empire that had established its centrality to begin with. As the Prussian empire, with Berlin as its capital, became consolidated in the last decades of the nineteenth century, Vienna began its cultural exploration of the inner world of man in literature, painting, and music. Freud's *Interpretation of Dreams* was published in 1900. Simultaneously there was a veritable explosion of lighthearted, escapist entertainment in the operettas and waltzes of Strauss, Lehár, and Suppe.

Influenced by a friend, Walter Pieau, who was an opera singer, Schoenberg, although perhaps still a "nonbeliever," converted to Lutheranism and was baptized on March 25, 1898, with Pieau present. We can only speculate about his reasons. Thirty-five years later, in Paris, after fleeing with his family from Nazi-dominated Austria, he converted back to Judaism in an official ceremony witnessed by Marc Chagall. Many of his greatest works from his final two decades were explicitly or implicitly sacred and Jewish. Among the many paradoxes and internal contradictions of Schoenberg's life was one he shared with many of the artistic comrades of his early life: the fact that his patriotic devotion to the culture of Germany and Austria from which he emerged did not prevent him from being forced from it as an outcast.

Another paradox is that it was the very reverence this famously "atonal" master had for the tonal tradition of his forebears that spurred the thoroughness of his extension of it. His own (tonal) *Theory of Harmony* is among the few truly stimulating books of music theory, and the only one that can also be read as a work of literature. Not only are his early works "tonal," even a number of his later works either are tonal or have pronounced elements of tonality.

Schoenberg's compositions are generally described as falling into four main periods.

1897–1908 Looked at in this way, the first phase of his work would begin with those first pieces growing out of Brahms and Wagner and the world of romantic tonality then at its zenith in the music of Strauss and Mahler and in the final song cycles of Hugo Wolf and would embrace his string sextet *Verklärte Nacht* (1899), the oratorio *Gurre-Lieder* (1901), the orchestral tone poem *Pelleas und Melisande* (1903) (which was written almost contemporaneously with Debussy's opera based—as is this tone poem—on the Maurice Maeterlinck play), the String Quartet no. 1 (1905), and the forward-looking First Chamber Symphony (1906); 1908 was the pivotal year in which, in his String Quartet no. 2, he first introduced passages without a tonal center into the middle of a tonal work.

1909–13 The year 1909 saw the completion of the song cycle *The Book of the Hanging Gardens*, in which key signatures were dispensed with altogether, opening up a radically new world and leading to such works as Five Pieces for Orchestra (1909), *Erwartung* (1909), Three Pieces for Piano, op. 11 (1909), Six Little Pieces, op. 19 (1911), *Herzgewächse*, op. 20 (1911), *Pierrot Lunaire* (1912), and *Die glückliche Hand* (1913), which have been called both "expressionist" and "atonal," although neither term pleased the composer. It was in this phase that Schoenberg spoke of music in rather expressionistic terms, writing, "art belongs to the unconscious." This was also the period in which he produced the bulk of his visual artwork and, surprisingly, in which he put on paper his understanding of the *tonal* system in *Theory of Harmony* (*Harmonielehre*).

1921–32 An internal search can be inferred from the compositional silence of the years 1913–23, interrupted only by the production of the Orchestral Songs, op. 22 in the years 1913–16. What followed in 1921 was the creation of a conscious organizing principle for this new nontonal realm: the "method of composing with twelve tones." The twelve-tone era represented an organizational and "tonal" breakthrough, a way forward that was fantastically fruitful for this artist. To this phase belongs the Serenade, op. 24 (1923), the Piano Suite (1923), Variations for Orchestra (1928), and the operas *Von Heute auf Morgen* (1928) and *Moses und Aron* (1932), among many other works.

1933–51 The last phase began with Schoenberg's flight from Europe and his establishment of himself as a teacher in the United States. An extraordinary heterogeneity characterizes this period, in which he affirmed his renewed connection to Judaism in such pieces as the *Kol Nidre* of 1938, *A Survivor from Warsaw* of 1947, and the *Modern Psalm* of 1950; created entirely twelve-tone masterpieces such as the Violin Concerto and the String Quartet no. 4 of 1936, and the Piano Concerto of 1942; and composed works such as the *Ode to Napoleon* (1942) and the String Trio (1949), which seem to synthesize the preoccupations of a lifetime—including the once-abandoned tonality—into a single opus.

The tone of Schoenberg's music was his own from early on. Neither Brahms nor Wagner had the unusual combination of temperamental traits that makes his work so strangely airy and vibrant, complex yet also transparent. The early songs that resemble Brahms seem less weighty than Brahms; they seem to float in space. And the more "Wagnerian" passages of the *Gurre-Lieder* seem somehow less earthbound than Wagner, more limpid, outward-opening, both more contrapuntal and more architectural.

It is almost as if the tonality in this first period of his work "resolves"—in some unanalyzable way—only provisionally, leaving one with a sense of being suspended in midair, as if the very force of gravity exerted by tonal principles had itself weakened. Or perhaps that is only a trick played by our contemporary ears, that when *we* hear these early works we imagine that he was already instinctively employing tonality in quotation marks, as it were, as a choice rather than as the only possibility.

Friends of the composer in all his phases commented on the speed and naturalness of his composing process. When he was writing, the ideas seemed to tumble out almost irrepressibly. Although, to be sure, there could be much struggle and willed construction involved, this was at bottom a music of inspiration, composed in concentrated bursts of energy. Even the two-hour *Gurre-Lieder* was entirely sketched out in short score in only thirteen months (March 1900 to April 1901). The pattern persisted throughout his life. The Prelude to the "Genesis" Suite (1945) was written in just a week. When he could not compose—and there were several long hiatuses in his evolution—he simply wrote nothing. Oliver Neighbour sees in this joy in work a key to the odd buoyancy of even his most disturbing creations: "His sheer zest in the making of music is one of his most persistent characteristics: it accounts for the feeling of resilience that accompanies his exploration of even the darkest regions of experience and tempers his findings."

ב

‖

TRANSFIGURED NIGHT

Many chamber works (including an important early string quartet perfected under Zemlinsky's guidance) and countless songs preceded the composition of *Verklärte Nacht* (*Transfigured Night*), generally considered Schoenberg's first major work. Having assimilated in these first pieces much of the language of Schumann, Brahms, Hugo Wolf, and Wagner, Schoenberg could trace himself back to the world of the original Viennese School—Haydn, Mozart, and Beethoven. Beethoven, it should be remembered, was still alive only fifty years before Schoenberg's birth.

By 1899, the year of *Transfigured Night*, Schoenberg's compositional mind was fully formed. Here are the transformations of themes, the complex polyphonic layerings, the sense of drama one will find in Five Pieces for Orchestra and later works, albeit still in a context that to our twenty-first-century ears sounds completely "tonal." Today *Verklärte Nacht* is performed with some frequency and pleases even those who dislike the rest of Schoenberg's music. To many listeners in its day, however, it opened up mysterious, alarming new musical vistas.

The early songs—nearly forty of them, counting those that were published as opuses 1, 2, and 3, and the seven that were published posthumously as "seven early songs"—chart an astonishing trajectory of growing exploration and sophistication. Leonard Stein has written of the imprint of Brahms and Hugo Wolf (whose last works appeared in 1897) on these pieces.* The introduction to "Mein Herz das ist ein tiefer Schacht," apparently written when Schoenberg was twenty, places us touchingly in the world of Brahms with its syncopated chordal right hand and beautifully crafted left.

*Although Wolf lived another six years, during which he worked on an opera, he completed no works after the Michelangelo songs of 1897. The already depressive Wolf suffered increasingly from physical and mental symptoms brought on by terminal syphilis, and he died in an asylum in 1903.

Its classical harmonic structure (music readers will note the V/VI–VI, V/V–V, I progression in the bass in measures 3–5) is worlds away from Wagner and presents the A-flat major tonality unambiguously, if also artfully. Perhaps we can detect Schoenberg the string quartet player in the nice "viola and cello" writing in the left hand of measures 3–4. "Mädchenlied" of 1897 shows Schoenberg's way with the assymetrical phrase lengths that he had studied in Brahms,

and the way the piano imitates and dovetails with the voice is wonderfully subtle.

As the songs became more contrapuntal they also became not only richer harmonically but also more tonally ambiguous. After a relatively quiet year (1898), Schoenberg had plunged back into work with settings of poetry by Richard Dehmel, whose writing had also been set to music by his friend, mentor, and soon-to-be brother-in-law, Zemlinsky. Dehmel, author of the collection *Weib und Welt* (*Woman and World*), greatly admired by the young Rilke, had also become well known because he had been charged in Berlin with "blasphemy and immorality." Forced to defend himself legally, he had issued a declaration of his views that included the statement "I believe that anyone who helps the human soul open its eyes to its bestial urges serves true morality better than many a moralistic accuser." His own work of the time was inspired by his passionate affair with a woman named Ida Auerbach, for whom he eventually left his wife.

Dehmel's erotically charged poems unlocked something in Schoenberg. The new songs brought together his Brahmsian and Wagnerian sides and pointed a way forward. In the intense and original—though, in the opinion of some, slightly awkward—Dehmel setting "Mannesbangen" ("A Man's Anxiety"), the proper classical cadences are gone, and in the two places where the dominant is reached, it does not resolve to the tonic. At the final cadence (measures 23–24) the dominant is skipped over—simply left to the imagination:

This ellipsis (as Berg would later refer to such cases) is of a piece with a harmonic style that uses as many ambiguous and altered harmonies as it uses those that would normally belong in the key, a style in which complex chords that are related chromatically and could be presented smoothly are sometimes starkly juxtaposed, as in measures 5–6:

One of the first chamber pieces to be described as "program music," *Verklärte Nacht* was inspired by Dehmel's 1895 poem of the same name. (It became the first in his collection *Zwei Menschen: Ein Roman in Romanzen*.) The poem tells of a married woman who walks with her lover in the night under the moon. She married before she knew what love was; she was lonely, and she wished to have a child. "Now life has taken its revenge," she confesses to him: she has fallen in love but is carrying a child by the husband she does not love. The man replies that their love "will transfigure the strange man's child. . . . You will bear the child for me, as if it were mine."

In addition to its narrative voice the poem contains, in effect, two monologues, the woman's story followed by the man's response, the response that "transfigures." Commentators have described the structure of the music variously as a kind of sonata, a large-scale rondo, a five-part form modeled after the five-part structure of the poem, and so on. But the composer's own notes make one thing clear: the shift from female to male is plainly projected in the music. The female monologue reaches a climax of despair with the return of the opening D minor material intensified into a tragic B-flat minor that makes one imagine her prostrate before her lover. This is followed by the first unsupported high string chords of the piece, a suspension of motion as the man prepares to answer, to lift her up. These suspended E-flat harmonies are answered by his warm opening melody in D major.

In the poem, the division into two parts is marked by the repetition of the idea of walking and the image of the racing moon in lines 2 and 20: "Der Mond läuft mit, sie schaun hinein" ("The moon races along with them, they look up at it"), "Sie schaut empor; der Mond läuft mit" ("She looks up; the moon is racing along"). Moonlit monologues haunt the work of Schoenberg, most memorably in *Erwartung* and *Pierrot Lunaire*. Dehmel's poem was itself inspired by a romantic moonlit tryst with Ida Auerbach. Recalling the evening in a letter to her he wrote: "Everything glowed." The incandescent coda to *Verklärte Nacht* captures this "glowing" in sound. (In later years the composer admitted that to some the Dehmel poem might now seem "rather repulsive.")

The composer's ability to find apt musical analogues for the moods of the poem could not be bettered and is clearly second nature. Listening to the woman's impassioned confession,

then her memory of loneliness,

we need no text to follow the emotional progression. (These thematic identifications are the composer's own.)

As in an opera, the unfolding succession of musical ideas projects the progress of moods and images in the (unheard) text, and the modulations from key to key have a dramatic meaning, often setting up a new paragraph so vividly that one half expects a voice to enter. And the string writing *is* often quasi-vocal; *Verklärte Nacht* is opera without words. Not surprisingly, the sextet, in its string orchestra version, became the score for a ballet, Antony Tudor's *Pillar of Fire.*

The transfiguration of the title is represented by the "transfiguring" of the ideas in the second half of the work. On the most obvious level, it moves from a succession of primarily minor keys in the first half to predominantly major ones in the second, and overall from D minor to D major. In terms of the themes and motifs, nearly every note in the second half can be traced to those of the first. The man has listened and rephrases the materials in a new light, and with a new lightness. In some cases the woman's desperate chromaticism is ironed out into a radiant major diatonicism; in others a falling idea becomes a rising one. The simple confidence of the man's new theme of rising fourths in the second part expresses an optimism not felt in the work's first half.

The work is an unfolding. Everything seems to grow out of the walking gait of the couple suggested by the opening pedal point, out of the ground on which they are walking— the note D and the steady tread of half notes and the rhythm of walking in the opening melody,

which when doubled in thirds evokes the two protagonists spiritually and literally in step. As in the later *Gurre-Lieder*, the piece begins and ends in a kind of pure, primal tonality, but here the harmonic language stays more or less within the boundaries of what was already known in *Tristan*. One idea connects to the next so naturally it is almost disconcerting to look more closely and realize how immensely subtle the connections are. (For example, in the two musical phrases on page 17, the third measure of the first outlines the opening melody of the work, and notes 3 through 7 can be reordered to form the melody in the second example, transposed up a major third.)

If, as in the inventions and fugues of Bach, everything that happens seems like a variant of everything else and it is difficult to imagine which ideas, other than perhaps the opening ones, came first, this makes sense in terms of the composer's working habits. Schoenberg's colleague and early biographer Egon Wellesz, points out how in the composer's early sketchbooks "every one of his thematic ideas is invented simultaneously with its counterparts" and notes that, in contrast to those writers who have to labor to combine their themes contrapuntally, Schoenberg had "to apply a good deal of energy in stemming the spontaneous fullness of his ideas." If we consider the expression on Schoenberg's face—both in his self-portraits and in photographs—we who did not know him can surmise that part of the intensity one senses in it comes from this furious inner activity, a constant branching out of musical associations, in which small shoots gradually grow into a tree. Later, as a teacher, he would instantly provide myriad examples of alternate ways of treating passages in a student's compositions, or whole pieces in classical style that illustrated a form or technique. One sees this fluency at work in the music not only in those moments of rapid wild invention but also in the interconnectedness of themes that probably sprang to mind quite naturally. No doubt in his tonal phase he carried the basic seeds of each work in his mind just as he would later carry his twelve-tone row forms, allowing relationships and combinations to germinate in his unconscious, ready to appear on the page when he sat down to write.

Here a melody with the cast of urgent speech and marked "wild,"

turns out to be a variant of many other motifs, such as:

and

Principles behind a lifetime of work: abundance from economy, "developing variation." As the piece unfolds, the themes
evolve and recombine as if from their own needs. The same is
true of the key relationships. We move seamlessly through a
chain of keys related usually by common tones, and modulations occur through musical trapdoors that are perfectly
natural yet unheard of before. Diminished triads and seventh
chords and augmented triads—"vagrant chords" as the composer dubbed them in his *Theory of Harmony*—often unlock
these doors, creating a magical feeling of tonal adventure. Yet
almost always we are unquestionably in a key, and when sudden chromatic shifts occur they are in clearly transitional or
climactic sections, in "Wagnerian" sequences that are elaborations of the work's themes. There is a recurrent grounding in
pedal points.

The overall progression of key areas would appear to be:
(first part) D minor–B-flat minor–F-sharp minor–F minor–
E major–modulating passage ("wild") through many keys and
back through D minor to B-flat minor–E-flat minor [second
part] D major–F-sharp major–E-flat minor–D-flat major–
F major–modulating as if to D major but arriving at D-flat
major–D major.

A falling cycle (primarily of thirds) that goes far afield is answered in the second part by one that stays within a narrower
compass of the rising thirds D to F-sharp and D to F, and the
keys a half step above and below D. In the first part, the
woman's description of her desire to have a child gives rise to
the first instance of a major tonality (E).

In some analytic notes written in 1932, Schoenberg
pointed to an overall plan of surrounding the tonic D with the
tonalities a half step above and below it, E-flat and C-sharp
(or D-flat), and even pointed to the same tendencies in in-

dividual themes. He also left contradictory evidence about whether this scheme was entirely intuitive or only partly so. In the 1932 notes he recalled being aware of the relationship between the end of the first part in E-flat, the beginning of the second in D major, the second part's important rising fourth theme in D-flat major, and the way that the music manages to modulate back into D major. All the other relationships that, with hindsight, seemed connected to these, however, he ascribed to "the diligent effort of my brain, working 'behind my back,' without seeking my approval." This scheme does explain a great deal about the work, including one of its most memorable "trapdoors," the dominant seventh chord on A, which leads (improbably) both from D major to D-flat and back from D-flat to D major. As Walter Frisch points out, the dominant chord of D doesn't really do its normal job of resolving into the tonic until we have returned to D by this very unusual tonal route. So another way of looking at the formal progress of the piece would be to say that the first part destabilizes and becomes more and more remote from D minor and that when D *is* finally reaffirmed in the second part, it has become major. How appropriate for the story in the poem!

The restrictions imposed by the six-part ensemble give the music an extraordinary transparency even when many ideas are intricately combined. The music breathes; every voice sings and is motific, but the harmonic motion is never hectic and affords many moments of rest. The piece is both lush and lucid. The final D major coda exudes a sense of profound relief and resolution. The tragic descending scale of the woman's lament becomes a thing of tenderness in major,

and the opening pedal point is combined with the original dotted walking rhythm in slow motion in the pizzicato cellos, while the moon of the upper strings shines in four distinct layers: two violas, one tremolo and the other pizzicato, and two violins, arpeggios in the second part and a serenely high-flying melody in the first. The radiant final D major harmony is achieved; suddenly the whole work seems the consequence of those opening low Ds. We have gone from the ground to the sky. *Verklärte Nacht's* half-hour length suddenly seems to have been but an instant.

The work received its premiere in Vienna on March 18, 1902. There were disruptions and fistfights in the audience that night, but there was also appreciation. Among those who would soon believe in the work and its composer was Gustav Mahler.

3

—————╫—————

DAWN:

THE *GURRE-LIEDER*

Behold the sun—
Golden-hued on the edge of the sky,
Lighting the east with morning dreams!
With a smile he climbs higher and higher
Over the waters of night;
Making golden shafts of light
Stream from his shining brow!

In 1900 Schoenberg contemplated entering a composition contest for piano-accompanied song cycles with settings of poems from the *Gurresange* by the Danish poet, novelist, botanist, and translator of Darwin, Jens Peter Jacobsen, a writer much admired by, among others, Joyce and Rilke. Zemlinsky, who was to be on the panel of judges, played through the first few for Schoenberg and, finding them "wonderful and truly original," agreed with him that, regrettably, "precisely on that account they would have little chance of winning the prize." Schoenberg's response was not to abandon the project but to expand it. The nine-song cycle with piano accompaniment that he had envisaged became a monumental two-hour work—part symphonic song cycle, part oratorio—for soloists, chorus, and one of the largest orchestras ever assembled. The huge orchestra necessitated the manufacturing of special music paper—forty-eight staves!—which the composer ordered. The brass section alone contains twenty-five players.

By the end of 1901 the *Gurre-Lieder* was essentially completed in piano score, but it would take Schoenberg another full decade to complete the orchestration and the work was therefore not performed in its entirely until 1913, after he had become known for a radically different kind of music. When the *Gurre-Lieder* was performed, it became the greatest public triumph of his life.

Much as Stravinsky's *Firebird*, written when that composer was twenty-eight, shows a mastery of its Russian tradition and points a way forward, this work, written when its composer was twenty-seven, emerges out of German lieder and Wagnerian music drama into something new. But *Gurre-Lieder* travels a greater distance, coming as it does exactly at the fulcrum of the century (*Firebird* dates from 1910) and spanning, arguably, compositional and orchestrational idioms sixty or seventy years apart. In addition, the late date of the orchestration of part 3 resulted in a shift in orchestrational method partway through the work: in contrast to the massed sonorities of the first two parts, the last section of the work is notable for its complex and subtly colored solo and chamber scoring. The piece seems to move forward in time as it progresses.

As he had in *Verklärte Nacht*, and as he would again in *Pelleas und Melisande*, *The Book of the Hanging Gardens*, *Erwartung*, *Die glückliche Hand*, and *Von Heute auf Morgen*, Schoenberg found inspiration in a story of thwarted illicit love. The *Gurre-Lieder* recounts the Danish legend of a twelfth-century king, Waldemar, who loves a beautiful young woman, Tove. Although she cannot marry him, not being of royal birth, she nevertheless bears him two children. The lovers continue to meet clandestinely at night at the castle of Gurre, which stands by a "silent lake," but when they are discovered the jealous queen has Tove murdered. Part 1 consists of a series of increasingly rapturous alternating arias between Waldemar and Tove, as Waldemar approaches the castle on horseback and the couple is reunited. This group of nine songs, preceded by an orchestral prelude depicting dusk and linked by orchestral interludes, is the fulfillment of Schoenberg's original song cycle plan. The final interlude illustrates the couple's ecstasy and is interrupted violently by a musical representation of Tove's death. In the tenth and last aria of part 1, a "wood dove" sings of Waldemar's inconsolable grief. We learn that he is, in effect, mad and will not let go of his beloved's corpse, carrying her coffin with him in the night.

In part 2 Waldemar curses and rebukes God (a theme that will find echoes in the blasphemous moments of *Pierrot Lunaire* and *Moses und Aron*) for taking away "a beggar's only lamb." In part 3 he roams the night in a wild hunt with an army of the dead, calling for Tove. ("My senses strive to give her form, my thoughts struggle to find her image," he sings, in lines that strangely anticipate *Moses und Aron*.) For fifty minutes the only voices we hear are male: Waldemar, his army (portrayed by three choirs—each divided into four parts—of male voices), the baritone-voiced peasant frightened by the ghoulish mob he sees, the tenor voice of Klaus, the fool, who provides ironically unsympathetic commentary, and finally a "speaker," who narrates the coming of day and the dispelling of the spectral visions of night, in Schoenberg's first use of *Sprechstimme*, a vocal technique between speech and song first used by Engelbert Humperdinck in his 1897 opera *Königskinder*. (Here, though, the speaker's part is more of a rhythmicized declamation, not true "speech-song" as would later be used in *Pierrot Lunaire*, since the speaker is not meant to suggest the notated pitches, only to take his phrasing from them.) Then the full eight-part chorus—male and female—enters to joyfully welcome the sun. As in the ending of *Verklärte Nacht*, a mystical contemplation of nature brings about a transfiguration. Waldemar's torment dissolves into a universal pantheistic awe.

This is particularly fitting since the author of the text, whose poetic telling of the legend of King Waldemar and his lover, Tove, was but one of many literary versions of this tale, was primarily a botanist. The music is suffused with the naturalist's vision, beginning and ending with sumptuous evocations of a benign natural world. Just as Jacobsen's poems abound in naturalistic detail so does the orchestral fabric of the music—in the only way music can accomplish this, of course, by a process of musical analogy. As we have seen, this gift for tone painting was evident in *Verklärte Nacht*, and it would be again in *Pierrot Lunaire, Erwartung*, and countless other works of the composer where one easily "feels" the elements invoked, as one feels here the hard-breathing horses in Waldemar's second song and the sea winds in Tove's second, to cite only two instances.

But this gargantuan work also contains much that seems, at least in retrospect, "Schoenbergian." Even the almost static opening of the orchestral prelude, with its sparkling E-flat-major-with-added-sixth harmonies, which is often compared to the beginning of Wagner's *Das Rheingold* (in which the E-flat major harmony is maintained for an astounding 135 measures), can also be fruitfully likened to the opening of *Pierrot Lunaire*. The transparent and magical scoring, the elevated register, the presence of repeating figures against a melodic line, even some elements of the tonality, quite evidently issue from the same imagination that would produce *Pierrot* eleven years later.

A comparison could also be drawn to Debussy (who completed his Nocturnes for Orchestra in 1899) and even to the opening of Stravinsky's *Petrushka* (of 1911) in the way—for the first twenty-two bars—a coloristic world of activity is set up out of the alternation of two major triads (E-flat and A-flat). These chords are the origin of the "added sixth" in the harmonies of the first measures as well as of the very abstract trumpet melody (suggestive of a fourth chord) at measure 7 (played here by the trumpet in F and later by the bass trumpet in E-flat, French horns, alto trombone, and lower strings, among others)

and they are sonorously superimposed (creating a ninth chord) when the lower registers are added at measure 14. (The new note F in this measure gives the A-flat harmony its own "added sixth.")

Schoenberg, *Gurre-Lieder*

Wagner, *Das Rheingold*

Also characteristic of Schoenberg is the ongoing variation and development of the ideas and materials mentioned in connection with *Verklärte Nacht*, so that in the first part as song follows song, an extraordinarily dense web of associations and cross-relationships is quickly built up. Alban Berg, in his hundred-page analysis of the *Gurre-Lieder*, points to elaborations of at least nine major themes from the preceding arias in the ecstatic interlude that precedes Tove's death and "The Song of the Wood Dove." The speed with which Schoenberg's ideas transform themselves, if not his overall musical method —which in much of this piece has its origins in Wagner's developments, sequences, and leitmotifs—is a lifelong hallmark of this composer. The ideas in *Gurre-Lieder* are in a constant state of becoming something else. To take as an example the very first prominent melodic idea in the trumpet, its many transformations and meanings culminate in its return in inverted form at the close of the work:

This compositional approach can make the work seem more like a symphony than an oratorio.

Another Schoenbergian trait is the tendency to compress and streamline transitions or to leave them simply implied, a tendency we noted in his early song settings. Harmonically this can result in strikingly new harmonic juxtapositions, which are interpreted by Alban Berg as elisions, for which the missing implied harmonies could be supplied and which the ear unconsciously does supply. Yet at what point do these elisions really constitute the parts of speech of a new language? After all, in verbal language what may be understood as an abbreviation in one era can become a new word form in the next. There are moments in this piece in which one can almost palpably sense that the harmonies and melodies employed have a new kind of autonomy and are no longer bound to any preconceived system.

If these are two of the reasons for the supposed difficulty of the composer's music, they also help account for its concision and energy. *Gurre-Lieder* is huge without being flabby.

Even in the through-composed song cycle of part 1, where the listener may be reminded of Wagner in many places, particularly in the music associated with King Waldemar, the orchestral opening and "The Song of the Wood Dove" seem to issue from a different spirit. In the introduction to the wood dove's lament, the half-diminished seventh chord—known to music students the world over as the "Tristan chord"—is given a strikingly "feathery" orchestration suggestive of a bird. It is then used thematically as a leitmotif in the song itself:

Here a chord familiar from the time of Bach as a chromatic decoration, emphasized in a strikingly new way by Wagner—

but still used by him as a dissonant chord that eventually resolves—behaves in a new manner: as a kind of musical object,
an idea in and of itself. The shift in meaning is one not merely
of degree but of kind: it is as if an adjective has become a
noun. This same chord later becomes an important element in
"The Wild Hunt" of part 3, where it is extended for so long
that one loses any sense of its connection to a tonal center.
The harmonies in this passage become so wayward as to seem
the work of a different composer from that of part 1 and to
lead to fearsome dissonances:

In this and other first-period works by Schoenberg such harmonic ambiguities and seeming anomalies are still being made
to fit, sometimes just barely, into conventional tonal logic. But
just because these harmonies are "prepared" and eventually "resolve" doesn't mean that something crucial hasn't changed in the
language. It may simply mean that the composer who has discovered them is still following the principles of voice leading he

has learned. The new reality may be that it is the novel harmonies and "vagrant" chords that have become the primary
point of interest or even of repose, and the "resolutions" and
"preparations," which are now increasingly only decorative, ves-
tigial remnants of an old musical grammar.

As in so much else of early Schoenberg (as well as early Berg)
there is a frequent emphasis on the augmented triad, the one
of the four basic triads that can be used in almost any musical
context and that will continue to figure prominently in the expressionistic works and the twelve-tone ones as well. Whereas
the diminished triad always suggests the possibility of tonal
resolutions—it is, indeed, in the words of one author, a "skeleton key" that can unlock eight different keys—the augmented
triad is a kind of floating ambiguity that can belong to conventional tonality:

Wagner, *Siegfried Idyll*

a whole-tone scale:

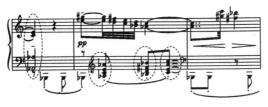

Debussy, *Voiles*

the language of chromaticism in transition away from tonal
functions:

Berg, Sonata

or a completely nontonal context:

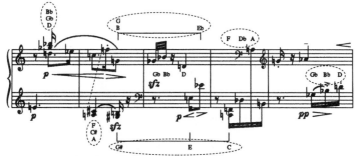

Schoenberg, "Waltzer" from Five Piano Pieces, op. 23

Alternating major and minor thirds piled on top of each other
tend to have tonal implications. Minor thirds by themselves
are bursting with a kind of potential energy; they want to resolve. But major thirds without minor can easily become neutral, stable, and abstract.

In terms of the storytelling itself, there is a schism as well.
A very modern—one might almost say postmodern—self-
awareness is created by the presentation of the story in part 3,
which becomes an ironic commentary on the grief-laden
lover's tale in part 1. And this part also comes the closest to
the edge of atonality.

In this work of summation and foreshadowing even the
composer of *Pierrot* can be glimpsed from time to time. There

is also more than a hint of cabaret and operetta in Klaus the jester's music and in the orchestral interlude that follows him:

And the nine-voiced song of Waldemar's shadowy men is particularly dense and strange, closer to the world of *Wozzeck* than of *Tristan*. But it is also miraculously well-imagined: Schoenberg, who had himself been the conductor of several workers' choruses during this period (in Stockerau, Meidling, and Mödling), knew the sound of massed male voices intimately. In fact, it was after a late-night party with the Mödling chorus that, climbing through the forest mists to view the sunrise at the top of the Anninger mountain, he first imagined the sound of the wonderous choral entrance of the sunrise music at the close of the *Gurre-Lieder*.

The botanist's vision attains its height in the "melodrama" of "The Wild Hunt of the Summer Wind" narrated by the speaker. Here the delicate orchestration brings us close to the quicksilver world of "Der Mondfleck" in *Pierrot* as the text moves from describing the tiniest of visible beings—gnats,

glowworms, ladybugs, spiders—and the awakening of summer's flowers to describing the flaming center of the solar system. At the words "Awaken, awaken, all ye flowers to joy" the
speaker becomes a singer, and his singing suddenly ignites the
voices of the enormous choir. The chorus sings, "Behold
the sun"*; the music blooms into an almost blindingly radiant
C major. For the final twenty-eight measures of the *Gurre-
Leider*, there isn't a single sharp or flat. Though not the same
major key as the opening of the work, it is prepared for in
much the same way—by saving the use of root position for
the climactic moment—and it, too, is embellished with that
thematic "added sixth"; it feels like a return to the work's, and
music's, origins: C, the center of tonality's solar system.

Curiously, the diatonic opening and these closing moments
of the *Gurre-Lieder* sound more modern today than the sections extending Wagnerian chromaticism. These passages are
not simply tonal; they are visions of tonality by someone who
already senses that there are musical alternatives to it. But
much of the work still seems more of a summation than an
anticipation, and listening to it one can be overwhelmed by a
sense of loss. It may not be too fanciful to see it as a long
farewell to the whole idea of a "heroic" romantic music and,
with it, to tonality itself. It is a stroke of genius that in the last
section the sense of farewell is reversed: that as the text describes the rising sun, and the full chorus enters for the first
and only time, a dense and tonally mysterious passage gives
way to the blazing sunlight of a major key. To us, listening
now, this triumph of "tonality" over the forces of death and
darkness brings with it some complex historical ironies and is

---

*The word *Sonne* in the chorus coincides with one of the few places in the work
where all ten French horns, six trumpets, bass trumpet, alto trombone, four tenor-
bass trombones, bass trombone, contrabass trombone, and contrabass tuba are
employed, after which they continue playing to various degrees until the end of
the work. See the full score, two measures after rehearsal number 92 to the end
of the score.

terribly moving. Here we are at the pivot of the century and arguably at one of the most fateful turning points in the thousand-year evolution of Western music. We now know that Schoenberg and much of twentieth-century music was progressing in exactly the opposite direction of this sequence of musical events: away from the tonal center and into a new way of hearing tones. The end of the *Gurre-Lieder* is history in retrograde, or, to paraphrase Debussy's description of Wagner, the dawn at the close of the *Gurre-Lieder* was actually a sunset. C major is being welcomed for what seemed then the very last time. The *Gurre-Lieder* was one final, almost orgiastically beautiful evening-length work, for staggeringly large forces, on mythic subject matter. For a long time after it, anyone composing such a piece would seem to belong to a bygone age. Perhaps because of this and because of the inevitable rarity of live performances, it has remained, despite its musical innovations and notwithstanding its rapturous first reception, in something of a time warp: a work associated more with the past it apotheosized than with the musical gifts of its composer.

4

BERLIN CABARET

One of the main reasons it took so long for Schoenberg to complete the orchestration of the *Gurre-Lieder* was that he had to earn a living. By 1902 he and Mathilde had a daughter, Gertrude, and in 1906 a son, Georg, as well. In 1903, at the age of twenty-nine, he assumed the role of teacher that he would maintain for the next forty years.

For a brief time in 1901–02 Schoenberg was a cabaret composer, conductor, and orchestrator. He was twenty-six years old and worked for an avant-garde theater company called Überbrettl in Berlin, modeled on the literary cabaret then popular in France. Inspired by the performances at Parisian nightspots such as the Auberge du Clou and the Chat Noir, the writer Baron Ernst von Wolzogen (later the librettist of

Strauss's opera *Feuersnot*) had set out to create a cabaret tradition in Berlin that would surpass the French intellectually. He formed a company to showcase sophisticated light entertainment created by adventurous poets and composers who could bridge the worlds of "high" and "low" art. Twenty years before the famously decadent Berlin cabaret scene of the 1920s, the Überbrettl company (so named because it intended to go "beyond" anything accomplished yet in the manner of the *Brettl*, a slang word—literally, "little boards"—for cabaret) built its own theater, designed in Art Nouveau style, and was briefly a forum for some of the most interesting artists of the time.

In 1900, the year he also began his *Gurre-Lieder*, Schoenberg, perhaps dreaming of financial rewards, wrote his own series of songs in the light but sophisticated vein of the material used by the Überbrettl. He drew his texts from the same collection, *Deutsche Chansons*, that the Überbrettl used. When Wolzogen was in Vienna he listened to Schoenberg play through them. The songs included the charming and racy "Gigerlette," "Der genugsame Liebhaber" ("The Contented Suitor"), and "Galathea" to a poem by Frank Wedekind, himself a cabaret performer, whose plays *Pandora's Box* and *Erdgeist* many years later formed the basis for Berg's *Lulu* (which in fact memorably quotes one of Wedekind's cabaret songs in its third act). But it was "Nachtwandler" ("Night Wanderer"), to a poem by Gustav Falke and orchestrated for piccolo, trumpet, side drum, and piano, that particularly delighted Wolzogen. He hired Schoenberg as a conducter and orchestrator. Schoenberg resettled in Berlin, and when the composer Oscar Straus moved on from his position of *Kappelmeister* (music director) for the theater, assumed that role as well.

During this period, working independently and for the Überbrettl, Schoenberg produced massive quantities of cabaret, opera, and operetta orchestrations, some six thousand orchestral pages of music in all, by composers such as Bogumil

Zepler and Heinrich von Eyken. Work on these pages, among other musical chores, took his attention away from those forty-eight-stave manuscript pages of the *Gurre-Lieder* score.

"Nachtwandler" was the only one of his cabaret songs that was orchestrated, and Schoenberg imagined that it might be something of a hit. In fact, it was performed only once, but it was certainly not just the "difficulty of the trumpet part," as Schoenberg later thought, that kept it from being a successful example of sophisticated popular art. Although the phrase structures and general style of the cabaret songs show that their models have been thoroughly enjoyed and absorbed, the mentality behind them is different. Uneasy with literal repetition, the composer can't help subverting the directness of the style with asymmetries of phrasing and momentary tonal ambiguities.

In the text of "Nachtwandler" a man happily strolls through the moonlit streets at night, arm in arm with Luischen (left) and Marie (right), preceded by a drummer and a trumpeter making a racket. The piccolo, trumpet, and snare each have highly individual and inventive parts, more illustrations of the text than parts of an "arrangement" of the song. The delightfully active piccolo obbligato suggests the cockiness and carefree mood of the lucky man who has a woman on each arm, while the rhythmical independence of the trumpet's fanfares convey the unruly nighttime noisemaking of the poem:

> *Jolly trumpeter blast it out*
> *So they leap out of their beds . . .*
> *Nightcaps flying all around.*

The drum meanwhile taps out a dextrous parody of march rhythms. The harmonies are occasionally diatonic, more often subtly chromatic. Here, where the melody could be harmonized by a simple triad, it is harmonized by two chords containing seven different tones, mimicking the sound of a drum.

There are unusual textures, such as the doubling of low piccolo with the piano left hand, and moments when the harmonic underpinnings are concealed in counterpoint. As in many other of his cabaret songs, the transitions become more intriguing than is common in the idiom. In short, the composer is more concerned with portraying the scene in a complex and multilayered fashion than in simply providing a clear-cut, repeating accompaniment for a melody that projects the text. "Nachtwandler" is the work of a complex musical mind working in the theater.

Even when a song is otherwise unremarkable for the cabaret context, its mixed intentions are betrayed by small details. For instance, in "Jedem das Seine," another marchlike song, the tune (A)

appears in diminution in the accompaniment while the singer introduces a subsidiary melody (B).

Later a variation of the subsidiary melody accompanies the
second phrase of the main tune (B).

And for a song in F major, the tonality at one point becomes
remarkably slippery:

The true home for these songs is the concert hall. Close in
spirit to Charles Ives's contemporaneous treatments of the
march, waltz, hymn, and carol genres, they are *about* the
cabaret as much as they are *for* it. They ironize the irony of
the idiom they imitate, and as everybody knows, two ironies
make a truth.

Not for nothing has the publisher put a photograph of
Schoenberg's designs for playing cards on the cover of the
Cabaret Songs (*Brettl-Lieder*). These cards could be used, of
course, but they are also *about* cards (see chapter 22).

Deep familiarity with lighter music was common to "serious" composers of the time. Webern had extensive experience
as a conductor of operettas in his younger days, but none of
the music appealed to him or seemed to influence his work. In
Schoenberg's case a lifelong respect for "lighter" music was re-

flected in such things as his regard for Johann Strauss's waltzes and Tchaikovsky's ballet music; his esteem and affection for the operettas of Franz Lehár, whom he knew in Vienna and stayed in touch with even after moving to America; and his later friendship with and admiration for George Gershwin. Writing shortly after Gershwin's death in 1937, Schoenberg took to task those who considered the American composer less than serious, by saying that what was essential about him was that he was an authentic composer—"serious or not"—unlike those who had simply learned to "add notes together" and were "only serious on account of a perfect lack of humor and soul." What's more, he considered Gershwin to have been an innovator.

A highly poeticized and sardonic form of cabaret performance is evoked by the rhythmicized declamation used in the *Gurre-Lieder*, and in the *Sprechstimme* of *Pierrot Lunaire*, and arguably even in the *Ode to Napoleon*. While speaking over music relates most obviously to the Parisian *diseuse* style, which was not in fashion in the German or Austrian cabaret of the time, it still evokes the world of the "little boards" in which Schoenberg found himself.

More generally, the lighter forms of dance, music-hall, and march music can be found throughout Schoenberg's expressionist and twelve-tone works, including *Erwartung, Pierrot Lunaire*, the Suite, op. 29, the Serenade, and *Moses und Aron*. (In *Moses* there is an unmistakable Viennese waltz impulse in the "orgy" scene and a Germanic march in the music accompanying the journey into the desert.) But in these later works there is no tension between style and substance, since the composer's total immersion in the composing process is taken for granted, and it is the element of parody and suggestion that is the delightful surprise. Arguably, in *Von Heute auf Morgen*, the twelve-tone "operetta" of 1929, there is again an unintended gap between the light tone of the scenario and the multileveled complexity of the score, which plunges the listener who is expecting a more conventional operetta into a surreal state of mind.

"Nachtwandler" itself seems an ancestor of the march movement of the Serenade as well as of the marching-band music in Berg's *Wozzeck*. These beautiful cabaret songs, which descend as much from Brahms and Schumann as from the music hall, anticipated by twenty-five years the sophisticated music theater style of Weill and Eisler.

5

COMING APART

When the Überbrettl disbanded in the summer of 1902, Schoenberg found work teaching at the Stern Conservatory in Berlin for the following academic year. By the summer of 1903, the Schoenbergs and their daughter were back in Vienna. The period between 1903, in which Schoenberg completed the symphonic tone poem *Pelleas und Melisande,* and 1909, the year in which he composed the Three Pieces for Piano, op. 11, Five Pieces for Orchestra, op. 16, and the monodrama *Erwartung,* was one of staggering stylistic change. It was also an exceedingly difficult period financially and, in the end, domestically. Compositions were often produced in the early morning hours before teaching. The musical works from this phase include the Six Songs with Orchestra, op. 8 (1904),

the String Quartet no. 1 (1905), the pathbreaking Chamber
Symphony no. 1 (1906), and the choral work *Friede auf Erden*
(1907) and culminate in two works that marked a fateful
turning point: the extraordinary String Quartet no. 2 of 1908
and the song cycle to fifteen poems of Stefan George, *Das
Buch der Hängenden Gärten* (*The Book of the Hanging Gardens*), of the same year. Taken together these works chart a
progression toward an ever more challenging compression of
musical thinking and toward the elimination of those elements of traditional harmony that no longer had a function or
meaning in the evolving new language. By the time one
reaches the Second String Quartet of 1908, a whole new way
of approaching harmony is being explored, even though the
work as a whole begins and ends in a key. In the song cycle,
one has reached a point of no return. Although there are triads
and seventh chords, they exist in a harmonious and beautiful
world that is simply not "tonal." There are no key signatures.
This is chromaticism without resolution in any previously understood sense. The completely unmoored endings of these
songs, where listeners to highly chromatic works of the day
were used to eventually finding some tonal bearings in a home
key, must have been particularly shocking at the time.

At the very same moment (1906) that his music was beginning to cross the frontier of tonality, Schoenberg had immersed himself in painting as well. Though largely self-taught
in this medium, as he was in music, he may have received
some instruction from a gifted young painter, Richard Gerstl
(1883–1908), but according to Gerstl, it was he who was
influenced toward a more adventurous style by seeing Schoenberg's work. Whatever the truth of the matter, the temperamental and headstrong Gerstl, whose work continues to be
highly regarded (he is considered by some to be the first German Fauvist), rented a studio in the same building in which

the Schoenberg family lived on Liechtensteinstrasse, accompanied the family on holidays, and painted alongside Schoenberg for a time. Mathilde also did some painting study with him, and before long she and Gerstl had begun an affair and eloped together.

It is likely, as some writers suggest, that in addition to the difficulties and financial strain of living with a person such as Schoenberg, the creative and emotional upheavals her husband was going through had made this a particularly lonely period for Mathilde. Some writers describe difficulties Schoenberg had even at the outset of their marriage "integrating [Mathilde] into the circle of his friends." According to Schoenberg's biographer H. H. Stuckenschmidt, theirs had been a passionate courtship. The romance had flowered in the summer of 1899, which the composer spent with Zemlinsky in the town of Payerbach (near Semmering), the same weeks in which he produced the intensely sensual Dehmel songs and *Verklärte Nacht*. We do know that after the birth of their children Mathilde was frequently ill. In the portraits of her by her husband from this time she looks weary and weighed down by cares. In *Mutter und Tochter*, painted by Gerstl, she seems to gaze meaningfully—perhaps angrily—at the painter, while her daughter, Gertrude, is the very picture of childhood melancholia. Of Schoenberg's temperment in his early thirties we can extrapolate primarily from what we know of him in later life. But as early as December 12, 1904, he wrote to Mahler: "Please forgive me, I do not have medium feelings, it is either-or!" Indeed, his early relations with Mahler were often strained by unexpected quarrels, after one of which both composers vowed to never see each other again. (They soon did.)

In her memoirs, Alma Mahler describes the thirty-year-old Schoenberg as original, "prone to paradoxes," aggressivity, and argument (and also as "suffering from inexhaustible Bohemianism," whatever that means). We can infer that this was a person who was impulsive, egotistical to the point of seeming "conceited" (to use a term Gustav Mahler once employed about him in irritation), a man driven from within, high-spirited but also splenetic, whose judgment could sometimes be sarcastic, contemptuous, and peremptory. (Before he came to revere Mahler, for example, he dismissed the idea of attending the Viennese premiere of Mahler's Fourth Symphony with the words "How can Mahler do something in his Fourth Symphony which he could not do in his First?") One can only speculate how frequently his scorn was directed against his wife. One can also only speculate whether more joy or stress resulted when the composer/breadwinner in a financially struggling family embarked on a second career in an entirely new artistic medium.

But whatever the causes of the extramarital romance (if one ever needs to look for "causes" in such cases beyond simple human nature), the family underwent a traumatic rupture and it was only at the urging of Schoenberg's student Anton Webern that Mathilde reluctantly returned to her husband and children.

This crisis eventually pushed the twenty-five-year-old Gerstl over the edge. In November 1908, he burned most of his works and notes and committed suicide by stabbing and then hanging himself. As a result there is little left of his work. Given all this, his laughing and slightly maniacal self-portrait of 1908 makes an unsettling impression.

In the midst of this appalling chain of events and while immersed in his experimental paintings, Schoenberg completed his Second String Quartet, itself a fractured work. There is also evidence that during this period he contemplated suicide himself, since he wrote out several wills. In one he expressed his regret at what he had not yet achieved. In another he seemed to separate himself from the events that had occurred in his life with the words "He who sticks to facts will not get beyond them, to the heart of things. I deny facts. All, without exception. For me they have no value; for I elude them before they can draw me down to them."

It is hard not to take this chapter in Schoenberg's personal life into account when encountering both the high anxiety quotient and the specific literary themes embodied in his musical works from the period 1909 to 1913. In addition, these events surely exacerbated his suspiciousness and his fear of betrayal, character traits that would stay with him his entire life. (Franz Werfel referred memorably to Schoenberg's "narrow-chested energy with fearful side glances.") A great deal of the good he achieved—as well as, paradoxically, a great deal of harm to his own reputation—issued from his tendency to surround himself with fierce loyalists. By all accounts he was someone who demanded that his own ironclad allegiance to those he considered friends be reciprocated unequivocally, and this included strictures against their consorting with those he considered his "enemies."

6

AN INNER COMPULSION

The Second String Quartet introduces a soprano part in its final two movements, an idea perhaps influenced by Mahler's
use of solo voice in his Second, Third, and Fourth Symphonies. For texts Schoenberg turned to poems by the German
symbolist poet Stefan George (1868–1933). The middle two
movements, the first of which contains a bizarre direct quotation from the children's nursery song "Ach du lieber Augustin,
alles ist hin" ("Oh, my dear Augustin, all is lost"), from which
some of the principal motives of the movement are derived,
were written during the marital crisis. The last movement's
text, George's "Entrückung," with its unforgettable line "Ich
fühle Luft von anderem Planeten" ("I feel the air from other

planets"), was set to some of the eeriest music yet composed by anyone. The movement has no key signature, many passages would be next to impossible to describe tonally, and the return at the end to the F-sharp major of the quartet's first movement does not dispel the sense that this music has indeed traveled beyond the bounds of the known musical world. Walter Frisch in his excellent study of early Schoenberg sees an "essential tonal-atonal conflict" at the basis of the entire quartet, which is epitomized by the floating, unearthly opening of the last movment. Here an eight-note atonal "subject" is treated imitatively with entrances a fifth apart (G-sharp, D-sharp, B-flat, F), while an important descending-fifth idea serves as a kind of support in the lower voices: tonal gravity and weightlessness are placed in precarious equilibrium. At the premiere the audience was so disruptive that the soprano completed the performance in tears. This work was also on the program that so excited the painter Wassily Kandinsky that he wrote to Schoenberg hoping to exhibit Schoenberg's music and paintings alongside his own artwork. This invitation, which led to the 1911 exhibition of Schoenberg's work mentioned in the next chapter, initiated their important friendship.

That the Second Quartet embodied a paradoxical situation—in which tonality was affirmed at important junctures, only to be disregarded during many of the intervening sections—troubled the composer deeply. This was the same ambiguity of language that he deplored in later years when he encountered it in the works of others (such as Paul Hindemith), when a confident major triad was tacked onto the end of an essentially nontonal work, and his criticism came to include this work of his own as well. In his essay "My Evolution," written in 1949, he explained the logic behind abandoning this inconsistent use of the old "tonality" thus: "It seemed inadequate to force a movement into the Procrustean bed of tonality without supporting it by harmonic progressions that pertain to it."*

It was increasingly clear to him that the ear did not demand of music that it return to a tonal center in order for the listener to perceive that the piece was over. Rather the contrary: as the sections in pieces in which tonality was "suspended" became longer and longer, thanks to those wandering and tonally ambiguous harmonies, it became increasingly arbitrary to "return" the music to a context that had not been, for the most part, its real basis. Since consonant harmonies were no longer being depended on as structural pillars in most of the work, why should they be used at the last minute as if they had been the guiding principle all along? The harmonic architecture was already being created by chords that in a traditional tonal context would already have *multiple* meanings.

However "natural" it was to Schoenberg and his followers to let go of the type of tonal anchoring that occurs at the end of the Second Quartet, they nevertheless had first to overcome their own incredulity at the prospect. Likening the disappearance of tonality to the falling of ripe fruit from a tree, Anton Webern wrote later of the struggles, doubts, inhibitions, and "panic fear" that nonetheless accompanied the composition of the first works to make the leap. It had been, in his words "so pleasant to fly ever further into the remotest tonal regions, and then to slip back again into the warm nest, the original key!"

In his 1933 lectures *The Path to the New Music*, Webern traces the development of the tonal system of two modes, major and minor, out of the original church modes (sometimes Webern uses the German word *Geschlecht*, which really means

---

*Incidentally, the word *procrustean* derives from the name of a legendary Greek robber who tortured his victims by placing them on his bed and stretching or maiming them to make them fit its length. From this comes its current meaning, as given in the *Oxford Concise Dictionary*, "seeking to enforce uniformity through violent methods."

"gender," to mean "mode": how nice to think of the two "genders" of major and minor) and then describes how the burgeoning complexity of the system led to the era of Wagner, Bruckner, Wolf, and Richard Strauss, in which major and minor effectively no longer existed. If in a major key one "borrows" a harmony that really belongs to the minor key that has the same tonic (as often happens, say, in a song by Schubert) one remains in a major key momentarily colored—overcast—by an influence from the minor mode. But even though a cloud of "minor" has passed over the tonality, one is still in major. If *most* of the harmonies are altered and borrowed, however, major and minor have been fused into an—as it were—androgynous whole. Such was already the case in much late-nineteenth-century music, even if, as Webern puts it, "most people didn't know." The ambiguity and fluidity of the music of the day was obeying an as yet undefined principle of order that made return to a "keynote" almost superfluous. As far as Webern's generation was concerned, "just as the church modes disappeared and made way for major and minor, so these two . . . disappeared and made way for a single series, the chromatic scale." As frightening, if natural, a progression as this was to the composers themselves, for the audiences of that time and later, the leap was still harder to make.

Schoenberg's stunningly far-ranging setting of a poem by Goethe, "Deinem Blick mich zu bequemen" ("Yielding to Your Glance"), composed in 1903, illustrates the transition to this stage. It is a piece in which the chromatic needs of each

voice take precedence over the use of codified harmonies, pure triads appear only fleetingly and almost as if as decoration of the more emphasized chords, and the tonal close feels—if not exactly "Procrustean"—like only one of many possibilities:

With the fifteen song settings that comprise *Das Buch der Hängenden Gärten* (*The Book of the Hanging Gardens*), Schoenberg's music finally made the leap, although in a remarkably subtle and intimate way, to a world without tonal resolution. This stunningly beautiful cycle occupies a special place in the history of twentieth-century music and of song literature, yet is seldom performed. Schoenberg had employed George's poetry first in his two songs of 1907 and the contemporaneous vocal movements of the Second Quartet. Amazingly enough, the texts Schoenberg chose for the new song cycle had been written by George (in 1894) out of admiration for the very same woman, Ida Auerbach (then Ida Coblenz), who later was the inspiration for Richard Dehmel's poem "Verklärte Nacht" and afterwards Dehmel's wife.

Stefan George considered himself a kindred spirit to Mallarmé and to Baudelaire (whose *Fleurs du Mal* he translated). Although written in strict, classically metric forms, his poetry explores an evocative and dreamlike inner world full of symbolism drawn from nature. From George's original *Book of the Hanging Gardens*, which tells the tale of a heroic Oriental potentate in love with a woman intended for his rival, Schoenberg chose fifteen of the more abstract poems, thereby eliminating most of the elements of the original story line and leaving only the emotions expressed by the protagonist and vague suggestions of a plot. Schoenberg's cycle charts a course from vague anticipation (poems 1, 2) and longing (3, 4, 5) to obsession (6, 7, 8), frustration (9), reverie (10), brief consummation (11), and finally doomed resignation (12, 13, 14, 15). In Schoenberg's "abstract" of the original poetic cycle, every element begins to seem symbolic, making it a kind of modern Song of Songs in which the "garden" has become almost as important as the "woman."

As for the musical language, few works sit so ambiguously between worlds as this one, and this, too, lends the piece a dreamlike quality. The exquisite vocal lines, built on thirds, and sonorous piano accompaniments, which are full of triads and seventh chords, suggest at every turn the great late-nineteenth-century German song tradition from which this music comes. But like the hero slowly drifting away from his beloved in a boat in poem 13 ("You lean against a white willow by the bank"), Schoenberg's music has torn itself loose from the shores of the old meanings. No longer guilty of the dual allegiances expressed in the 1903 Goethe setting or in the Second Quartet, it has crossed over into a completely nontonal realm.

Although melodies and fragments return from time to time throughout the cycle, the very flexible forms of the songs and the form of the cycle as a whole are distinctly at odds with the structures of the poems. So, too, the vocal part interprets the meter of the texts very freely. As H. H. Stuckenschmidt says in his biography of Schoenberg, "George's strict metres are as it were unmasked by Schoenberg. . . . Schoenberg's sounds and

rhythms shine behind this order and disclose the spiritual or-
ganism which hides behind it."

For the first performance, on January 14, 1910, Schoenberg wrote a preface for the program that included these lines:

> In the George Lieder I have succeeded for the first time
> in approaching an ideal of expression and form that had
> hovered before me for some years. . . . I am following an
> inner compulsion that is stronger than education, and am
> obeying a law that is natural to me, and therefore stronger
> than my artistic training.

But in the note Schoenberg also expresses his worry that even
those who have supported him up until now will oppose his
new work. Indeed, he implies that entering this new musical
domain has required courage and an overcoming of resistance
on his own part.

As strong an "ego" as he must have had, Schoenberg never recovered from the reception many of his first works received.
Early opposition reinforced his sense of being embattled and
caused him to think of others in stark terms, as either adherents or detractors. The Viennese audiences were vociferously
opinionated and violent, and their frequent hostility to his
work contributed to his decision to accept a post in Berlin in
1912 and to move back there with his family. Viennese concerts turned into battlegrounds on many occasions. One fervent admirer of Schoenberg's and a member of his circle, first
as a student and later as an assistant and archivist, was an official of the public railway system named Josef Polnauer. His of-
fice, according to friends, was full of musical scores instead of
books. Polnauer was a reassuring presence at the concerts because of his size and strength. At the premiere of Berg's Seven
Early Songs, he was cut in the face by a knife while coming to

the defense of Gustav Mahler. Mahler had turned to silence a loudly protesting man sitting behind him in the audience. When the disgruntled audience member upped the ante by saying to Mahler the equivalent of "I hiss at your unspeakable symphonies, too," Polnauer jumped into the fight and was cut. (Apparently he wore the resulting scar proudly for the rest of his life.) Though the use of knives in concert brawls was uncommon, this type of incident was not. An admirer of the time recalled having sometimes to get Schoenberg "out of a concert hall by a back entrance" and to "shield him with our very bodies against all the things that were thrown at him." After a performance of *Pierrot Lunaire* a musician member of the audience pointed at Schoenberg and shouted, "Shoot him! Shoot him!"

A contributing factor to hostile audience reaction was surely the unevenness of the performances themselves. Schoenberg came up with a novel idea in 1908 when he gave ten open rehearsals of his First Chamber Symphony. At the premiere on February 5, 1907, in Bösendorfer Hall, the work had caused a commotion of hissing, whistling, seat banging, and noisy departures. Here he conducted a stellar ensemble in patient rehearsals in which each voice in this complex yet formally lucid work could be separated out and combined with the other voices in turn. The rehearsals won over many skeptics, and after the final one, at which the work was performed twice through, the hall erupted in cheers. Alban Berg wrote to his wife that it was an overwhelming experience and that afterwards he felt "ten years younger." Perhaps the seeds were planted here for the Society for Private Musical Performances of ten years later.

Schoenberg family, Berlin, 1913

A NEW FORM
OF EXPRESSION

1909 — 13

7

f A R B E N

I must believe: this is something.
　　　　　　　　—Schoenberg, in a letter of June 16, 1910

No analysis or musical explanation is as helpful to an intuitive understanding of Schoenberg's music during the period 1906–12 as is a viewing of his paintings from that time, which was the height of his painting activity. (He continued to draw with paper and pencil throughout his life but painted only occasionally after 1912.) This is not to say that the paintings necessarily "say" the same thing as the music in another medium. Rather their impact is immediate and provides one with a human understanding of the composer, one might almost say an instantaneous personal contact with him. Although perhaps crude in some technical respects, the paintings and drawings have retained their immediacy.

The artworks can be divided roughly into three groups:

portraits (primarily self-portraits), more abstract visionary expressions, and realistic works from nature. In addition there are the designs for the sets and characters of *Erwartung* and *Die glückliche Hand*, as well as assorted sketches, caricatures, and doodles. During the period when Schoenberg actually hoped to earn an income from the works, forty of his paintings were shown in a small one-man exhibit in Vienna in 1910. Later some of his work was exhibited alongside that of painters such as Franz Marc, Wassily Kandinsky, Henri Rousseau, and Egon Schiele. Gustav Mahler anonymously purchased some of these paintings to help support the painter/composer.

In the self-portraits one sees a face that changes radically from work to work in many of the externals—often drawings done within the same year seem to depict a man of entirely different ages, for example—but in which the look of the eyes, the shape of the hairline, and to a great extent the intensity of mood are constants. As art historian Eberhard Freitag writes, "the facial expression often seems disturbed or uneasy, and the slightly crookedly drawn mouth always stands out as a common physical characteristic." As one looks at image after image one feels as if one is witnessing a search of some kind. The mind is digesting the impressions of what it sees reflected back by its own eyes from the mirror—reflected back into those very eyes. For a man with such an involvement in his own inner life, is there not also evidence here of a search for reassurance that he is still physically there or a search to understand what remains of his identity from day to day? In more than twenty of the self-portraits the staring head simply floats in space, unconnected to neck or body. Many of the heads melt into pure form and color. By contrast, those that show his neck, and an attractive rendering of the upper portion of a jacket, collar, and tie, convey a sense of relief in the grounding of daily reality. A few images are in profile. Particularly arresting is a brush-and-ink drawing in which his face and gaze are turned upward, with dark bands of ink striped down his neck (see ch. 23).

Schoenberg was particularly preoccupied by the idea of the emotional impact of color and color combinations. In her memoirs, Alma Mahler describes the rooms in the Schoenberg's home in 1915 as each having a distinct intellectual atmosphere and "an individual color." Certain of Schoenberg's works have a blatant color scheme giving them the boldness that can be found in art by children. Associations between sound and color led him to design sets and costumes for his stage works and to provide detailed instructions as to the lighting required for specific moments. In *Die glückliche Hand* he conjoined the two art forms even more specifically by notating in the score itself an exact progression of color changes to accompany an orchestral interlude that itself was meant to mirror a psychological progression in the main protagonist (see ch. 13). In the study in orchestral color, "Farben," that forms the third movement of Five Pieces for Orchestra (see ch. 7), a painterly impulse seems almost palpable. This music draws attention to his explorations of timbre—the subtle mixing and overlappings of instrumental tone color, the "chamber scoring"—which characterize so much of his work even for large instrumental forces and with which a parallel can be drawn to his explorations of visual color. In the backgrounds, clothing, and faces of many of his portraits, for example, one is struck by the freshness and subtlety of the hues, which often are novel blendings of paint and carry with them a strange emotional charge.

Schoenberg was never satisfied with his realistic works from nature, in which he was well aware of his technical shortcomings, calling them "five-finger exercises." On the other hand, he believed in his self-portraits and "gazes" (*Blicke*) sufficiently to seriously consider pursuing a career as a painter. Later he explained his term *gazes* by saying that he never saw faces at all but, "because I looked into people's eyes, only their 'gazes.' "

To his wife's stepfather, Carl Moll, he wrote in 1910 about his sudden exploration of painting: "I must believe: this is something. At first glance it must seem strange that I assume that someone who can do nothing is suddenly capable of doing something. . . . It is, with me at any rate, routinely the case."

It appears that Schoenberg did not see either Kandinsky's or Kokoschka's paintings until at least 1911. In later years he disclaimed any direct influence from them. (Other painters who come easily to mind for comparison are Franz Marc, Egon Schiele, Edvard Munch, and Vincent van Gogh. Schoenberg came to particularly admire the paintings of Gustav Klimt.) Nevertheless, when Kandinsky heard Schoenberg's music for the first time he had a shock of recognition that he had encountered a kindred spirit wrestling with uncannily similar issues to the ones he was facing in painting. Kandinsky was himself an amateur musician (he played the cello and the piano) just as Schoenberg was an "amateur" painter, and both men drew parallels between the two art forms.

Kandinsky and Schoenberg were linked not so much by their styles of painting as by their sense of mission about the future of art and the unwavering authenticity of everything they did. They had both experienced a revelation about liberating the materials of their art from their old functions. In terms of his painting style Schoenberg seems to have more in common with Kokoschka, Schiele, Marc, and Munch than with Kandinsky, whose work would appear to be more formal, objective, universal, even "cosmic" than psychological and subjective. Kandinsky painted only one portrait of any kind in his entire oeuvre, and no self-portraits. Interestingly, he preferred Schoenberg's "realistic" work to his "gazes" (which Kandinsky called "visions"). Nevertheless, he wrote penetratingly and admiringly of both sides of Schoenberg's work in his article "Schoenberg's Pictures," which was first printed as part of a festschrift presented to Schoenberg at a concert on February 29, 1912, and he selected and personally translated portions of *Harmonielehre* for publication in a Russian exhibition catalog. In addition to exhibiting Schoenberg's paintings, he published some of them in his *Blaue Reiter Almanach*, alongside the score of *Herzgewächse*, op. 20, and an article by Schoenberg.

Kandinsky's *On the Spiritual in Art* was published concurrently with *Harmonielehre*. Like Schoenberg, he became particularly involved during the years 1909–14 in explorations of issues common to all the arts and sought to synthesize them. Like Schoenberg, he worked on trailblazing works of expressionist theater. He considered the notion of the "emancipation of the dissonance" to be consistent with his own new theories about color and in his writings showed a profound interest in the subject of "color hearing," buttressing his views with references to the research of a contemporary psychologist (a certain Dr. Freudenberg, who also had ideas about the relationship between the senses of smell and hearing), the theories of the scientist and composer Leonid Sabaneyev, and the color-and-music experiments of Alexander Scriabin, among others. He referred to the nonnaturalistic painter as using colors "according to their inner sound" rather than for their academically "accurate" mimicry of appearances.

At the moment of encountering the composer (1911), Kandinsky was at a remarkably analogous crossroads in his work. He had been spending much of his time living and working in the village of Murnau in southern Bavaria, and his paintings had begun to change, with the colors taking on what seemed a life of their own, independent of the real world, and the representational shapes becoming more like emblems and remnants than like images meant to be clearly read by the viewer. In 1908 he had had an epiphany: he realized, seeing one of his own paintings lying on its side in the dusk, the eloquence of the pure shapes and colors he had made, devoid of their comprehensibility as representation. Years of searching for a way to express the power of color and form, the power of seeing, reinforced by the experience of viewing the works of Monet and later the Fauves, who had obscured the recognizability of their subjects, had led Kandinsky to this momentous discovery: representation was a distraction from the essence of his paintings. This was an extention of Matisse's statement that whatever is not essential to the picture is in fact detrimental to it.

A look through Kandinsky's output from 1908 shows a continual process of evolution and growth while notions of comprehensibility and literalness ebb and flow. That is to say, there are canvases that appear to be entirely abstract as early as 1910, the year of the well-known "first abstract watercolor," but symbols and realistic forms or distillations of these forms recur throughout his work, almost in the way that remnants of tonal harmony recur in Schoenberg's. One can trace the evolution of certain shapes—such as the figures of riders on horseback of which he was so fond (these riders coupled with the blue of Franz Marc's horses inspired the name "Der Blaue Reiter")—from paintings like *The Blue Mountain* (1908–09), where three horses and riders in unrealistic dappled colors are clearly delineated in the lower frame of the picture, to *Study for Composition II* (1910), where the eye needs some time sorting out in a similar foreground area the shapes of two seemingly sparring riders on horseback—here strangely elongated and somewhat obscured—to the lunging ("tangled") lines in the upper left of the glorious *Composition IV* (1911), which we can read as similar dueling riders primarily because Kandinsky made notes on what was in his mind when he painted them. Once we see his notes, we of course recognize the "blue mountain" in the center of the painting as well.

How many specific images must be encrypted in these and other paintings from the time! Indeed, Kandinsky's own descriptions show how much more frequently he drew his abstract-looking shapes from images of real things than one might have thought. Many of the fascinating figures and constructions in his later work are compressed versions of motifs found in the earlier. To the viewer this may be experienced as an uncanny rightness in the shapes, which seem to derive somehow from a reality we share but which, like events in a dream, mean something we can't quite put our finger on. An analogy can be drawn between these derived shapes and the compression of historical musical elements found in twentieth-century music.

But even at this stage in his work, Kandinsky distinguished between "Impressions," which were based on external reality, and "Improvisations," which came from the imagination alone. He used the term "Compositions," a word he revered, for work based on internal processes but built up over time through preliminary sketches.

Much as it is tempting to draw a parallel between the dissolution of tonality and that of "representation" in music, there is no external reality from which the sounds in music are drawn—hence there is no realism possible in music (discounting the actual bird calls in Messiaen's music or the use of sounds from daily life, such as car horns, animal cries, and the like, in the "*musique concrete*" by electronic composers such as Pierre Henry and Pierre Schaeffer). The distinction Kandinsky makes between "outer" and "inner" reality can't be made in music, which is abstract already, tonal music just as much as nontonal. When composers have conscious feelings and impressions in their minds while composing, it is not truly possible to say that these very impulses have become embedded in the notes they have written. To be sure, we know when music has an urgency of tone. But how could we know, if he had not mentioned it in his writings, that many of Webern's early works were written under the impression of his mother's death? Could we possibly imagine, without the assistance and sleuthing of music scholars, that passages in the first movement of Berg's Violin Concerto were connected in his mind to a love affair he had had at the age of seventeen with a servant girl in his family home (particularly since he directed our attention elsewhere in his dedication)?* The conscious notions behind a work of music are like girders used during the construction of a building that are removed when the building is completed. Even the artist may not recall what—if anything verbalizable—was in his or her mind during the writing.

An analogy can be made between the processes involved in creating abstract painting and in creating *all* music, of whatever kind, between the way in which the inner thoughts of a composer and the specific images in the minds of visual abstract artists are subsumed—dissolved—in the materials of their media, resulting in a kind of "hidden iconography" known, if known at all, only by the artist. For this reason, Kandinsky's descriptions of his paintings sound like descriptions of what it feels like to compose and come closer than any music analysis I have ever read to capturing a sense of a composer's instinctive molding of materials:

> Composition IV, 1911
> Subsequent Interpretation
> . . . 2. Contrasts
>   of mass to line,
>   of the precise to the indistinct,
>   of tangled lines to tangled colors and the main
>   contrast: pointed, sharp movement (battle) to
>   bright-cold-fresh colors

---

*The young woman, Marie Scheuchl, gave birth to an illegitimate daughter, Albine, from this union. See George Perle, *The Operas of Alban Berg*, vol. 2, Berkeley: University of California Press, 1985.

3. Overflows
    of color over the outlines . . .
4. Two focal points:
    1. tangled lines,
    2. molded summit of the blue . . .
    Picture With White Border, 1913
    . . . Thus, clarity and simplicity at the upper left,
    blurred dissolution with gloomy little disintegrations at
    the lower right. As so often with me, two centers . . .

At the lower left there is battle in black and white, which is separated by Naples Yellow from the dramatic clarity of the upper left corner. The way in which the black, indistinct spots welter in the white, I call "inner seething in unclear form."

"Dissolution with gloomy little disintegrations," "inner seething in unclear form": these phrases could describe moments in Schoenberg's Five Pieces for Orchestra. "Inner seething in unclear form" could describe the flutter-tongue growl by the four muted trombones and tuba at the close of the first piece, for example, while "dissolution with gloomy little disintegrations" perfectly evokes the final clarinet gurgles, eerie tremolo chords "*am Steg*" in the basses, and stopped French horn chord in the last three measures of the fourth piece, a disintegration that follows the tremendous buildup of excitement at letter 9 and the huge crash in the second beat of that bar. "Overflows—of color over the outlines" could describe the "smudging effect" noted below in the "Farben" movement between letters 4 and 5.

In January 1911, Kandinsky returned in a state of high excitement from hearing Schoenberg's music for the first time, in a concert that included the Three Pieces for Piano, op. 11. He set to work painting an "impression"—*Impression III—Concert*—of it. After making two preliminary studies in which the grand piano, the musicians, the audience members, a chandelier, and the perspective lines of the stage are discernible, he produced a large oil canvas in which what one perceives as the sound itself—represented by a bold yellow swath—seems to envelope the performers and audience, and the piano has become a monumental black slab, like a giant note head, intersected by a shaft of white-yellow-gray light. He then wrote to Schoenberg a letter introducing himself:

> What we are striving for and our whole manner of thought and feeling have so much in common that I feel completely justified in expressing my empathy.
>
> In your works, you have realized what I, albeit in uncertain form, have so longed for in music. The independent progress through their own destinies, the independent life of the individual voices in your compositions, is exactly what I am trying to find in my paintings.

A correspondence and a close friendship ensued. Schoenberg wrote to the painter: "You are such a full man that the least vibration causes you to overflow."

With Franz Marc, Kandinsky was in the process of putting together the first of the two Blaue Reiter exhibitions, which was held from December 18, 1911 to January 1, 1912, and the first (and, as it turned out, only) Blaue Reiter almanac, which eventually appeared in mid-May 1912. Schoenberg's work was represented in both.

In 1910, when Schoenberg was thirty-six years old, the painter Max Beckmann (1884–1950) was twenty-six.

Robert Delaunay (1885–1941) was twenty-five.

Paul Klee (1879–1940) was thirty-one.

Gustav Klimt (1862–1918) was forty-eight.

Wassily Kandinsky (1866–1944) was forty-four.

Oskar Kokoschka (1886–1980) was twenty-four.

Käthe Kollwitz (1867–1945) was forty-three.

Schoenberg, *Portrait of Alban Berg (1885–1935)*, undated

Franz Marc (1880–1916) was thirty.

August Macke (1887–1914) was twenty-three.

Piet Mondrian (1872–1944) was thirty-eight.

Edvard Munch (1863–1944) was forty-seven.

Emil Nolde (1867–1956) was forty-three.

Henri Rousseau (1844–1910) was sixty-six and in the year of his death.

Egon Schiele (1890–1918) was twenty.

In Schoenberg's visual artwork, force of conviction, coupled with a kind of rawness of execution, renders the viewer a participant in the process of making. "Beauty" seems but a by-product of the attempt to convey an inner impulse. It is interesting to see where particular emphasis is placed on the external details. One particularly satisfying essay at "realism" is his portrait of Alban Berg. The only full-length self-portraits by Schoenberg are those where he is seen "in reverse" (see p. 305). The rest are generally haunting and haunted close-ups. When contrasted with these rather harrowing self-portraits, the full-length oil of Berg exudes a confident serenity. Here Berg's height is emphasized by placing him next to the tall bureau, on which he is leaning; by the verticality of the canvas and his occupying it almost completely; and by the strong verticals of the bureau's side, the door frame, and the frame of the painting of the house behind him, with its vertical columns. (It is also worth noting half humorously the possibly unintentional metaphorical import of the "supporting" bureau, which could be a symbol of Berg's teacher. It is hard to imagine the work of the younger composer without the older, who did, in addition, teach him for free his first year.) Furthermore, the picture itself is immense, 175 x 85 centimeters as opposed to the painter's customary 40 x 30 centimeters. The house in the painting on the wall—suggestive of classical times, symmetry, architecture, and of artistic production—puts the young and dapper Berg in

Schoenberg, *The Burial of Gustav Mahler* (*May 22, 1911, in Vienna*), **undated**

the context of the ages, and the finished elegance of the work and its strongly balanced structure, in which the younger composer seems to fit in such a relaxed and intimate manner, radiate warmth and, one might almost say, confidence in his future. (On the evidence in their correspondence, however, Schoenberg had more conflicted feelings about the promise of Berg than he did about his student Webern.) The handsome and sensual Berg, with his flowing dark hair and self-consciously artistic clothes, can also be seen as embodying his own romantic, idealistic, and worldly musical esthetic.

Another "realistic" painting of musical significance is *The Burial of Gustav Mahler*, painted shortly after the event, which gave rise also to the final piece of the Sechs kleine Klavier-

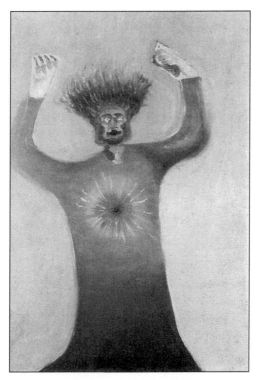

Schoenberg, *Hatred*, undated

stücke, op. 19 (see ch. 10). The windswept group of mourners are shown bowing over a womblike open grave.

It is hard to present hard evidence that these are the paintings of a composer, but intuitively this rings true. Sometimes (as in *Hatred*, above), the gestures have the impact of the orchestral outbursts in Five Pieces. In a few works, music and image come together, as in the caricature of a pianist of 1921. Here the body of the pianist loops upward like the unfolding phrase of music she is playing. The implied music is that of Bach, the name emblazoned on the piano. It is the contrapuntal music of Bach that the artist/composer described as producing its material not by development but "by a procedure rather to be called unraveling," as in a canon that, though

Schoenberg, *Caricature,* 1921

written "in one single line, yet furnishes various sounds." The upward gazing, somewhat animal face of the performer seems both comically self-satisfied and genuinely enthralled. The absurdly elongated, winding torso suggests, along with the contrapuntal unraveling of the Baroque music she is producing, her pleasure in the process, at the same time as it pokes fun at the romantic gyrations of showy performers.

Particularly striking are the images in which the human form appears partly disembodied, dissolving into abstraction, as in *Tears.* The forehead takes on a life of its own in the undated *Gaze.* The seat of the "inner compulsion" so dear to the artist seems to roil with power and looks almost like a spaceship about to blast off from the brown earth below it.

These "visions" remind one of the looming, seemingly un-

Schoenberg, *Tears*, undated

tethered sound shapes in the new music and form an interesting parallel to the notion of harmonic "elision" posited by
Berg in connection with the *Gurre-Lieder* (see ch. 3). What is
left out is unnecessary, as it is supplied by the viewer's imagination. There are also those paintings that leave all representation behind, like *Vision* (p. 76). To say that these images
"sing" is perhaps not simply a figure of speech.

Schoenberg's *Blaue Selbstporträt* (*Blue Self-Portrait*) of 1910,
while it could only be of Schoenberg and by Schoenberg, also
attains the abstraction of an anonymous mask (see p. 77). The
expression is less actively troubled, more distilled than in
many of his similar works. The eyes stare perhaps less glar-
ingly, but with the touches of red in the inside of the right
eye's lower lid adding to the sadness of their expression. The
blue-gray face is highlighted with streaks of white and patches
of orange that reflect the lovely, glowing peach-orange background. The two discrete mats of hair sit awkwardly on the
head, making one unusually aware of the skull underneath. In

Schoenberg, *Gaze*, undated

fact, if one blocks out the sides of the head and the hair, the skull is revealed as outlined in orange. There is something odd and overly protruding about the brain in the forehead. The bald top of the head is pointy. One senses both warmth and coolness in the face, whose slate-blue color is at one with that of the top of the jacket. A furnacelike intensity is suggested by the chimney-shaped nose. The mouth and nose tilt ever so slightly downward to his right, and the lips seem less full on this side, the same side on which the fleshy right ear with its prominent lobe is visible. The left ear is not concealed; it is simply missing. The white shirt collar is lit as if from below by streaks of pure white, which then gleams on the lower and upper lips and in the whites of the eyes.

In its directness there is also a faintly childlike quality to the painting. In their search to go beyond the "properly" representational for spiritual expression and to tap into a more instinctive type of motivation, Kandinsky and Marc expressed a strong interest in the art of the untrained and included in their

Schoenberg, *Vision*, undated

hopes for the Blaue Reiter group that the work they believed in
be displayed alongside masks made by untutored artists, Is-
lamic carpets, and the art of children. The Swiss-born Paul
Klee, who had only just begun exhibiting his work, enthusias-
tically reviewed the first Blaue Reiter exhibition for a Swiss
monthly journal, *Die Alpen*. He was particularly sympathetic
to the artists' innovative juxtapositions of their own work with
"primitive beginnings of art, such as you would expect to find

Schoenberg, *Blue Self-Portrait*, 1910

more in ethnographical collections." Shortly thereafter, Klee and Kandinsky became friends, and works by Klee became an important part of the second Blaue Reiter exhibition in February 1912. Certain techniques in Klee stemming from his interest in children's art—unsteady and wavy lines, exaggerated

Schoenberg, *Red Gaze,* 1910

Man Ray, portrait of Schoenberg, 1930

outlines, smudged colors, doodling, naively approximate geo-
metrical shapes, etc.—became a permanent part of his technical repertoire. Klee spoke in words almost identical to
Schoenberg's when he said, "[The artist] does not attach such
intense importance to natural form as do so many realist critics. . . . For he places more value on the powers which do the
forming than on the final forms themselves." During the years
of his painting activity, Schoenberg expressed a similar view:

> We want to see what the work of art has to give and not its
> external stimulus. . . . The exactness of rendering the action
> is [as] irrelevant to its artistic value as the resemblance to
> the model is for a portrait. A hundred years later no one

Schoenberg, *Hands*, 1910

will be able to check the likeness, but the artistic effect will always remain.

In his avowed following of "inner necessity stronger than any upbringing," Schoenberg sought a sophistication beyond training and also perhaps, *beneath* training.

The bluish face in the 1910 self-portrait suggests the subject's intensity, while also possessing a kind of iconic passivity. Oddly comforting in its unblinking awakeness, in its unforced steadiness of look, it conveys strength without tension in its expression, a calmness, a transcendence.

It is chilling to look at the outline in orange of the skull, however, and then compare the picture with the terrifying *Red Gaze*. It is almost as if the Red Gaze lies beneath the blue one. Both pictures date from 1910, the period of *Erwartung* and the Five Pieces for Orchestra. The *Blue Self-Portrait* bears a striking resemblance to the photographic portrait by Man Ray taken in 1930, during the years of Schoenberg's work on *Moses und Aron*. There is a perceptible shift in the feeling that emanates from the person depicted in the two images. The intervening years have deepened the intensity and strengthened the resolve in this face. But in both portraits, the gaze will not let you go.

In assessing Schoenberg's artwork, critics and fellow painters have run the gamut from derision to enthusiasm. The paintings have been considered early examples of "outsider art" by some, remarkable in their ideas, if amateurish in execution. Yet John Russell calls the *Blue Self-Portrait* "one of the great self-portraits of our century." Schoenberg "keeps nothing back," writes Russell. "This painting gives nobility to the notion of self-awareness." Contrasting him with professional painters, Russell feels that Schoenberg is neither "on stage," as Kokoschka is in his portraits, nor crying out to us "in self-pity" as is Schiele in his. Nor does he place himself within some defining context. Rather, he simply exists.

The playwright S. N. Behrman wrote in a memoir of the immensities behind Schoenberg's eyes. Robert Craft in his diary entry for July 5, 1950, spoke of Schoenberg's "pained, too sensitive face, difficult to look into and impossible not to look into." Stravinsky observed that "his eyes were protuberant and explosive, and the whole force of the man was in them." Max Deutsch, an early Schoenberg pupil, said that "his face was eyes" and that with "Schoenberg's eyes [looking] at you, you disappeared." The theme of eyes haunts much of Schoenberg's work, too. Jelena Hahl-Koch points out the emphasis on eyes in both *Erwartung* and *Die glückliche Hand* and describes the eyes in Schoenberg's portraits as "so strong in expression and dominating and intensive in their effect, that one can find only little to compare with them in the whole history of art."

In his concentration on the inward states of his subjects, Schoenberg has often been described as a member of the expressionist movement. But living closely with artworks described as "expressionistic" and with those called "neoclassical" makes one question whether these terms have any lasting meaning. The formalistic neoclassical works begin more and more to resemble their creator, to become idiosyncratic and personal, while the expressionistic ones begin to seem time-less, impersonal, and pure.

A visitor to this composer's catalog of visual works is struck by the variety of means and techniques attempted, by the un-evenness of the execution, by the utter directness and sincerity of the expression—but most of all by the number of times a powerful result is achieved, often, as here, in the difficult chal-lenge of capturing one's own likeness and facial proportions from seeing their reversed reflection in a mirror. The mirror-ing inherent in self-portraiture resonates with Schoenberg's more general tendency to symmetry and to replication of ideas through transformed repetition, reversing (retrograde), and inversion (turning upside down). In the *Hands* we see a kind of mirroring that could directly relate to *Moses und Aron*: the indissoluble union of two like but also opposite things.

A reverse image of another sort appears in Schoenberg's well-known painting of himself as seen from behind, strolling away from the viewer, wearing his brown suit, walking stick in hand. This was one of three Schoenberg paintings exhibited in the first Blaue Reiter exhibit in 1911. Here the "gaze" is not shown, although those who knew Schoenberg describe the portrait as an uncanny likeness. He is seen turning his back, as it were—perhaps on us, or on himself painting the canvas, or on the outmoded past and half-formed solutions of the pres-ent, on the well-trodden path, or on those who turned their backs on *him* by not hearing him. The possible interpretations are numerous. Perhaps he is just walking away. Yet it is a self-portrait; he is showing one of the ways in which he sees him-self. At the premiere of the *Gurre-Lieder*, in response to the thunderous ovation of the audience—this being the greatest public triumph of his life—he turned his back on the ap-plause, rejecting it in the name of all the more recent work that had been so roundly dismissed.

...

But the self-portrait as seen from behind is an exception, as are the profiles. Primarily Schoenberg looks at himself, and at us. And the frontality of these self-portraits and gazes is the frontality of the man and his work. This was a life and art of facing things. The rawness and straightness of the look reminds one of the writer Paul Rosenfeld's words: "If we ourselves see anything in Schoenberg's career, it is nothing if not the development of a man according to the law of life which compels us, if we would live and grow, to become ever more fully and nakedly what we essentially are."

The artist claimed not to possess the nature of a real painter—who would truly "look" at "the whole person"—grasping instead only the "soul" and capturing it out of his own nature, not by imitation of other artists. The staring faces in these paintings pose the paradox of "idea" and "style" that so preoccupied their author and that received its most extensive expression in the opera *Moses und Aron*: the so-called soul of a subject (idea) can after all only be depicted in some concrete form (style).

If there is a deeper consolation to be found beneath the disturbing surface of much of his music and painting—and to me there is—it lies in the universality of the extreme states of the psyche that are depicted; here Schoenberg uses his own face to depict and confront our common humanity.

8

---‖|‖---

LISTENING TO

FIVE PIECES

FOR ORCHESTRA

Of the works written between the Second String Quartet and the first twelve-tone essays of the 1920s, there are few that are not vocal and whose forms are not therefore, at least in part, determined by the course of the text. Of these the Five Pieces for Orchestra, op. 16, composed in 1909, are unique in approaching traditional concert length. One might choose these pieces to represent Schoenberg to an audience that is wary of him, not because they are "easy" to listen to but because of their obvious mastery and emotional power. (In fact, one New York Philharmonic subscriber died during the New York premiere of the work, which was conducted by Mitropoulos.) This is music of Mahlerian depth of feeling, music one could almost—almost—imagine Mahler himself writing had he lived to pursue the direction of the nearly atonal passages in the Adagio of his Tenth Symphony. There is variety and range here, too: explosiveness (movements 1, 4), tenderness (2), serenity (3). Listening to it after viewing Schoenberg's paintings of the time one could conceivably conclude that the intensity of the paintings and that of the music are comparable. But one would also have to conclude that the music is the work of an artist in whom the possibilities are greater. This is as seamless and beautifully wrought a work as any produced in its day. Part of the effectiveness of the paintings, as unimprovable and riveting as they are, seems to result from the artist's having simply eliminated all he could not do. The author of Five Pieces for Orchestra is in complete command, holding power in reserve, with a myriad of options at his disposal.

In 1912, at his publisher's request, the composer gave the five movements specific titles:

1. "Vorgefühle" ("Premonitions")
2. "Vergangenes" ("The Past")
3. "Farben" ("Colors")
4. "Peripetie" ("Peripeteia")
5. "Das obligate Rezitativ" ("The Obbligato Recitative")

In the Five Pieces for Orchestra the listener can sense what the composer meant when he said that an artist carries within him "the pulse of the world." The first movement's taut energy and instantaneous development of the tiniest of the ideas stated in the first few measures create a feeling of crisis, and a global more than a personal one. The headlong motion of the movement is due in part to the use of ostinati (short, obsessively repeating figures, often in the cellos and basses), the propulsiveness of the important dotted rhythmic motive, and the wild instability created by simultaneous layers of rhythmic activity in 3/8 and 4/8. After the first twenty-two measures introduce the ideas in small instrumental groups, the remainder of the movement (105 measures) consists of a kaleidoscopic layering of these materials over one ever-present sustained chord (D–A–C-sharp). The explosion at letter 10, marked by the tam-tam stroke, pits a five-part eighth-note canon in the strings against quarter-note and half-note versions of the same tune in flutter-tongue trumpet and trombone. The ending superimposes the sustained chord in growling flutter-tongue muted trombones and tubas with the main three-note ostinato of the piece in the cellos and double basses. This is both an ending and an upbeat. In fact, the whole movement, with the exception of the passage between 14 and 15, has the character of a leap in the air.

The second movement, drenched in memory and nostalgia, is where the leap lands. Its opening two phrases (A), grounded

by D-minorish tonality, open out into a brief subsidiary section (B) that floats over a pedal point F-sharp in the celeste,

then sinks back into a reorchestrated statement of the beginning. A longer subsidiary section (C) ensues

that develops all the melodic material previously heard, eventually reaching a quiet whirlpool of repeating figures that themselves derive from the same melodies: canons in the celeste, an ostinato in the flutes, and eventually a nine-part canon of staccato sixteenth notes in the winds. Then this subsidiary section is expanded further with its melodies in augmentation and inversion. The return to the opening (A) refers back to all of this, combining the essentials of the opening music with the F-sharp pedal and tunes of (B) and the ostinato figures and augmentations of (C), compressing many recollections into a single moment, as one can in a film montage. But how to describe the strange evening spell cast by this piece, with its mix of song and stasis, poignant string melodies and repeating lonely celeste figures? As I listened to it the other day, sitting in a parked car in my small town, schoolgirls getting off the bus passed me, chatting and giggling, then a mother with three children hurried by, a couple looked into the window of the Spectacle Shop, pointed to something, and entered. Bathed in the sounds of "Vergangenes," these sights took on a dreamlike sadness.

"Farben," with its overlapping reorchestrations of repeating chords, anticipates the strange meditative calm and radical simplicity of the last of the Six Little Pieces for Piano. But since the chords do change and "progress," the effect is also like that of a pulsating chorale or hymn. The method of reorchestration also progresses and changes. It is hard not to think of metaphors while listening. The overlappings suggest the inhalations and exhalations of breathings, or waves—with the same chordal rock washed by changing groups of timbres. An alternative title for the piece was "Morning by a Lake," and Schoenberg referred to this figure as illustrating a "jumping fish."

Perhaps this movement represents the closest the composer Schoenberg ever came to the painter Schoenberg. There is even a moment (between 4 and 5) when the "colors" seem to run into each other and smudge.

The jumping-fish motive stays at the same pitch in its upward and downward forms throughout the movement, often

joined by harp, celeste, or harmonics, creating an effect suggesting glinting light.

The first chord (which is also the final one) as well as the rest of the harmonies are new kinds of musical objects: chords

that would have previously been considered dissonant but that now give off a warm, stable, Rothkoesque resonance and move not because they have to but because they choose to. There are three phrases of chords with two moments of suspended activity. At first the piece seems to progress from one static point to another, pierced by twinges from the jumping-fish idea and a low-register two-note figure in fifths (which moves downward in steps over the course of the piece).

The first phrase ends with a version of the opening chord transposed down a whole step and held in the low register by four cellos and contrabassoon. In a moment reminiscent of the Adagietto in Mahler's Fifth Symphony, the harp picks out the pitches of this chord as the motion is resumed. In the second phrase, an undeniable forward tug is felt as the uppermost note of the chords inches to its highest point. The rate of the overlappings then increases and becomes rhythmically and orchestrally fantastically intricate (the moment of "running colors"), as the harmonies sink back to the opening chord once again. As this chord is sustained in harmonics, the two-note figure is heard in the flutes and clarinet and a derivation of it is played by piccolos, harp, and celeste. The third phrase is once again more rhythmically regular, but orchestrally remarkably subtle and luminous. The piece ends on the harmony with which it began. The final three chords almost form a palindrome with the first three:

The movement can be followed by listening to the soprano voice of its "chorale" only:

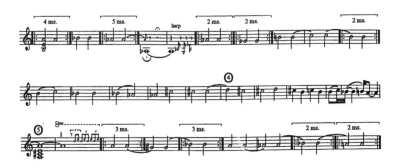

In movement 4 one returns to the crisis of movement 1. "Peripeteia" is defined as "a sudden change of fortune, in drama or in life" (*Oxford Concise Dictionary*). Here is a piece of music that would make an extraordinary interlude in an opera. The most heterogeneous of the Five Pieces in terms of characters, of ideas, and even, seemingly, of tempo (it sounds as if it is alternating between a fast and a slow tempo), it is actually in a single unchanging tempo and is made up of only a few basic ideas, of different rates of activity, strikingly varied and transformed. The three most obvious motifs are all heard piling on top of each other in the eruptive coda: a repeated-note figure, a slow-moving chromatic brass "smear" (as Robert Craft calls it), and a jagged ascending line (which is played at three different speeds in the coda). It is the frequent shifts in orchestration, rate of activity, and "mood" that give the movement its theatricality. Eight episodes can be easily discerned.

As exciting as the piece is in the context of opus 16, coming after two of the composer's most haunting creations, its effect is perhaps blunted. To this listener, at any rate, movement 4 becomes a revelation, listened to by itself.

After its most episodic movement, opus 16 ends with its most homogeneous one, a highly contrapuntal (generally five-to-six-part) organlike statement, in which the leading melodic line is passed continually from one register and instrumental group to another. The 3/8 rhythmic pulse lends the movement a tone of almost waltzlike regularity, of dailiness, at first, which makes the grandeur and prophetic intensity it amasses near the end all the more powerful. At its apex one feels as if the music is trying to burst its bonds, trying desperately to reach us. Then the urgency dies down and we are left with a hint of the overlapping chords of "Farben," ending in the world of that movement with a final exhalation on this sonority:

"The Obbligato Recitative" exudes a terrible world-weariness.

If movement 2 represents "The Past," perhaps it is possible to think of movements 1 and 4 as the active "Present," and 3 as "Eternity" or "Timelessness." In this interpretation, movement 5 addresses "The Future."

9

PATHS TO (AND IN)

ERWARTUNG

But you know the path and also a goal: must your path lead to your
goal? . . . Isn't the most important thing that you, on a path, are striv-
ing toward a goal?"
    —From Schoenberg's handwritten inscription in the copy of his
                       Harmonielehre given to Kandinsky

"I was seeking . . ."
                                        —Erwartung, *final line*

The Second Quartet formed, perhaps even described, a transition to a phase of Schoenberg's work characterized by phenomenal intensity, adventure, and expressivity, a phase that
includes several works that are among the high points of
twentieth-century music: *Erwartung*, the Five Pieces for Orchestra, and *Pierrot Lunaire* among them. If the quartet
formed a kind of bridge toward a new idiom, *The Book of the*
Hanging Gardens somehow seems to be the piece that floats
like an island between the old and new shores. Beginning with
his works of 1909, Schoenberg was in territory new not only

to him but also to music itself. He had achieved great mastery in his previous phase, having also fully absorbed the German-Austrian tradition from Bach through Mahler, and his works of this second phase—variously called "free atonality" or "expressionistic," for want of more precise terms—are the products of an extraordinary imagination and discipline set free; they possess a wildness and precision conceivable only after the achievement of mastery in a more codified form. Although musical principles and procedures can be deduced from these pieces now, they remain resistant to musical analysis; even Schoenberg himself claimed to understand and recognize certain aspects of their construction only when he studied the music in later life. That this music has an unprecedented density does not make it anarchic, however. On the contrary, one of the keys to understanding Schoenberg's work in this phase is to see to what extent it is, despite superficial appearances, a continuation of tradition. As Stravinsky said of his own musical explorations, the music in these works "obeys laws not yet written."

The plot of the monodrama (opera for one singer) *Erwartung*, the text for which was written by a medical student, Marie Pappenheim (whose portrait Schoenberg also painted), contains many of the elements of the traumatic Gerstl episode: an affair, jealousy, anxious waiting, a corpse that is discovered. It is a dreamlike, perhaps psychotic monologue set in a forest where the protagonist—a woman—searches for her lover, eventually discovering his dead body; it ends with her unfinished sentence "I was seeking . . ." The paths in the dense forest where the woman searches for the body of the man she may in fact have herself killed were meticulously drawn by Schoenberg in beautiful pen-and-ink and watercolor sketches.

While the search undertaken on these paths seems to us, in retrospect, to have both autobiographical and artistic overtones, we shouldn't underestimate the role played by the librettist in determining its nature. According to Schoenberg, the text was written under his direction, but in later years Pappenheim herself, who lived until 1966, claimed the text and all of the ideas behind it as entirely her own. The then-young doctor—whose cousin, Bertha Pappenheim, had been a patient of Josef Breuer's and was the basis for "The Case of Anna O." in Breuer and Freud's 1895 work *Studies on Hysteria*—had already written poetry reflecting her eerie view of the dead. These lines about a corpse, from her poem "Seziersaal" ("Autopsy Room"), which appeared in Karl Kraus's magazine *Die Fackel*, instantly evoke the world of *Erwartung*:

> *His mouth is pale and his eyes weary,*
> *as one who stares nightly into the darkness. . . .*
> *How sadly his desire wafts about me.*

Her description of her writing process suggests a trust in intuition and instinct (as well as a focus on small fragments of expression) that would have found an echo in Schoenberg's own views about art at that time: "I wrote lying in the grass, with pencil, on large sheets of paper, had no copy, scarcely read through what I had written. . . . I always wrote . . . without censorship. . . . Between the verses [I jotted down] other thoughts."

Schoenberg made significant alterations to Pappenheim's original text, including eliminating the more literal references to the murder of the woman's lover. Much as he had in his selections for *The Book of the Hanging Gardens*, he shifted attention away from clarity of narrative and toward the expression of emotions freed from their literal origins. In so doing he may have also radically altered the text's meaning. From being a realistic study of the plight of a woman in a state of hysteria, a plight that might have been avoided had the woman been less emotionally tied to her lover, it became a more purely emotional expression of the unconscious mind.

Schoenberg wrote much of his music at a feverish pace. He usually could not successfully complete a work once he had abandoned it. *Erwartung* was composed in just seventeen days!

In this work we are faced with what one might call dream form or psychological form. The piece begins as if already in progress. This is the beginning perhaps only in the sense that we have begun hearing it. It ends by seeming to evaporate— an ending like no other—but not without creating a further sense of "expectation" that the music will continue or start again from "the beginning."

Auden writes that the soul has no sense of humor. *Erwartung* seems to take place in the soul or the mind and is not a performance or theatrical offering to the audience, like the theatricalized song cycle *Pierrot Lunaire*. It is magical, luminous, eerie, marvelously varied—but without a social face; it does not have the irony or detachment or potential humor of *Pierrot*. It seems to be something that is happening to the protagonist, not to us. We participate by identifying with her dreamlike state.

A dream eliminates transitions; in a dream we find ourselves somewhere, we don't show ourselves how we got there. In a dream we do not need to establish character or identify ourselves. We already know who "I" is. A dream is not concerned with the development of an idea, or even with remembering itself as it passes. All these things also seem true of *Erwartung*, which gives the sense of taking place in a continually shifting present. In the audience of the theater, we find ourselves listening to this piece, and after only a very few notes we are simply in it. Like the protagonist, we often feel lost, but we also periodically find ourselves in very distinct places. Nevertheless, we are continuously captivated, even entranced. We have the dreamlike sensation of having been "here" before, since the intimate, psychic states evoked here—the terror, the confusion, the aloneness—instantly remind us of our own.

Schoenberg's new language was ideally suited to evoking such visionary states. Although, in the words of Oliver Neighbour, certain elements of "traditional practice"—such as thematic and motivic development—survived in this phase of his work, they took new form, making "swifter transformations and more abrupt contrasts" possible. Even more importantly, the independence of simultaneous musical events made possible by the lack of tonality permitted Schoenberg to present conflicting and "seemingly irreconcilable" textures and ideas at the same time, creating music that seemed to mirror the mind's own capacity for complex counterpoint.

He was, of course, still perfectly capable of presenting his materials in a more formal manner, one that creates a sense of logical progression and therefore, by extension, draws the listener's attention to the piece of music as an art object. But in *Erwartung* he obliterated any obvious signposts of the structure. The beginning:

plunges us into a fluid world in which one moment seems to blend into the next, much as the shifting orchestral colors do. The ideas and harmonies of this opening do indeed return again and again throughout the piece, and often in the very same key and with the same pitches. But the sense of form is deliberately obscured, so that one forgets that one is listening to a musical "work"; one enters the mental state of the protagonist and doesn't consciously think about musical materials. Throughout the score the singer returns obsessively to that first note in the oboe (C-sharp), as if to a sore tooth. Consider these many transformations of the opening oboe tune:

Though written "at white heat" (in Robert Craft's phrase), the piece clearly distinguishes the shifting mind states of the woman in an ongoing fabric of sensuous, evocative music that, while rent in several places—most notably at the "grand pause" where the woman swoons after discovering the corpse of her lover (measure 158)—never breaks. In the vocal part, the disjointed shards of thought in the text are set to tiny scraps of song, but these nevertheless cohere and connect and carry the listener forward.

Waves of seeming panic are balanced by the several lengthy passages of sustained lyricism in which texture, phrasing, rhythm, and vocal intervals reflect the woman's comparative lucidity. These passages include this hymnlike moment, which begins the long speech addressed to the corpse at measure 201:

The more angular and fragmented vocal lines evoke the woman's hysteria, the panic of seeking what she may in fact already know. By contrast, actual memories of her lover are suffused with the impulses of Brahmsian lieder and even waltz—fragments of "real world" music, such as these:

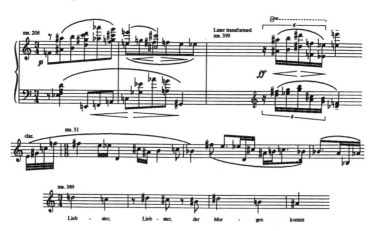

By such variety of writing does the accomplished (and sane) composer depict a once-whole character in a state of dissolution. To those who know Berg's *Wozzeck* (which was completed in 1922), the world of that opera's music—particularly for the scenes that take place in the woods—is vividly prefigured. *Wozzeck*, too, uses the orchestra to illuminate its central character's disintegration. Fragments of music from the "common world"—marches, tavern piano music, etc.—form a real-life contrast to music evoking psychological turmoil. The descending minor to major third motif of *Erwartung* foreshadows Wozzeck's "Ach Marie" motif. Like Wozzeck, the woman in *Erwartung* is—in the heightened sensitivity of her anxiety—touchingly observant of the details of nature around her. Among the things she notices are the silver tree branches (measure 5), the warmth of the night (measure 10), the cricket "still singing its love song" (measure 18), a rustling in the trees (measure 75), the moonlight (measure 92), and the lonely quiet of the moonlit road (measure 126), all of which are depicted in an impressionist manner in the score. For example, the mention of the cricket is accompanied by a repeating dissonant ostinato in the celeste and tremolo sul ponticello violin; the reference to the lonely road is sung against a single sustained chord in the woodwinds, trombones, and cellos.

Erwartung has no dialogue and virtually no external plot. Yet understanding it really requires hearing it as moment-to-moment theater. How is the listener—particularly one unable to read music—to learn to love these beautifully wrought bits of song, these desperate outcries? Perhaps the advent of CDs and tapes may help. One way to get to know the music is to follow it a minute at a time, text in hand, hearing it not as a generalized type of music but as a specific narrative in sound.

As dreamlike as *Erwartung* is, its structure and the way it establishes a sense of musical place is remarkable. The midpoint of the work is marked by the woman's recognition that the corpse is indeed her lover. Her cry of "*Hilfe*" ("Help") stretches an octave and a minor seventh, almost her entire range, from B to C-sharp (these are notes from the melody in the work's very first measure):

The cry reaches out to the world beyond the forest, to the audience itself, but only emphasizes her isolation.

The second half of the piece, then, is addressed to the lover's body, or at least in the conscious presence of it. Here perhaps her state of mind is reversed. Where there were scraps of "sanity" in the first half, here there is a greater proportion of continuous music, interrupted by moments of panic and disorientation. A moment of dead calm is achieved at measure 263 when she leans over to kiss her dead lover—the moment when she makes contact with external reality—at which a sustained eleven-note chord based on the work's opening harmony sends a chill up the spine of at least this listener. This is followed by a truly morbid bassoon melody in its highest register.

One gets a palpable sense of Schoenberg's genius when one reads the text for this moment by itself and then listens to its setting. This is one of the many moments of fixed stasis in the work, where the frantic darting to and fro of the anguished music becomes locked in a kind of tonal catatonia. It leads to a passage of mounting hysteria, which culminates in a complete breakdown of syntax. "No, no . . . my only love . . . not that . . . Oh, the moon is swaying . . . I can't see . . . ." At the words "my only love" (measure 315) there is a suggestion of both *Tristan* and the world of cabaret music:

Another climax, in both text and music, and one supportive of a feminist interpretation of the words (that in some sense the woman's hysteria is the result of her having no outlet for her emotions other than through a man and no place in the world other than with one), occurs when the woman declares, in rhythmically strict sustained tones, "Fur mich ist kein Platz da" ("There is no room for me here") (measure 350). After this she returns to the texture and manner of the first hymn-like passage of the corpse's discovery. Only now one has a physical sensation of the music's exhaustion, of being at a point not far from the end. This is partly the result of the formality of the phraseology and the nature of the vocal line. It is as if the angularity and rapidity of shifts characteristic of the piece were itself exhausted, leaving this tired remnant of traditional song. (This parallels what happens at the end of *Pierrot Lunaire*.) This is also a moment of truth for the protagonist, perhaps a moment when she is most in touch with external reality. She sings in an idiom closer to the familiar world of lieder, closer to traditional, externalized, social expression—the expression of a singer who can finally tell the audience who "I" is.

Erwartung achieves its many moods with writing of exquisite detail. There is, in a sense, no generalized "atmospheric" writing, only extreme visionary clarity. (This is one reason the music seems not to have aged.) Points of repose—or at least of orientation—are created by the many passages of static harmony or ostinati. Schoenberg was fond of repeating patterns in this period of his work—little idées fixes as in the opening of *Pierrot*, the second movement of Five Pieces for Orchestra, the third of the three tiny pieces for chamber orchestra of 1910. In *Erwartung* one finds ostinati used both to build and to release tension and excitement. In a work in which change has been occurring so continuously they are musically reassuring, but only partly so. Perhaps they act on our imagination a bit like clearings in the forest. We can see the sky but not a way out. Psychologically they remind one of the intense stares characteristic of Schoenberg's portraits. Music suggestive of rushing conflicting thought is interrupted by moments that are almost hypnotically locked in one place. In the transition from the third to the fourth scene an unchanging tremolo chord in the strings is combined with two different ostinati—in bassoon and flutes—against which trumpet and piccolo play a searing high melody. This musical object looms forward in an enormous crescendo to an accented chord in the brass and then, with the tune absent, gradually diminishes in volume. The repeating figures and the background harmony create an effect of musical tunnel vision—there is internal motion without external motion.

It is not possible to separate the psychology, the music, or the artistic meaning of this piece. (An aspect of Schoenberg's mystery is that his works seem inescapably rooted in his psychological makeup yet at the same time objective.) The idea of paths or a path—of finding one's path—is certainly an artistic as well as a personal notion at this time in Schoenberg's life. (Later, in 1927, he wrote a play about another kind of path called *Der biblische Weg*). The forest can be seen as the dark wood in which the nightmarish events of the preceding year in his personal life occurred. But it can also represent the uncharted forest of art, in which there is a search for a new form of expression.

10

WRONG NOTES

Though I have worked all my life in sound, from an academic point of view I do not even know what sound is (I once tried to read Rayleigh's Theory of Sound *but was unable mathematically to follow its simplest explanations).*
> —Igor Stravinsky, *Memories and Commentaries*

No art has been so hindered in its development by teachers as music, since nobody watches more closely over his property than the man who knows that, strictly speaking, it does not belong to him.
> —Schoenberg, *Theory of Harmony*

I played the wrong *wrong notes.*
> —Thelonious Monk

Charles Rosen refers to the consistent use of a common trichord (a group of three pitches) that is a recurring source for the prevailingly six-tone harmonies in *Erwartung*: a note surrounded by a perfect fourth below and tritone above, or its reverse (a fourth above and a tritone below):

This characteristic Schoenbergian sound also appears as an important thumbprint in works as early as *Pelleas und Melisande*, where one hears it as perfect fifth and diminished fifth in the context of a minor chord:

Yet shorn of an explicitly tonal context, as in the "Entrück-ung" movement of the Second String Quartet,

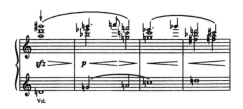

it still suggests the toniclike stability of the perfect fifth with, as it were, a lowered fifth or raised fourth degree attached to it. The most stable with the least stable, this strange pair of inter-vals seems somehow to cling to the tonality that it helps to undermine.

One can pose the question: When, exactly, does the origi-nal reference point for this sound lose its pertinence?

As one travels down the road from a mountain, the moun-tain's shape recedes, becoming eventually a dot; but the viewer knows that it is still a mountain.

A mountainlike shape is placed on a canvas; the painter entitles the work "Mountain." A mountainlike shape is placed on the canvas; the painter entitles the work "Form." A dot is placed on the canvas; the painter entitles the work "Mountain."

The cat walks across the piano keys; the ear that hears the notes has heard them before, only differently, in a context more deliberately ordered. But notes are beautiful. The cat, while certainly musical, is no composer. Yet the uncomposed notes have an unsuspected potential and beauty.

You play a dominant seventh chord; you add notes; you change notes; soon none of the notes are the same, yet perhaps you still hear the chord as "acting like" a dominant seventh, because of the power of memory and of the ear's ability to sort out, substitute, "read" into sounds, because those of us alive today will never forget how these same twelve tones of the chromatic scale were used in music employing major and minor keys. Even if we did forget, such music is with us every day.

Beethoven preceded Schoenberg, and it will never be the other way around.

In their wonderful book about Stravinsky, *The Apollonian Clockwork*, Louis Andriessen and Elmer Schönberger quote Thelonious Monk complaining after a concert: "I played the *wrong* wrong notes." Watching Monk playing the piano in the film *Straight, No Chaser*, one sees the concentration of a composer: the choices rejected, those made, the sense of responsibility, the all-out effort up until the last note to keep pushing further, to add, to surprise, to leave out, to find the right wrong notes. One sees a composer working at a rapid, intense pace, not with pencil and paper but at the piano itself.

At his desk, Schoenberg also worked at a rapid pace, and during the period we are discussing, in a near-trance state, believing passionately that art should come primarily from the unconscious.

What if Schoenberg's music had been improvised? What if it belonged to the world of "free jazz"? Or more realistically, what if the technical aspect of Schoenberg's music had been kept secret when it was first introduced? Would it have more easily found a following if it had been presented as a form of spontaneous expression?

Many jazz musicians, most notably Duke Ellington, have revered Schoenberg. Played in a jazz context at the Village Vanguard in the late 1970s by Paul Jacobs (alongside jazz-tinged pieces by Rzewski, Bolcom, and others), the opening sliding four-note chords of Schoenberg's twelve-tone opus 33a sounded like harmonies found under the fingers of a progressive jazz pianist, the quicker flurries of pitches like brilliant impromptu riffs, the songful phrases like wisps of melancholy soulfulness. The very first time I had heard the piece, in a classroom, I had been handed a sheet showing its row forms and asked to put the appropriate number above every note in the piece. This "analysis," which led to neither comprehension nor pleasure in the piece, connected itself in my mind with the title, opus "THIRTY-THREE" "A," and it was some time before I could look at the title without associating it with the effort it took to decode that strange mathematical puzzle.

What did Monk mean by the "*wrong* wrong notes"?

J. S. Bach was accused of creating fearsome dissonances in his church organ improvisations. Mozart could surprise the listener with anguished discords that seem as unprepared as they are accented (for example, in the "Dissonant" String Quartet, and the Fortieth Symphony). In Robert Schumann's *Kreisleriana*, op. 16, we find this passage

in which the bass notes and chords concur with those in the right hand but change at the "wrong" time, momentarily creating such harmonies as:

Although the ear understands the process and knows what the "right" version would be, it also registers the deliberate unease created by the dislocation. This is a kind of distortion we usually think of as typically *twentieth* century, right things in the wrong places, as in those portraits by Picasso in which the features of the face are repositioned and read to us as both wrong and expressively "right" at the same time.

Charles Ives in some of his music conveyed the sounds of mishaps, clinkers, out-of-tune violins, the sounds of unsynchronized playing; he meticulously notated the moments when a player gets off by a sixteenth note in a band performance, trailing comically and dissonantly behind the beat (his father had been a marching-band leader in the Civil War and an inveterate musical experimenter), or the clashes of simultaneous performances, or the sound of discordant (because undisciplined) group singing in a hymn where the fervor of the choir exceeds its skill—out of which he created art, capturing the joyfully anarchic sound of the orchestra tuning up and the mayhem of a hundred musicians playing different things at the same time, but in a way that one wants to listen to again and again because there is precision, vision, and science behind it. It isn't *actually* anarchic, it *expresses* the anarchic. Ives spoke of wanting to play the notes "in the cracks between the keys."

In a different spirit, Stravinsky rewrote classical harmonies in the "wrong" way, strangely rehearing them, superimposing what used to be juxtaposed, compacting what used to be linear, cutting and wrapping around itself a once recognizable shape. At such moments he suggests cubism. One could "sort out" some of Stravinsky's passages (such as the opening of the second movement of his "Dumbarton Oaks" Concerto) but the process would be more complex than in the Schumann example referred to above. Not only are there realignments, elisions, substitutions, but there is an element of collage as well: the addition of incongruities comparable to the pasted strips of newspaper or signlike lettering ("TABAC") found in the work of Braque.

Stravinsky composed directly at the piano. He said that he listened carefully to his "mistakes."

Then there are the "wrong" notes of composers such as Prokofiev, who wrote tonal music that proceeded in an essentially traditional manner, with the addition of flavorful distortions and substitutions.

Bitonality can create the illusion that one is hearing two strands of music, one of which *would* be right if it were simply transposed into the key of the other. Milhaud carried the principle out for long passages, such as one in *Saudades do Brasil* that begins like this:

But even small touches of bitonality can be intelligible. In the march music in Berg's *Wozzeck*, the accompanying C-sharps and G-sharps would harmonize correctly with the melody in the first measure if they were Ds and Gs, so the C-sharp and G-sharp are "wrong" in a clearly logical way that the ear instictively grasps:

The "wrong" notes in Schoenberg are of a still different kind. What does one make of the opus 11 piano piece,

where the seemingly unrooted chromatic melody is heard against the backdrop of an oscillating minor third in the left hand that sets up a D-minorish gravitational field? Yet how could anything sound more "right"? What is one to make of this passage in his Piano Concerto, op. 42?

Here the accompanying piano figure is slavishly unsupportive of the melody. (The twelve-tone principle involved is called "combinatoriality," the use of rows in which the inversion produces the contents of the two halves of the original series in reverse order.) This lack of harmonic euphony between melody and accompaniment lies at the heart of the charge that Schoenberg's music is more theoretically than aurally based. These wrong notes are "wrong" in a way that differs profoundly from the wrong notes of Stravinsky, Prokofiev, Monk, and possibly Ives, as well. Yet they, too, originate in the instincts of a great composer's ear, not his theories.

In a noteworthy article on Schoenberg's "atonality," British musicologist Hans Keller argues that Schoenberg never ceased to hear tonally—that the secret of the strange comprehensibility of his melodies and harmonies is that they are "foreground" deviations from a tonal "background." In fact, he maintains that if you play a passage from a twelve-tone work such as the Third String Quartet very slowly, you can fill in mentally the tonal subtext that is being subverted and bypassed, in the same way that you can sense the rhythmically foursquare version of a series of phrases by Mozart in which there are implied compressions, extensions, or artful ellipses. In this interpretation, Schoenberg's "wrong" notes are the "right" ones because of their tonal implications, however submerged. Keller would seem to be suggesting that in this music the intervals, far from being arbitrary or deprived of their original meaning, are all the more expressive because of the suppression of their resolutions and meanings.

Following his argument through to its logical conclusion, he states that the so-called return to tonality in Schoenberg's late works is no return at all but simply an allowing back into the "foreground" of some of those tonal implications.

This position would seem to suggest that some of Schoenberg's notes are ultimately to be heard as in some sense substitutes, signposts, summaries, or bridges, but not as the "right" ones. To this listener, at least, no amount of filling in or chromatic harmonization can make any of the notes of the right hand in the above example from opus 11 (for instance, that big sonorous D-flat) seem less strong and important than the supporting D–F in the bass. Or vice versa.

Intriguingly, there *are* literal "wrong" notes in the twelve-tone works, notes that violate the row order, where the composer simply lost his place or was inattentive. When he was asked about such places Schoenberg never changed the notes back to the "right" ones. He respected the deeper instinct that had led to the error.

II

SIX LITTLE PIECES

Sechs kleine Klavierstücke, op. 19, is a set of six tiny pieces
containing a total of seventy-two measures, lasting roughly five
minutes. In density of compression they bear comparison with
Webern's Six Bagatelles for String Quartet, op. 9 (1911–13)
and Berg's Four Pieces for Clarinet and Piano (1913). For the
Webern pieces, which last a total of three and a half minutes,
Schoenberg wrote an introduction in the score that was defiant
and poetic, expressing a support for the music that was clearly
tinged with the pain of anticipating that it would have very few
sympathetic listeners. Schoenberg begins with the observation
that even though "the brevity of these pieces is a persuasive advocate for them, on the other hand that very brevity itself requires an advocate." He continues by describing the brevity in

Webern as "concentration," as if a novel were expressed "in a single gesture, joy in a breath." An important line in the paragraph that follows is this: "These pieces will only be understood by those who share the faith that music can say things which can only be expressed by music."

With these words Schoenberg shows the same protectiveness of music, the same belief in its untranslatable eloquence, and the same fatigue at hearing it described in terms of its ability to evoke other art forms or even real events that Stravinsky expressed in his famous statement "Music is powerless to express anything at all."

Composers often rightly and understandably retreat to a position behind their sounds, letting the sounds do the talking. Sometimes if they say anything at all, it is to describe the technical aspect of their work. It is the music that matters, after all, the music and the emotion to be found *in* the music itself, and who cares what emotions motivated it?

Nevertheless, in each new artistic language, no matter how technical its description, a new world of feeling is given form, and that world must correspond in some way to the artist's inner world, otherwise he or she would not be creating it. For example, it is obvious that a specifically personal and twentieth-century feeling is expressed by the gestures of Martha Graham's choreography. Her celebrated "contraction" is not simply a "device." In the same way there is a new world of feeling in the works of Schoenberg from 1910 to 1913. There is a new world of feeling in this phrase, for example (from piece no. 1), as traditional as is its rhythm, texture, and use of the piano:

It is a phrase that begins at its high point melodically and at its most tense harmonically. The two first chords are the most dissonant, the third—containing only thirds—is more euphonious, and the fourth contains an appoggiatura that resolves into a diminished triad. The phrase traces a downward sigh and release of tension. In its visceral character, and almost queasy chromaticism, it is of 1911, and it is imbued with the feeling of that time and of its author. Schoenberg expresses this better than I can when he says in *Harmonielehre* (*Theory of Harmony*):

> That which is new and unusual about a new harmony occurs to the true composer only [because] he must give expression to something that moves him, something new, something previously unheard-of. His successors, who continue working with it, think of it as merely a new sound, a technical device; but it is far more than that: a new sound is a symbol, discovered involuntarily, a symbol proclaiming the new man who so asserts his individuality.

Among the "new and unusual" sounds, in these epigrammatic pieces, and a sound expressive of its time, is the sound of silence itself: the power of the spaces between the notes. For Webern this became a definitive discovery. Concision, brevity, purity, extreme sensitivity to timbre and pitch, to vibration and silence became permanent hallmarks of his work from here on in. For Berg and Schoenberg this was somewhat less the case, although the chamber music–like quality of Schoenberg's writing and his love of quietude is one of his most obvious characteristics. (In fact, he always counseled his students that when they were writing loud passages they should consider whether these might not be more eloquent played softly.) In Berg's *Lulu* and in Schoenberg's later works, there is a return to the long, arching melodic line and expansive form. Webern's music remained epigrammatic, although never to the extent it was during this period of his writing.

One is tempted to compare Schoenberg's own Six Pieces to brief poems in which each word carries tremendous weight, but this comparison will go only so far. One would read such a poem more slowly and carefully than one would read a poem less dense, whereas these pieces are to be played in the tempi indicated. To think of each note or phrase as more weighty than "usual," is to suggest something overly precious and ponderous. These are exquisite and limpid little pieces. They are not fragments or bits of something that might have been more extensive; they are short, complete expressions, deeper than they are long.

Pieces 1 through 5 were all composed in one day, on February 19, 1911. The sixth was written on June 17, under the impression of Mahler's funeral, which had occurred on May 21. (Mahler died on May 18.) Following this event Schoenberg also painted his haunting picture *The Burial of Gustav Mahler*.

In the absence of major or minor key tonality, we have extreme concision, along the lines of the three incomplete pieces for chamber ensemble that he composed in 1910. We are in an intimate, private realm, worlds away from the public gigantism of the *Gurre-Lieder* (or of the works by Wagner and Mahler that that oratorio emulates). This is music of short phrases and episodes, passages of contrasting textures that, instead of covering a page, can be as brief as a few notes or as a single chord progression. This music also contains beautiful voice leading, melody, and accompaniment, expressive gestures of many familiar kinds, sensuosity, formal clarity—in short, many features familiar from previous eras of music. To say that "tonality" is entirely absent here would not be quite true. Several of the pieces do gravitate around a central sonority. The opening and closing phrases of each piece sound and feel like beginnings and endings. Every piece ends with a gesture of unmistakable finality, and three (nos. 1, 3, and 5) end with a pair of chords mimicking a tonal cadence. The overall journey of the work as a series of evocative moments would be felt by almost any listener of any age.

The first piece is the most orchestral and diverse, suggesting the dreamlike world of *Erwartung*. Shorn of its accompaniment, the soprano line could be the opening of a melody by Brahms (in B major)

and among the other seeming suggestions of "B major" are the right hand in measure 7

and the last bar,

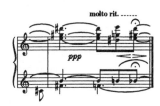

which, with the removal of three notes, could be rearranged to make:

The lyricism of the longer lines surrounded by fleeting counterpoint and shards of harmony remind one of transitional
music tied to visual incident in a stage work, and the chromaticism of more than a few moments carries a hint of Wagnerian longing:

Depending upon what one considers to be a unit, there are
approximately a dozen episodes in this seventeen-measure
piece, and they are so suggestive that one finds oneself trying
to tie them to an imaginary scenario. What glimmering apparition appears at measure 7, chased away by whom or by
what thought at measure 8?

As in *Erwartung*, there are patterns of tension and release,
"confusion" and "lucidity," as when the tremolo chord of
measure 9 subsides into a held chord, suggesting an abating
anxiety that makes possible the deep breath of silence at measure 12. A small, hymnlike moment emerges from this (measures 12–13), a more explicit "song," only to collapse back
into the prevailingly mysterious tone (measure 15).

The alternating chords at measure 3, which act as a kind of cadence to the first two phrases, are transposed upward and extended in the final cadence of the piece, and the small tune in the left hand of measure 3 is now drawn out to fold back into the notes of the opening melody. (In this form it resembles the opening of Berg's Piano Sonata, completed in 1908, during his studies with Schoenberg.) This ending maintains the feeling of a cadence, of closure, and, in every respect but pitch, is identical to an ending that one could find in a thousand Baroque and classical era works. But the contemporary sense of closure achieved here leaves the tonality and the questions implied by the music unresolved:

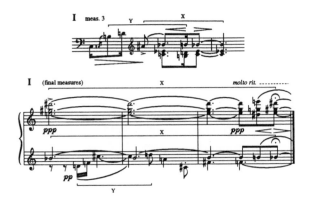

It is striking that this rich and romantic opening piece is not followed by five short pieces in a similar vein but by five that trace a progression: through the contrastingly cold and economical second, the broadly lyrical third, the choleric and compressed fourth, the fleeting and sadly retrospective fifth, to the bell-like sixth. These six pieces are held in perfect balance—perfectly balanced and permanently strange, one might add. Only the first contains changes of meter. The varieties of textures explored in the first piece are taken up by pieces nos. 3, 4, and 5, but by none in the same diversity. The idea of a repeating sound with B as its uppermost note recurs in pieces nos. 2 and 6. The last piece can be viewed as an expansion of the first measure of piece no. 2—three repeating chords, two rests, and a fourth repeat of the chord. In this reading, the two eighth rests of piece no. 2, measure 1, become measures 7 and 8 of the last piece.

Piece no. 2 is the polar opposite of piece no. 1. Made of almost nothing but thirds, it also contains a few different rhythmic values: eighth notes, quarters, dotted quarters, and half notes. While 1 was fluid and mercurial, 2 is dry and stark. While there was one interrupting static moment in 1 (the left-hand chord in measures 8–12), there is but one bar of quick harmonic motion in 2, which otherwise contains the core sound of the major third G–B in every bar. Piece no. 2 starts with a dripping faucet, the "drip-drip-drip-rest-rest-drip-rest-rest" of this third, sounding exactly like a Mozart or Haydn accompaniment figure, and when the "tune" enters at the end of bar 2, it confirms G major for the first two eighths before becoming its real, nontonal self.

Why does the opening G–B third sound so perfect after the

chromaticisms of piece no. 1? At least in part because the same sound in the same register is contained in that static section in piece no. 1. It is also contained in the very first gesture of that piece as well. (In fact, so are the notes of the strange tune in measure 3 that Haydn would never have written.)

This piece plays with thirds—the old building blocks of traditional harmony—as if they were a set of child's toy blocks. The last chord piles one on top of the other into what again seems like a tonal "pun," a cadence on "C" that contains the original G–B third, now seeming like a "dominant." This little teetering tower (technically a fifteenth chord) is a kind of object of contemplation and feels temporarily restful.

II

Piece no. 2 also seems a bit of a palindrome. If one thinks of the last measure as a coda and reads the piece backwards, starting with measure 8, it becomes clear that the piece divides into two halves that roughly mirror each other. Looked at in this way, measure 5 seems a kind of mirror/repeat of measure 4; and the moment of darkness at measure 6—when the rising thirds swallow up all the notes of the earlier (non-Haydn) tune, while adding a new note, C-sharp, and come to rest on that dense chord (which also derives from the tune)—is a variation of measure 3. From here on the right hand returns to the G–B of the opening, but with the rhythm clipped of one note and reversed, while the left hand descends with major thirds to that fifteenth-chord "tonic."

Piece no. 3 startles us with its rich right-hand chords played forte against a very melodious left hand playing pianissimo. This surprising acoustical effect works beautifully, and the left-hand melody is all the more expressive for being the only instance of octaves in the piece. How rich and fresh the octaves sound! The first harmony is very close to the building-block chord that ended piece no. 2, and it also catches a fistful of the notes from the dark chord heard in measure 6 of that piece. The sensitively contrapuntal phrase in measures 5–6, which starts with the identical G–B that permeates piece no. 2, is in the spirit of the hymn-like statement near the end of piece no. 1 (measure 13). Then the voices thin out; the octaves are gone; we are down to a single line and then again there is a quasi-cadential pair of chords:

(The bass line B-flat to E-flat reverses the two opening bass notes of the movement; the first chord is a dominant ninth chord; the final chord is identical to the first chord of the piece transposed down a major third.)

Piece no. 4 is volatile, the eruptive climax of the set. A detail near the end of piece no. 3,

a sustained tone punctuated by a staccato chord, bears fruit here:

In this piece there is a veritable catalog of different rhythmic values, a dynamic range from pianissimo to fortissimo, and an instability of tempo caused by two ritards, all within a mere thirteen measures. The pileup of thirds that ended piece no. 2 forms the basis of the opening melody and much of the harmony. The ending greatly telescopes the opening, giving it a feeling of great violence:

Just as he created great weight of sound with the quiet left-hand octaves in piece no. 3, Schoenberg manages to create an ending that seems like a "bang," with only the single note B:

Piece no. 5's retrospective character is something that I feel as a listener, but I am not sure I can explain it. The piece seems to hearken back to piece no. 1, but hurriedly, as if running out of time. The 3/8 flowing rhythms recall the opening's 6/8, as do the sustained lines set against fleeting sixteenth notes. Comparing the openings also shows a family resemblance. The breathless romantic phrasings of measures 4–9 resemble the hesitant declarations of piece no. 1. The little alternating chords at bar 7 and the "cadence" at the end also seem to come from that piece. Measure 12 to the end could be seen as a variation of piece no. 1's measure 13 to the end:

The language of thirds beginning at bar 9 reminds us of the thirds in piece no. 2, the opening and coda of piece no. 4. There are clear references back to the alternating cadential chords in piece no. 1:

It seems safe to say that this is a piece of a developmental character, a hearkening back.

Mahler was buried in Grinzing Cemetery on May 21, 1911, at his request in the same grave as his eldest daughter, Putzi. His funeral must have left those present profoundly affected. In spite of the difficulties created by his autocratic personality, he had clearly been viewed by a large circle of artists as a central figure, a link not only to the greatest composers of the past but, through his own monumental and highly original works and through his courageous advocacy of the artwork of the younger generation, to the future. To sense this one has only to read of the scene on December 9, 1907, at the Vienna train station when an already ailing Mahler and his wife began their journey to America, where he was to conduct the New York Philharmonic. More than two hundred artists, composers, singers, and other friends were there, among them Schoenberg, Berg, and Webern. Many were in tears. Surprised, Mahler moved through the group shaking hands. In a sense Schoenberg began saying good-bye to Mahler at that very moment. His own period of crisis commenced shortly afterwards. Mahler's work, too, contains many *Abschiede*.

One can speculate that for Schoenberg Mahler's death represented not just the end of one great composer's life but the end of a good deal more. The bells in opus 19, number 6, seem somehow to convey this.

Piece no. 6 comes from a different world than the previous five pieces, echoing no. 1 from a great distance, catching some of its sounds. A few of them are the fourth chord of measure 1:

I

VI

The neighbor note D-sharp–E–D-sharp from the last measure of piece no. 1:

The baritone-range solo line at measures 10–12 in piece no. 1:

Perhaps we hear an echo of the pedal chord D–E-flat–G–B in the chord progression at measure 8 (which reminds me of a beautiful flower being pressed)

 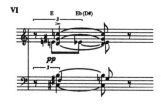

or perhaps only an echo of the cadential formulas and abundant half steps of these pieces, all crushed into one harmony.

There are two tolling bells at first, high, and middle range. The notion of alternating chords itself seems suggested by those chords in measure 3 of piece no. 1. A third bell tolls a fourth chord between the first two, at measure 5. This connects the bells even more clearly to measure 3 of piece no. 1, since the B and B-flat are in the same registers as they were in that measure:

That drop of a minor ninth paves the way for the solo line at measure 7, which also begins with that interval. This tiny fragment of lamenting chant seems oddly related to the "non-Haydn" tune of piece no. 2:

Then the coffin is lowered—or so it might seem to the listener. (This is the "pressed flower" chord progression. It contains the E–D-sharp, too.) Now the pianissimo bells: first high, then middle, and then two low tones, one deep, the second deeper, played pianissimo ("*wie ein Hauch*"), the only time, with the exception of a few octave doublings in piece no. 3, that this register is reached in the set.

It is not known if Schoenberg had seen the score of Mahler's Ninth Symphony when he wrote this piece. It is possible.

Berg may have seen the score as early as 1910; in an undated letter to his wife, Helene, he wrote of it that it was permeated by thoughts of death. But the letter probably dates from 1912, if not later. The first public performance of Mahler's Ninth did not occur until June 26, 1912.

The final movement of the Ninth becomes attenuated to the point of evoking nonbeing. It, too, ends with four PPPPs, reducing its themes to echoes and whispers. The first movement of the symphony begins in D major, with this ostinato figuring prominently,

over which the violins sing:

The sixth of the Little Pieces begins with this chord:

Among the most prominent themes in the finale of the Mahler is this one,

which in the final measures is reduced to

Schoenberg, opus 19, number 6:

The last notes of the symphony:

And of opus 19:

We also shouldn't neglect to note that the bell chords of piece no. 6 outline the G–B of piece no. 2:

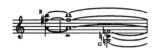

Evidence that G–B forms a reference point throughout the six pieces is not hard to find (at the ends of pieces nos. 3 and 4, for example), but whether this is the result of a conscious or unconscious order I couldn't say. Whether or not Schoenberg himself could have reconstructed his process of work in an analytical way, I also don't know. Even in as systematic a piece as his Variations for Orchestra, a twelve-tone work, he found reconstructing the idea behind a variation that he had temporarily put aside extremely difficult.

Whatever the underlying logic of these pieces, Sechs kleine Klavierstücke, ninety years after its composition, remains a haunting, seemingly indestructible set of gems.

Gustav Mahler

12

THEORY OF HARMONY

The young artist . . . believes that his work is at no point distinguishable from what is generally found to be good in art; and all of a sudden he is violently awakened from his dream, when the harsh reality of criticism makes him aware that somehow he is not so normal after all, as a true artist should never be normal; he lacks perfect agreement with those average people who were educable, who could submit wholly to the "Kultur." —Schoenberg, *Theory of Harmony*

The uproar continued, however, and a few minutes later I left the hall in a rage; I was sitting on the right near the orchestra, and I remember slamming the door. I have never again been that angry. The music was so familiar to me; I loved it, and I could not understand why people who had not yet heard it wanted to protest it in advance.

—Stravinsky on the first performance of *Le Sacre du Printemps*

Not long after the belated premiere of the *Gurre-Lieder*, on February 23, 1913, caused a euphoric fifteen-minute standing ovation, a concert of the newest music of Schoenberg, Berg, and Webern in the same city on March 31, 1913, gave rise to fistfights and shouting matches and ended with a portion of the audience physically storming the stage. In an ensuing lawsuit a doctor testified that in his opinion the music presented was "enervating and injurious to the nervous system."

Meanwhile Schoenberg's massive *Harmonielehre* (*Theory of Harmony*), which he had worked on alongside his radical compositions of 1910 and 1911, and in which he explicated his understanding of the tonality he was leaving behind, had been published by Universal Edition. The five-hundred-page *Harmonielehre*, a personal theory of harmony, is a unique combination of philosophical and practical writing. As befits the work of a man who, let us recall, even developed an individual way of holding a pen, *Harmonielehre* takes nothing for granted. Even such staples of theory texts as the circle of fifths are presented in a novel way, and many technical definitions and explanations are rethought.

Schoenberg starts from scratch, tracing the organization of the major-minor key system from a single tone (*Klang*), which is itself already a composite sound containing a complex series of overtones. From here he progresses all the way to a discussion of modulations to distant keys, the use of unusual harmonies, and eventually the chromatic scale itself as the basis for composing. Through his skepticism about received wisdom and his ever-active inquisitiveness of mind, he thus opens the door toward other types of tonal systems based on other scales and toward systems in which the word *tonality* itself would have to be redefined. (Schoenberg never accepted the term *atonal* as a description of his work.) What he seems to most abhor are ways of writing that only pretend to be using the old tonality, those nontonal pieces that display a tonal "coat of arms," as he puts it, at convenient cadential points, simply as a mannerism.

Significantly, when he introduces near the end of the book what were then still rather outré materials—such as the whole-tone scale or chords constructed of fourths—he always traces their development from their first introduction in conventional tonal contexts, wrestling with their justification in a quasi-ethical manner. He demonstrates, for example, how the use of the whole-tone scale as an independent entity (in the works of Debussy and others) was preceded by its use as a series of passing tones over augmented triads and as the result of augmented triads moving in contrary motion over each other. Thus, the ear first became habituated to their use in a context in which they functioned tonally and then accepted them when they were used independently for their own sake. In discussing whole-tone chords he shows how they can function as dominants and how they can smoothly resolve into more conventional harmonies. He states that the first appearance of new sounds have an impressionistic effect expressive of "a mood of nature" and that they are "an omen of possibilities . . . enveloped by a mysterious luster." But whether he believes that these functional uses of a novel harmony or scale always precede its more impressionistic use, or in fact follow it, is not entirely clear, since while he makes a point of saying that they first appear as a result of a "powerful expressive urge," in every case he illustrates how they can derive from voice leadings in a conventionally tonal context. In his discussion of fourth chords, for example, he shows how he himself employed them in a relatively conventional context in *Pelleas und Melisande* (1902–03) and later as true thematic and structural material in the Chamber Symphony no. 1, op. 9, of 1906.

"Against my will—I still remember, even today, that I hesitated to notate this sound. The clarity with which it forced itself upon me, however, made it impossible for me to dismiss it." Thus speaks the reluctant radical.

About these very fourth chords Glenn Gould says: "The theory of dissonance within the system of tonality is that it must be derived from and resolve into, in fact be an embellishment of, a fundamental progression. . . . Schoenberg is here examining the consequences of relating dissonantly conceived chordal progressions to a basic triad harmony, not simply extracting closely related dissonances from triad harmonic functions."

Put another way, perhaps in this transitional phase of Schoenberg's work, he was still managing to find a tonally defensible way to employ nearly "atonal" harmonies, ways modeled after the more bizarre moments in the works of the masters, when extreme chromatic harmonies defying conventional analysis resulted from smoothly logical voice leadings. What Schoenberg clearly could not defend, however, would be a hybrid language, cobbled together simply for emotional effect.

Near the end of his book, Schoenberg attempts to confront issues raised by chords with six or more different pitches, arguing in the case of an eleven-tone chord from *Erwartung* that, because of the orchestration and the way the pitches are arranged, the ear sorts out the sound into groups that constitute "previously known forms" or that suggest a resolution that does not need to be heard to be understood.

He goes even further toward the metaphysical in describing a chord progression of Alban Berg's: "That it is correct I firmly believe. . . . Even the spacing is obligatory. . . . Laws apparently prevail here. What they are I do not know." Yet the seeds of a new kind of organization can also be found in the next lines, about the unanalyzable Berg chord progression, which "seems to be regulated by the tendency to include in the second chord tones that were missing from the first, generally those a half step higher or lower. . . . Then, I have noticed that [in this new harmonic idiom] tone doublings [and] octaves seldom appear" lest they become overly emphasized and come to resemble a quasi-tonal root.

These lines remind us that in feeling their way toward the twelve-tone idea, Schoenberg, Berg, and Webern were guided by an instinctive avoidance of octaves and pitch repetition, recognizing that all the notes of the chromatic scale needed to be treated as equals if the gravitational pull toward a tonal center was to be avoided. Webern records in *The Path to the New Music* that while composing his tiny Six Bagatelles for String Quartet, op. 9, he would check off each pitch from the chromatic scale as he employed it, finding that the piece seemed to have been completed when the last pitch was sounded. No wonder those first nontonal works were so brief! The chromatic scale had become the new measure of wholeness, and in the longer works the "inner ear" led the composers to avoid repeating a pitch until the other twelve had sounded.*

Throughout *Harmonielehre* the composer/theorist paves the way toward the moment when the old tonal scaffolding can be removed from beneath the new sounds, revealing a music of linear and vertical beauty obeying as yet unknown harmonic laws. In his chapter on the chromatic scale as a basis for tonality he comes right out with it: "We are turning to a new epoch of polyphonic style, and as in the earlier epochs, harmonies will be a product of the voice leading: justified solely by melodic lines!" He also points out, as sooner or later any teacher of basic music theory has to, that our notation would be more accurate—at least for much twentieth-century music—if it gave an independent symbol for each of the twelve pitches and not seven note names with five sharps or flats. The seven note names come from music that employs seven-note scales.

About cadences he writes: "The ceremonious way in which the close of a composition used to be tied up, nailed down, and sealed would be too ponderous for the present-day sense of form to use it. This precondition that everything emanates

---

*Perhaps it is not too fanciful to think of tiny pieces like the ten-measure third movement of Webern's Three Little Pieces for cello and piano, op. 11, as twelve-tone pieces made of the basic set stated once.

from the [fundamental] tone can just as well be suspended, since one is constantly reminded of it anyway by every tone." Or later: "Nothing is lost from the impression of completeness if the tonality is merely hinted at, yes, even if it is erased. . . . It may be perhaps that we simply do not yet know how to explain the tonality or something corresponding to tonality in modern music."

The idea of "something corresponding to tonality" may slip by almost unnoticed by us, but at the time of writing it can only have caused astonishment.

No music-theory book is more sensible and commonsensical in its explanations than this one, and none relies more faithfully on the empirical evidence presented in works by the masters. Yet none is more subversive of what it explains or more on the side of creative intuition:

> The evolution of no other art is so greatly encumbered by its teachers as is that of music. . . . The theorist, who is not usually an artist, or is a bad one (which means the same thing), therefore understandably takes pains to fortify his unnatural position. . . .
>
> To hell with all these theories, if they always serve only to block the evolution of art and if their positive achievement consists in nothing more than helping those who will compose badly to learn it quickly. . . . The laws of art consist mainly of exceptions.

From the very first chapters on the major scale, Schoenberg reminds the pupil that while it is essential to learn the basis of tonality and how to produce it, it in no way constitutes an "eternal law": "Let him know that the conditions leading to the dissolution of the system are inherent in the conditions upon which it is established."

In flagrant contrast to the tone of most music-theory texts—indeed to textbooks generally—material is presented not as faceless, incontrovertible fact but rather as something embedded in the human condition itself: "Let the pupil learn by this example to recognize what is eternal: change, and what is temporal: being."

Equally importantly, one sees from the outset that one is learning the carpentry of music—not the laws of creation itself. "The order we call artistic form is not an end in itself but an expedient. As such by all means justified, but to be rejected absolutely wherever it claims to be more, to be aesthetics."

Interspersed with the very first presentation of major and minor triads are observations about what constitute order and beauty in art, Schoenberg averring that it is a delusion to think that an artist's goal is to create beauty. Only the "compulsion to produce" a work yields a result that can eventually be found to be beautiful. He speaks of order not as necessarily the obligation of the artist but more as something the listener wishes to find, and is likely to find, just as we find order in the manifold complexities of nature. In the first edition of the book (1911), written alongside *Erwartung* and *Pierrot*, he actually says that beauty does not presuppose order. In the revised edition (1921), emended alongside work on his first twelve-tone compositions, he says that while art may not be able to do without "order, clarity, and comprehensibility," these qualities can be found elsewhere than where we have previously found them. This is surely a crucial distinction and shows that in the intervening years Schoenberg had found the need to be more consciously aware of the guiding principles behind his composing.

About "beauty" he writes: "Beauty exists only from that moment in which the uncreative begin to miss it. Before that it does not exist, for the artist does not need it. . . . To him it is enough to have said what had to be said; according to the laws of *his* nature." In these words Schoenberg calls to mind Charles Ives's view in *Essays Before a Sonata*: "My God! What has sound to do with music! . . . What it sounds like may not be what it *is*."

Schoenberg's colorful wit and sense of play are rarely absent from this Janus-like text, and they confirm the impression of sprightliness given by the portrait of him in Dika Newlin's charming diary of her student days, *Schoenberg Remembered.*

Speaking of augmented sixth chords and other unstable harmonies that can move in many different directions, he writes:

> Later the pupil will best take all these vagrant chords for what they are, without tracing them back to a key or a degree: homeless phenomena, unbelievably adaptable and unbelievably lacking in independence; spies, who ferret out weaknesses and use them to cause confusion; turncoats to whom abandonment of their individuality is an end in itself; . . . but above all: most amusing fellows.

Here Schoenberg views a chord type exactly as he might a chess piece that can move in any number of ways. (For a description of the chess game that he designed himself, see ch. 22.)

Eminent common sense is also seldom, if ever, absent. Declaring the term *dominant* (as the term used to designate the chord built on the fifth degree of the scale) a misnomer, he writes: "If anything dominates, it can only be the fundamental tone. . . . If the tonic follows the dominant, it happens only in the same sense as when a king sends his vassal . . . on ahead to make appropriate preparations for his arrival. Then the king does in fact follow his man. The vassal is there, however, because of the king . . ."

Deploring the term *circle of fourths* as a description of the circle of fifths viewed counterclockwise, he points out that, after all, "C to G is a fifth upward or a fourth downward, and C to F is a fifth downward or a fourth upward. Therefore I pre-

fer to call this opposite direction The Circle of Fifths downward." The circle of fifths itself is described as a series of con-
centric circles expanding outward from the original tonic.

His chart of the chords that have common tones is visually
illuminating. It also closely resembles those for the games he
designed and for his twelve-tone writing.

Reading the book one is brought into a musical workshop
in which everything to do with music is taken apart and ex-
amined afresh. This includes the technical terms themselves,
some of which are deemed so misleading that the author simply changes them.

Schoenberg's examples of harmonic progressions often take
on an odd look by comparison with those in more standard
texts, since he tries seemingly every solution to every situation to see where it might lead. Indeed, he explores tonality
as if it had never been used before, and already in the spirit
of twelve-tone music. Here are the charts and musical games,
the exploration of the complete range of possibilities, the almost ethical view of proper voice leading. His words point toward a music of beauty, logic, lyricism, and liveliness of
counterpoint in which the chromatic scale is the primary field
of operations.

In his excellent essay "Schoenberg and the Origins of
Atonality," Ethan Haimo observes that the text of the *Harmonielehre* and the examples in it accurately mirror Schoenberg's own early work, in which Haimo finds a musical style
"employing the traditional vocabulary of tonality (triads and
seventh chords) and traditional syntax (no parallel fifths,
proper resolution of sevenths, and so forth) without defining
or establishing the tonic as the referential sonority by means of
harmonic progression." In other words, Schoenberg's view of
tonality, as laid out in *Harmonielehre*, is already pre-atonal,
in the sense that, although he places great stress on the connections between chords, the harmonic progressions themselves are no longer "aimed for a tonic." Fascinatingly, this

description also perfectly suits those of Schoenberg's late works, which return to the use of triadic materials but use them in an almost serial manner. Haimo also points out that "because he was largely self-trained, Schoenberg was capable of seeing possibilities that might have been suppressed had he had a more traditional education." It is also probably fair to say that, as an autodidact, Schoenberg had a particular need to present himself as one who was thoroughly "schooled" in the art and that he took particular pride in himself as a teacher, like an orphaned child who has a deep need to be a parent.

Haimo's insight is profound. Perhaps Schoenberg was only partly conscious of how far he had already come. Perhaps he had always been Schoenberg, from the very beginning.

If one could extract only the philosophical and aesthetic portions of the book it would furnish the general reader the opportunity to get to know Schoenberg the man and artist much in the way that one comes to know Charles Ives from his colorful, cranky, transcendent *Essays Before a Sonata*. Indeed, *Harmonielehre is* Schoenberg's *Essays*: a self-explanation displaying his mastery of the past, a show of erudition entitling him to claim an authority equal to that of any potential critic, a declaration of his traditionalism and his reverence for his heritage alongside an expression of the fierce integrity behind his innovations. The book makes a case for an approach to new musical materials that has the same logic and thoroughness as the tonal system, not one that simply apes some of its external characteristics but ultimately makes no sense. At the moment of his most difficult transition, it gave evidence— to himself and to others—that the strangeness of his new work was the result of his reverence for the materials and history of music, not a rebellion against them. The book can be seen as the text accompanying the Second String Quartet, explaining both the strangeness of its tonality and the gradations by which that tonality disappears. Already in *Harmonielehre*

Schoenberg speaks of passages in classical-era works that exhibit "*schwebende Tonalität*," tonality that fluctuates ambivalently between two keys, and "*aufgehobene Tonalität*," tonality that is temporarily lost altogether.

The book is also a portrait of tonality itself in transition, a tonality suffering from what Gould calls "an organic disorder" undermining its health. The imagination brought to bear on chord progressions, cadences, and modulations is already one that has experienced Strauss, Mahler, Debussy, and early Bartók, one that defines dissonances, significantly, as "the more remote, more complicated" relations to the fundamental tone, not as another species of interval entirely. Had this text been written during the transition from the Renaissance to the Baroque period, instead of at the dawn of twentieth-century music, and had it become a standard text, perhaps a composer such as Gesualdo would have formed our first notions of harmonic "common practice."

Taken as a whole, then, *Harmonielehre* is no mere theory text for harmony students. In fact, as the basis for harmony study it should perhaps be read in conjunction with other texts, which, while they might be less inspiring and less literary (there being none more literary than this one), might also be a simpler, plainer, less personal point of departure. The Dubois texts and the exercises written by Nadia Boulanger for her students, for example, have a kind of Shaker-like purity that gives them wide application for a musician who might turn in almost any direction. (A parallel to Boulanger's unpublished harmony manual in the literary realm might be Strunk and White's *Elements of Style*.)

Clearly the author of *Harmonielehre* considers himself a custodian of all that has gone before and, to his mind at least, is no revolutionary. Near the end of the book he addresses this idea explicitly in a beautiful passage:

It has never been the purpose and effect of new art to suppress the old, its predecessor, certainly not to destroy it. . . . The appearance of the new can far better be compared with the flowering of a tree: it is the natural growth of the tree of life. But if there were trees that had an interest in preventing the flowering, then they would surely call it revolution. And conservatives of winter would fight against each spring. . . . Short memory and meager insight suffice to confuse growth with overthrow.

13

P I E R R O T

*Schoenberg said that music was repetition—repetition and variation.
And he said variation is also repetition with some things changed and
others not.*

—John Cage remembering Schoenberg's teaching

In 1912, Schoenberg was commissioned by a Viennese actress,
Albertine Zehme, who had studied voice with Cosima Wagner
and had appeared in plays by Shakespeare and Ibsen, to compose a work that she could recite with piano accompaniment,
a set of "melodramas"—recitations with music. The work that
resulted was a setting of poems by the Belgian symbolist Albert Giraud. The "accompaniment" grew into an ensemble of
five instrumentalists playing a total of eight instruments in
ever-shifting groupings. For the reciter's part Schoenberg re-
lied on that manner of performance between speech and song

called *Sprechstimme*, in which the performer only suggests the pitches of the fully notated vocal part while executing the rhythms, phrasing, and dynamics precisely; occasionally, and tellingly, there are notes marked "*gesungen*," which are to be sung normally.

Ever the questioner of musical habits, the composer had first come close to the idea of *Sprechstimme* in his 1899 setting of Hugo von Hofmannsthal's "Die Beiden," which he marked "less sung than declaimed . . . like reading about an old picture." From the *Gurre-Lieder* to *Pierrot*, to the *Ode to Napoleon*, to the *Modern Psalm*, various degrees of *Sprechstimme* can be found in his work. In *Pierrot*, the combination of this half-sung voice with intensely melodic and evocative music creates a world that seems to define for all time the feeling of the uncanny first conjured up in the last movement of the Second String Quartet. The singing of the flute, with the pizzicato violin and the raindrop staccatos of the high-register piano, establishes a magically disquieting mood in the very opening bars of the piece. But what truly pushes it over the edge into the world of the sublimely bizzare is how that music combines with the singer who isn't quite singing. Here a kind of universal madness has been fixed on paper with clarity and art.

Albert Giraud's *Pierrot Lunaire* comprises fifty poems. Originally in French, they were translated into German by Otto Erich Hartleben. Each poem follows the rondeau form of three stanzas, of four, four, and five lines (thirteen lines in all), in which lines 1 and 2 are repeated as lines 7 and 8, and the first line also returns as the final line. For example, the first poem:

> *Den Wein, den man mit Augen trinkt,*
> *Giesst Nachts der Mond in Wogen nieder,*

Und eine Springflut überschwemmt
Den stillen Horizont.

Gelüste, schauerlich und süss,
Durchschwimmen ohne Zahl die Fluten!
Den Wein, den man mit Augen trinkt,
Giesst Nachts der Mond in Wogen nieder.

Der Dichter, den die Andacht treibt,
Berauscht sich an dem heilgen Tranke.
Gen Himmel wendet er verzückt
Das Haupt und taumelnd saugt und schlürft er
Den Wein, den man mit Augen trinkt.

The wine that only eyes may drink,
Pours from the moon in waves at nightfall,
And a spring flood overwhelms
The still horizon.

Desires, shivering and sweet,
Are swimming without number through flood-waters.
The wine that only eyes may drink,
Pours from the moon in waves at nightfall.

The poet by his ardor driven,
Grows drunken with the holy drink.
To heaven he rapturously lifts his head
And reeling sips and swallows the wine
That only eyes may drink.

(translation by Ingolf Dahl and Carl Beier)

Schoenberg selected twenty-one of the original fifty poems for his "opus 21." (The number-conscious author was no doubt also aware that the number 21 appeared reversed in the year of composition.) Special significance is accorded this and other numbers in the work. Pierrot is first mentioned in measure 21 of the song "Der Dandy," for example. The work as a whole is grouped into three equal parts of seven poems each (the title page reads "Three Times Seven Poems by Albert Giraud"), and there are seven notes in the score's most important theme. Schoenberg's fear of the number 13 (a phobia known as triskaidekaphobia) was demonstrated in some works by his numbering measures as 12, 12a, and 14. This surely caused him to place the poem "Enthauptung" ("Beheading") as number 13 of this set. Fortunately, it did not prevent him from setting the texts themselves, each of which contain thirteen lines.

It is worth noting that, despite the protests and considerable critical disfavor it received, audiences tended to love *Pierrot Lunaire* in the days of its first performances. But one wonders how many listeners have been brought to the work through recordings alone. It is first and foremost an experience, a piece suggestive of the cabaret milieu in which the composer had briefly worked. Also—and it may seem simplistic to say so—like much other music (Wagner, for example), it is infinitely more intelligible, and therefore more enjoyable, when heard in its entirety than when excerpted. Listening to recordings people can stop at any time, and often do, particularly if the music presents challenges. Hearing the first movement of *Pierrot* only by itself, how could one know that this strange song is only the beginning of a progression and that the progression is not just of individual songs but of groups? The key to following the work's progress is to hear it as a group of three sections ("three times seven") of roughly equal length, not as twenty-one short movements.

A portrait of the poet as lovelorn commedia dell'arte character: Part I introduces us to Pierrot's eerie, lonely world. Part 2, which begins with "Nacht," grows darker, more grotesque and satanic. Part 3 begins with a lament on the part of Pierrot's old cohorts that he has become too modern, sickly, and "sentimental" and ends with his returning to his commedia dell'arte homeland, Bergamo, and a wistful echo of old times (with echoes of the "old" world of tonality in number 21). The last piece is the only one in which all eight instruments are employed, and in the remaining twenty the precise instrumentation is never duplicated, despite the use of only five instrumentalists.

The density of the music increases in the second part and is at its height at the beginning of the third, only to lighten again at the end. The score indicates an increasing tendency for the songs to follow each other without pause as the piece progresses, but there are also numerous additional cases where the ending of one song prefigures the beginning of the next. The first part ends with "Der kranke Mond" ("The Sick Moon") for voice and solo flute, and after a pause the second part begins with "Nacht" ("Night") and the maximum timbral contrast: piano in its lowest register, bass clarinet and cello in their lowest registers. An extended coda appended to the penultimate song of part 2 refers back to "Der kranke Mond" by adding bass clarinet, viola, and cello to much of the flute line from that song. (This was the last section of *Pierrot* Schoenberg composed.) This interlude moves without pause into the final song of part 2.

The twenty-one poems chosen by Schoenberg are permeated with Christian religious imagery presented in a surreal and sardonic fashion. The most blatant instance of religious parody is in "Rote Messe" ("Red Mass"), in which Pierrot, acting as priest, rips out his own heart and offers it for Holy Communion. Appropriate to the "blasphemous" nature of the text, this is the one movement that uses all three of the available secondary instruments: piccolo, bass clarinet, and viola, alongside cello and piano.

The originality and inventiveness of Schoenberg's instrumentation were admired even by the work's detractors. From this piece of music and a very few others of the time emerged a new conception of what could constitute a twentieth-century instrumental ensemble. A surprising list of composers attended the premiere performances, Stravinsky, Ravel, and Puccini among them. Stravinsky, who had only just completed the sketch score of the music for *Le Sacre du Printemps* on November 17 (the orchestral score would not be completed until March 1913), attended rehearsals and the fourth performance of *Pierrot* on December 8, 1912. On the train from Switzerland to Berlin, Stravinsky worked on the score for *Le Sacre*. He was also in the process of completing his own *Three Japanese Lyrics* and composed the last of the songs after hearing *Pierrot*. The attempts of several authors to trace the delicately complex figurations and final choice of instrumentation of the Stravinsky songs to the influence of Schoenberg's melodrama leave a mixed impression. On the one hand, some parallels can be drawn, and there are some visual correspondences between instrumental textures seen on the page. But the two pieces are worlds apart to the hearer, and the listener hardly exclaims "Aha!" upon hearing the Stravinsky work next to the Schoenberg, as he does when placing numerous moments in Stravinsky next to those by other composers (Mozart, Verdi, Mussorgsky, Tchaikovsky, Debussy, to name a few). Many composers, including Ravel, Debussy, and Bartók, also thought they detected Schoenberg's presence in Stravinsky's *The Nightingale*.

In any case, this *was* the one period when the two composers were face-to-face and on amicable terms. While Stravinsky was in Berlin, Schoenberg and his wife, Mathilde, attended a performance of *Petrushka*, sitting next to the Russian composer, and they also received him in their home more than once. On February 13, 1913, Stravinsky referred to the Austrian composer in a *Daily Mail* interview as "one of the greatest creative spirits of our day." There is no question that he enormously admired *Pierrot Lunaire*. He saved the program and ticket stub from the performance for the rest of his life. (He had sat in the left part of the hall, row 5, seat 5.) Years later he called the piece "the solar plexus as well as the mind of early-twentieth-century music" and described his meeting with its composer as "the most prescient confrontation of my life."

Schoenberg's relationship to numbers has its sublime and its ridiculous aspects. The number 12, with which his name is forever associated, is one less than the number of which he had a morbid fear. In addition to routinely skipping over measure 13 in his work, he renumbered page 13 as well, claiming that if he numbered it correctly he was sure to make an error on the page or experience some other bad consequence. (An instance he cited was page 13 of his Violin Concerto, the point in the score where his work was interrupted by a three-week illness and where he later made a mistake in the numbering of measures.) He removed an *A* from the spelling of Aaron's name in *Moses und Aron* so that the title would not contain thirteen letters. Schoenberg did not consider such habits superstition (*Aberglaube*), insisting that they were a matter of belief (*Glaube*). One of Schoenberg's first literary efforts was entitled "Aberglaube." (In Jewish tradition, incidentally, the number 13 is considered lucky, associated as it is with the age at which a bar mitzvah or bat mitzvah occurs, the age at which David was anointed as future king, and the thirteen attributes of God.)

Born on the thirteenth of September, Schoenberg feared that he might die on Friday the thirteenth, and in fact he did (July 13, 1951).

The seven-note "Pierrot" tune heard in the piano at the beginning of *Pierrot Lunaire* with pizzicato violin accompaniment returns in many different guises throughout the work, usually with its basic shape and rhythmic pattern intact—at varying speeds, of course. To some extent, *all* the pieces in this set emerge from this little tune made up primarily of thirds:

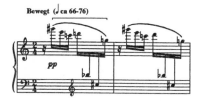

Here are only a few of the numerous guises in which it returns in subsequent movements:

no. 2, "Columbine"

no. 7, "Der kranke Mond" ("The Sick Moon")

no. 9, "Gebet an Pierrot" ("Prayer to Pierrot")

no. 15, "Heimweh" ("Homesickness")

no. 6, "Madonna"

no. 8, "Nacht" ("Night")

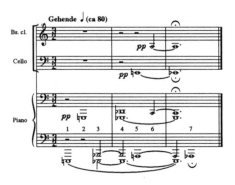

no. 21, "O alter Duft" ("O Ancient Scent")

So used does one become to the tune in all its forms that the rhythm alone evokes it:

Even the first three notes of the rhythm evoke it:

And we still recognize this rhythm as "motific" even when it is fragmented:

This perception alone makes us complicit in Pierrot's obssessive "lunacy."*

"Chromaticism" is a strange description of nontonal music that is so dominated by the thirds and triads of its principal theme. The work seems almost a demonstration of how little needs to be altered in tonal materials for them to lose their gravitational pull. If one alters the registers of the opening notes, one feels almost maddeningly near a key center. It seems only a short step from the world of the whole-tone scale, which can be formed by two parallel augmented triads, to this same melody (compare the Pierrot melody with the Debussy example on p. 31). This quality of ambiguity—being close to something familiar but also conceptually far from it— is matched by the vocal ambivalence of *Sprechstimme* and perfectly suits the twilight world of the little drama, whose tone lies between comedy and tragedy. Schoenberg's biographer

---

*In his diary for 1913, Paul Klee refers to a performance of "Schoenberg's mad melodrama *Pierrot Lunaire*" as one of the signs of a resurgence of culture occurring in Munich, adding, "Burst, you Philistine, me thinks your hour has struck!" (*Diaries, 1898–1918*, ed. Felix Klee, Los Angeles: University of California Press, 1964, p. 276).

H. H. Stuckenschmidt recounts the composer's trying to lighten Mrs. Zehme's overly tragic delivery in rehearsal by standing behind her and reciting with her in rhythm:

Don't despair, Frau Zehme, don't despair.
There is such a thing as life insurance.

In the last two songs, the aquatic barcarole "Heimfahrt" and "O alter Duft," the thirds not only dominate but are used more harmoniously to emphasize Pierrot's nostalgia and to bring the work to a becalmed, resigned close. Of the seven (!) instances of "*gesungen*" passages in the vocal part, five are—or outline—thirds, and the other two repeat pitches from these. There are no "*gesungen*" passages in part 3.

In addition to heralding the composer's renewed interest in traditional formal techniques—such as passacaglia ("Nacht") and canon ("Der Mondfleck")—*Pierrot* contains some wonderful little parodies. The most obvious of these are the two waltzes—number 5, "Valse de Chopin," with its romantic melodies, and number 16, "Gemeinheit," which suggests a giddy marching band in 3/4 time—the rhapsodic serenade for cello and piano (number 19), and the rippling and drifting barcarole in 6/8 (number 20). Number 12, "Galgenlied" ("Gallows Song"), which is only thirteen (!) measures long and accelerates increasingly in tempo beginning at the seventh, lasts only a matter of seconds and suggests both a nursery rhyme and a crazed cabaret patter-song.

The apex of complexity and composerly virtuosity is probably reached in number 18, "Der Mondfleck," in which, at lightning speed, a fugue unfolds between the piccolo and clarinet, and a canon between the violin and cello, both of which reverse themselves midway—just at the point where Pierrot finds the little fleck of shiny moonlight that he cannot rub out—presenting the first half of the piece in exact retrograde.

. . . then he finds it—
Just a snowy fleck of shiny moonlight
On the shoulder of his black silk frock-coat.

Wait now (he thinks), 'tis but a piece of plaster,
*Wipes and wipes, yet cannot make it vanish!**

Simultaneously, the intricate piano part, which appears at first hearing to be playing some kind of sparkling, tangled three-voice invention, spiked with occasional marcato chords, is actually producing note for note the piccolo and clarinet canon approximately twice as slowly (that is, in augmentation). With this process taking twice as long as the wind canon, the piano continues moving forward, augmenting the wind's first half of the piece, throughout the retrograde occurring in the rest of the ensemble, and arrives at the pitches of the piccolo's and clarinet's midpoint at the instant they complete their retrograde.** Meanwhile, the voice sings its poem straight through to the end, of course. "Der Mondfleck" takes approximately

---

*The German text reads:

        Er . . . findet richtig—
        Einen weisen Fleck des Hellen Mondes
        Auf dem Rucken seines schwarzen Rockes.

        Warte! denkt er: das ist so ein Gipsfleck!
        Wischt und wischt, doch—bringt ihn nicht herunter!

**The reader with a score handy will find the piccolo line beginning in the piano's left hand in measure 2 and becoming its highest voice in the piano in the last bars of the piece. The clarinet line does the reverse, beginning as the top voice in measure 1 and ending as the final notes in the piano's left hand. Along the way, the two parts cross each other more than once, with the "clarinet" remaining below the "flute" definitively after measure 14. There are a few discrepancies between the pitches in the piccolo/flute parts and the piano augmentations, as well as between a few details of the first half of the piece and its retrograde, but while noticing these tiny discrepancies, one also can't help noting how, in maintaining the exact pitch sequence of the first half of the wind parts in the piano while the winds play those pitches in retrograde, Schoenberg has come very close, ten years before soldifying his "twelve-tone method," to writing in a twelve-tone manner here.

fifty-five seconds to perform, and listening to it can only be compared to some primal and animal experience, such as suddenly finding oneself outside under a vast black sky filled with stars or unexpectedly looking over the edge of a cliff.

In fact, all the pieces in "Pierrot" are uncannily evocative of the subject matter and details of the poems, as illustrative of the texts as a movie score. Schoenberg makes us see the moonlight shining onto white linen in the darkness in "Eine blasse Wäscherin" (number 4), a movement for flute, clarinet, and violin only. We hear the "gigantic black butterflies blot out the shining sun" in the passacaglia "Nacht" (number 8), a piece in which the treble instruments seem to be eclipsed by the instrumentation of bass clarinet, cello, and piano, all playing a proliferation in different tempi of sinister three-note figures in their lowest registers. Here is a piece about which one can truthfully pronounce: This has not been said in music before.

Todesängst (fear of death) is depicted in number 13 ("Enthauptung"), naturally, in a passage that has been wonderfully described in this way: "Experience almost too bewildering for the human mind to encompass is given an appropriate representation."

One hears the "crystal sighing" in "Heimweh" (number 15) and the gently flowing stream of "Heimfahrt" (number 20). One senses the loss of, and longing for, ancient times in "O alter Duft" (number 21).

Although at first Schoenberg had expressed lack of enthusiasm for the project, things changed once he started to compose, and, to her credit, Mrs. Zehme adjusted to the expanding financial requirements of the work. Starting with a song setting in which he added the clarinet to the piano accompaniment ("Gebet an Pierrot," which eventually became number 9), he worked with phenomenal intensity and speed, as he had on *Erwartung* and would on many later occasions, adding instruments to his conception until the ensemble came to five play-ers. He completed most of the work in less than two months, and many of the movements in a single day.

Pierrot, with all its phenomenal craft and traditional forms and devices, is essentially a gigantic leap into the unknown. In his journal of the time Schoenberg wrote: "I think I am ap-proaching a new kind of expression. The sounds become an almost too animal and immediate expression of sensual and spiritual emotions." This is a musical world described by the composer George Perle as "the essential chaos of free atonal writing, with neither key centers nor serial organization. And it is precisely through this feeling of chaos, of being on the verge of the breakdown of everything familiar, that Schoen-berg is able to take us in *Pierrot Lunaire* as far into the world of the unconscious as music can ever penetrate."

By turns haunted, delicate, and strong, this work can per-haps best be seen as a rarefied, enchanted form of the irony Schoenberg's cousin remembered finding it difficult to appre-ciate in him as a child. It seems to suggest a way of life, a view of the underside of things.

Pierrot Lunaire left a beam of moonlight on the shoulder of twentieth-century music that could not be brushed off.

14

DIE GLÜCKLICHE HAND

> *"For a long time I have been wanting to write an oratorio on the following subject: modern man, having passed through materialism, socialism, and anarchy and, despite having been an atheist, still having in him some residue of ancient faith (in the form of superstition), wrestles with God . . . and finally succeeds in finding God and becoming religious. . . . It is not through any action, any blows of fate, least of all through any love of woman, that this change of heart is to come about."*
> —Schoenberg to Richard Dehmel, December 13, 1912

Pierrot Lunaire, surely one of Schoenberg's greatest works, also marked the beginning of a transitional phase in his compositional method, from those deliberately intuitive expressions of the unconscious, such as *Erwartung* and the Five Pieces for Orchestra, to his more "systematic" works using the twelve-tone approach. Although composed almost without sketches, and therefore with relative spontaneity, *Pierrot* also utilized many traditional forms and techniques, embedding a new, seemingly uncharted language of tones within at least some familiar architectural shapes.

Since he worked on *Die glückliche Hand* over a period of

three years, beginning it before *Pierrot*, in 1910, and completing it afterwards, in 1913, its gestation charts this evolving notion of musical order and his increasingly conscious control over his compositional process. As Joseph Auner points out, Schoenberg wrote most of the earlier sections without precompositional planning, relying on his instincts (his disciplined and informed instincts, that is), but wrote some of the later sections, such as the quasi-fugal passage that begins the third scene, from detailed sketches. In short, while still creating music of breathtaking newness and "visionary" character, he was internally moving toward a specific "way" of working that could be articulated and more generally applied.

Neither twelve-tone nor sacred in its subject matter, *Die glückliche Hand* can still perhaps be viewed as a kind of precursor to *Moses und Aron*. The theme of the dreamer-artist-seeker unable to reconcile his otherworldly visions with worldly fulfillment is sounded here for the first time explicitly. The otherworldly vision in this work is a beautiful young woman dressed "in a soft deep-violet garment, pleated and flowing" who has a "graceful figure" and "yellow and red roses in her hair." The mocking voices of the half-sung, half-*Sprechstimme* male-female chorus that frame the work anticipate the sound and texture of the voices from the burning bush in *Moses*, and the defeat of the man—his loss of the woman—that they articulate at the end of the opera could be a description of Moses' defeat, too:

> You know how it always is, yet you remain blind. . . .
> Once again you fix your longing on the unattainable. Once
> again you give yourself up to the sirens of your thoughts,
> thoughts that roam the cosmos, that are unworldly but
> thirst for worldly fulfillment!

If one examines all of Schoenberg's vocal and stage works, it becomes clear that this is the most frequently encountered literary theme. While in his early work the idea of the irreconcil-

ability of the spiritual with the worldly was expressed in romantic terms (the unattainable beloveds in *The Book of the
Hanging Gardens, Erwartung,* and *Die glückliche Hand*), after
his reconnection with Judaism the theme became explicitly religious (*Jacob's Ladder, Moses, Modern Psalm*). During this period in which Schoenberg was not yet employing sacred
subject matter and had not yet formulated the principles of
twelve-tone writing, one can still see strong elements of both
in his work, even if they were not yet recognized as such by
him, just as one can see in his early tonal language signs of his
future atonal language.

That the representation of the unattainable is embodied in
music that is itself dense and tangled is no accident. Although
it is beautifully constructed and so headlong in its progress
that it seems even shorter than it is, *Die glückliche Hand* is neither "simple" nor "nice" music. Like the music of *Moses,* of *Kol
Nidre,* of the last movement of Five Pieces for Orchestra, it is
as unflinching as the gazes of the composer's contemporaneous paintings and at times reaches peaks of intense complexity
and dissonance. Yet it is precise and transparent in its intri-
cacy, and the orchestration is lush and full of color. It is as ex-
hilarating and exciting, as stunningly and naturally expressive
as a painting by Vincent van Gogh.

The allegorical "plot" resists easy summary. Only a small
percentage of the libretto is given over to sung or declaimed
text, the bulk of it detailing actions and giving explicit stage
directions and indications of lighting changes.

The main moments are these:

Scene 1.   The man is face down on a dark stage, with a fantastic animal crouching on his back, its teeth in his neck. The
chorus, whose eyes alone are visible, sings with pity lines such
as "You know how it is, yet you remain blind."

Scene 2. The stage enlarges and bright sunlight shines on a portion of it. The man sings to the apparition of the beautiful woman (at whom he never looks directly), who offers him a goblet. As he drinks from it, her expression turns from great sympathy to hostile indifference. As the man stretches out his arms to her, a gentleman appears and the woman smiles at him and rushes into his arms. She returns only to reject the man again, but, not recognizing that she is gone, he sings, "Now I possess you forever."

Scene 3. A rocky landscape. The man climbs out of a ravine to a grotto where workers toil in a kind of workshop. Saying "that can be done more simply," he places a piece of gold on an anvil and strikes it with a heavy hammer, producing a glittering diadem. The workers prepare to rush angrily at him, but the stage suddenly darkens and the workshop disappears. At this point there is an enormous crescendo of light and storm, which is mirrored in the man's expressions. Suddenly the woman, half naked from the waist up, is seen in the grotto. The man tries unsuccessfully to climb up the rocks to reach her, singing, "Beautiful vision, stay with me." The gentleman appears briefly, leaving the missing part of the woman's dress behind him. When she puts this on, she continues to elude the man's beseeching grasp and gives a man-sized stone a slight push with her foot. The stone, which resembles the "fantastic animal" crouched on his back from the opening of the opera, falls on top of the man, as the mocking laughter from scene 1 is heard from the chorus.

Scene 4. The man is lying as at the beginning, with the stone on his back. The chorus (whose faces are now visible, tinged with blue light) sings, "You seek to lay hold of what will only slip from you when you grasp it. . . . Do you only understand what you hold?" (The light on their faces reddens.) "You poor fool!" The stage darkens and the curtain falls.

By comparison with *Erwartung*, which mirrors every fluctuation in its heroine's hysterical spirit like a seismograph, *Die glückliche Hand* is more continuous and even so has a form that is more molded and sectional. Like some of Schoenberg's later, more classically modeled twelve-tone works, it contains a few literal repeats, as well as small motifs that are emphasized enough for the listener to recognize them as such. From the first instant one feels that one is in the theater. Even a description of the opening scene's music might convey this:

Tiny introduction Very emphatic repeating figure in bassoons. (A real "beginning"!)

Measure 3 Voices of the chorus enter whispering in *Sprechstimme*, six men, six women, at first in two equal parts, then dividing further. At the same time (and for the duration of the scene) there is an ostinato in the timpani; small solo instruments stand out in short phrases: bass clarinet, piccolo, solo cello, bassoon, clarinet, violin, oboe.

Measure 9 The orchestra continues over the pulsing ostinato as some of the voices start to sing: first soprano, then bass, then alto. Now there are six separate vocal lines.

Measure 12 Three male lines in close dissonant harmony sung in rhythmic unison are answered by a similar texture in the three female lines. When not singing, the voices resume various types of rhythmicized speech. The sung trios answer one another at shorter intervals. Then soprano and tenor sing in canon. (During all of this the ostinato continues.) There is a long, ornately descending clarinet line. The voices in unison declaim: "Und kannst nicht bestehn!" ("And you cannot win out!") Then, dying away, soprano and tenor sing over the others, speaking, "Du Armer!" ("You poor fool!") The orchestra shudders; the harmony is static; there are repeated chords in the strings, all very soft.

Measure 26 Suddenly there is loud, angular brass band music. Harsh, mocking laughter from the voices, joined to a sustained dissonant chord, is suddenly cut off, leaving a quietly plaintive melody in the cellos and intimate chamber scoring. The man's first notes are sung.

Die glückliche Hand is such an original and powerful piece that it has to be heard to be believed. No one could possibly guess its impact from the text alone. It is also as much a *Gesamtkunstwerk* as anything by Wagner, even if, at roughly twenty minutes, it is less than a tenth as long as a Wagner opera. Schoenberg conceived and wrote the text and music, made preliminary designs for both the sets and the costumes, gave detailed bar-by-bar instructions for the stage directions in the score, and, most unusually of all, created a specific musically coordinated outline of the lighting. In scene 3 a "crescendo" of light through an exact range of colors is meticulously marked in the score.

Written for large orchestra, a small chamber chorus of six female and six male voices, a solo baritone singing the part of the protagonist (called simply Ein Mann), and two nonsinging actors, the work was originally intended as a "male" companion piece to the "female" *Erwartung*. The first performance, in October 1924, involved over a hundred musicians and required an enlargement of the orchestra pit at the Volksoper. Reviews and audience reaction ran the gamut from wild enthusiasm to complete rejection. Some of the reviews professing incomprehension still made some valid observations, such as that the composer evoked from the orchestra "solo and ensemble sounds never heard until now" and that light becomes a "part of the emotional experience."

The chorus, which sings at the beginning and ending of the work only, never sings simultaneously with the man. For his part, the man comes closest to an aria only in the second scene. He sings two short utterances in each of the next two parts of scene 3, after which there are no vocal lines for fifty-two measures, and in the last section of the scene he sings a few short phrases amounting to only six measures.

Roughly speaking, an outline of the musical form would look like this:

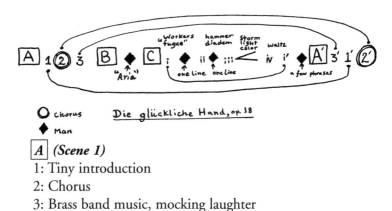

A (Scene 1)
1: Tiny introduction
2: Chorus
3: Brass band music, mocking laughter

B (Scene 2)
The Man, lyrical; chamber scoring; after pause at measure 72, he addresses the woman

C (Scene 3)
i: Orchestral interlude starts like a fugue, fortissimo. (This passage, with its clear 4/4 meter, memorable tune, containing many repetitions of tones, and Beethovenian rhythm, represents a daring allusion to a past style.) Then, after a breath, the orchestra continues with very delicate scoring leading up to

man's interruption, singing, "Das kann man einfacher" ("One can do that more simply").

ii: From measure 103 to measure 120, orchestra alone. Elements of the fugue subject return. A massive crescendo accompanies the man's raising of the hammer, and the sound of the hammer blow (at measure 115), a gigantic twelve-note chord made up of thirds, is unmistakable. As the man raises the diadem set with precious stones from the cleft, measures 115–24, there is a single unchanged chord sustained in the winds throughout and a glittering orchestration emphasizing celeste, glockenspiel, string trills, and rippling clarinet lines. During this, the man sings, "This is the way to make jewels." At measure 125, as a transition, we have a brief recall of the moment that preceded the mocking laughter at measure 24.

iii: From measure 126 through measure 151 we have the light/color crescendo combined with a wind crescendo and an orchestral passage of increasing complexity, in which nevertheless there is a three-note melodic fragment that recognizably reappears over and over again. During this crescendo of light and storm, according to a note in the score, "the man reacts as if both emanated from him." The progression of colors is dull red, brown, dirty green, dark blue-gray, violet, intense dark red turning to blood red, mixed increasingly with orange, bright yellow, glaring yellow. When the storm breaks off and the bright yellow light dims to a pale blue, the orchestral complexity and volume are dramatically cut, leading to

iv: Measures 156–66. A plaintive waltzlike passage, with the violin carrying the melody, accompanies the entrance of the woman, partially naked from the waist up, and the appearance of the gentleman, who holds the missing portion of her dress.

i (reprise): At measure 166, the music returns to the meter, rhythm, character, texture, and some of the materials of the fugal section, over which the man (trying to climb the rocks to reach the woman) now sings, "You, you! You are mine . . . you were mine. . . . Beautiful vision, stay with me." This culminates in a fast passage (at measure 195) during which four trombones intone the obsessively repeated melody of the light crescendo music. This connects directly with

$\boxed{A'}$ 3 (reprise): The return of the loud brass band music accompanied by mocking laughter.

(Scene 4)

1 (reprise): The introductory repeated bassoon figure over the timpani ostinato, followed by an orchestral passage in unison rhythm derived from the fugue subject, and a further reiteration of the timpani ostinato, sinking to a low trombone chord (measure 214).

2 (reprise): The chorus returns, divided at first into three spoken parts, primarily accompanied by fluid and mysterious orchestral music and not by the ostinato. Measure 224: after a breath in the music, for the first time in the piece all six parts in the chorus sing simultaneously, a kind of chorale in inverted canon between the female voices and the male. At measure 240 they collapse back into a texture that is part sung, part whispered *Sprechstimme*, like sections of the opening chorus. As the orchestral texture thins (at measure 245) they sing a beautiful two-measure phrase in quiet dialogue (no *Sprechstimme* here). The orchestra dwindles down to the same low trombone chord (measure 248) heard at measure 214. There is an emphatic fortissimo line in the cellos, a strangely exquisite moment in violin and harp as the chorus once more intones, "Du Armer." The soprano alone is left singing these words over choral *Sprechstimme*. The low trombone chord sounds again (measure 252) and there is one last outburst—only four and a half beats long—in strings and trumpets. The work ends quietly, with a feeling of suspension of time (created by the static alternating figure in strings, among other things) that anticipates the ending of Berg's *Wozzeck*.

A startling parallel to much of what Schoenberg was trying to do in this stage work is to be found in Kandinsky's *Der gelbe*

Klang (*The Yellow Sound*), which the painter began working on in 1909 with the composer Thomas von Hartmann, a fellow Russian and a follower of the Armenian mystic and musical folklorist Gurdjiev. Although Kandinsky's text was published in *Der Blaue Reiter*, the work was not produced in Kandinsky's lifetime and Hartmann's music remained a sketch.

Kandinsky's text is even more abstract than Schoenberg's, with the spoken or sung words occupying an even more minimal role. His fifth scene is all "movements, noises, and colored light," almost as if he were seeking to turn one of his paintings into a work of theater. In both works lighting is given an unprecedented function, but while Schoenberg's "light crescendo" is tied to expressions on his central character's face, as if brought about by his thoughts and emotions, Kandinsky's directions for light seem intended to create, as Jelena Hahl-Koch says, an "absolute play of form purged of all comprehensible content" that will act directly on the imagination of the viewer.

While both artists were trying to dismantle the traditional logic of theater in order to give the audience an experience that transcended the worldly, it appears that Schoenberg's approach was the more psychological and thematic one, as it was in his painting.

To address for a moment the issue of why this and so many other works by Schoenberg repelled a good part of its audience, we need first to remind ourselves that music itself has a unique power to disturb, that the wellsprings of its power to delight are also the source of its power to appall. The evanescent character of its substance, the mystery of its internal laws to nonmusicians, the potentially disturbing metaphorical nature of sound production—which mimics speech, breathing, the beating of our hearts—and the incomprehensibility of the connection between the physical principles involved and the emotions aroused, all make for a situation in which the listener feels vulnerable and seeks familiarity and what he or she takes to be signposts of order.

Then, too, in the words of Stravinsky, music is given to us as the only way in which we can truly "digest time." Music has a unique way of making us experience existing, and this can be both joyous and frightening.

In Hebrew the word for *awe* is the same as that for *fear*. Mozart can strike terror in the heart.

I deliberately used van Gogh as a point of reference earlier because, as alarming as certain elements in his paintings are, and in some cases as emblematic of the artist's disturbed mental state, viewers are not as alarmed by van Gogh's paintings as listeners are by Schoenberg's music. The impression of a painting can be instantly escaped; we possess the ability to close our eyes without even looking away. But to escape music one must leave the space in which it is being played, attempt to hold one's ears, or reject it outright.

Schoenberg was, of course, in the process of deliberately dismantling and reaching beyond the routine "signposts" that distanced the listener from the impact of the sounds. His process of motific development was now so compressed, for example, that one could sense only intuitively the onrushing cohesiveness of his musical thinking and could not have the reassuring distancing experience of being able to think, "Ah, yes, there is that familar tune being bandied about." It can be argued that in this music the density of thinking of a Bach, Beethoven, or Mozart was being revived and the listener was at the mercy of music as demanding and therefore threatening as the work of those masters, but now employing hitherto transitional, marginal, or outlawed combinations of rhythms and tones.

Die glückliche Hand, for example, is one of the first pieces to explore the melodic beauty and expressivity of "dissonant" intervals such as major and minor sevenths and ninths. Here we see the idea of the "emancipation of the dissonance" in action:

This is a new way to present a simple chromatic scale. The point is not only that these dissonant intervals are used melodically but that, freed from their tonal context (in which it would be quite a challenge to make such a melody seem plausible), they have become intensely expressive and beautiful and need no "resolution" to be legitimized. No longer expressive decorations for diatonic melodies and harmonies, they are now central; they are the matter at hand.

The language is disorienting in myriad other ways as well, including such fundamental breaks with convention as having an enormous orchestra used as a resource for soloistic chamber scoring to create delicate colors and effects or having the central operatic character sing so little and in such an unheard-of manner.

I also believe that at least as early as *Die glückliche Hand* one can see overtones of Jewish musical and sacred traditions in Schoenberg's music and that these might even help account for the hostility and incomprehension engendered by his work.

After all, as has become increasingly clear, many of the features that astonished and alienated the first listeners of much innovative "new" music in the twentieth century derived from folk or sacred traditions that were in fact thousands of years old. Some of these traditions were native to the composers using them. Others, such as the Balinese gamelan music that influenced Edgard Varèse and John Cage or the Ghanaian drumming studied by Steve Reich, were appropriated by composers looking outside their own cultures for inspiration.

The whole notion of a specifically Jewish cultural heritage

takes on an unfortunate character within a historical period in which "racial characteristics" were cited as reasons for genocide. Photographs and documents pertaining to Schoenberg were featured prominently in the so-called "Degenerate Music" exhibition in Düsseldorf in May 1938, alongside those connected with Hindemith, Weill, Berg, Webern, and Stravinsky. A recording of *Pierrot Lunaire* was broadcast, while a wall placard pronounced it "*Hexensabbat*" ("witches' Sabbath") music.

But I am talking not of DNA molecules carrying memories of ancient scales and customs but of the songs, prayers, ideas, feelings, and practices passed down through culture and absorbed both consciously and unconsciously.

We know from studying the evolution of jazz that characteristics from wildly divergent sources can merge in the creative minds of artists to form something new. Without African rhythmical procedures there would be no jazz. Schoenberg believed that the idiom or "style" of a piece of music was simply the result of the working out of its ideas. In his famous essay "Style and Idea," he dismissed "style" as an a priori notion. He also did not believe in the conscious attempt to exploit folkloric elements in music in order to achieve a "nationalistic" idiom through the artificial injection of superficial stylistic traits. In a 1934 article, he wrote that a genuine American art music would simply emerge naturally: "a genius will compose and will not worry about what is demanded or expected of national music by the experts; but then, suddenly, all these symptoms [embodied in folk traditions] will be present (though others, too)."

But it seems fair to say that, while the music lying behind Schoenberg is first and foremost the tradition of Bach, Beethoven, Wagner, Brahms, and Mahler, there may also be, at least unconsciously, the tradition of the music associated with Judaism. (In the sounds of Schoenberg one does not particularly sense, say, the English choral tradition that so influenced Benjamin Britten or the Russian folk traditions and music of the Russian Orthodox Church that lie behind the work of Stravinsky.)

As Alexander Ringer points out in his authoritative book, *Arnold Schoenberg: The Composer as Jew*, the Jewish music Schoenberg would have heard growing up was a very word-based style of singing in which prayers were chanted—either at home or in the temple—in a rhythmical but unmetered manner. After all, despite his unreligious upbringing, Schoenberg's mother did come from an Orthodox family of cantors.

Some descriptions of the complexity and mystic rapture of group singing in temple sounds remarkably Schoenbergian. The following is a description of Hasidic chant: "The leader of the prayer used to exclaim each verse with mystic fervor. The congregation repeated it with the same power and profound emotion but with minor changes and in a faster tempo. This congregational response shifted key centers frequently, unconsciously creating an atmosphere of unbridled, almost primeval, religious fervor." If we listen to the choral opening of *Die glückliche Hand* and imagine that this is a piece of *sacred* music we can certainly relate it to this description. We hear music that is half spoken, half sung; we hear voices in conflict, in unison; we hear solo flowing melodies emerging out of a web of choral sound; we hear "mystic fervor," "shifted key centers," something "primeval." It is not all that difficult to imagine the high tenor solo that emerges out of the interlocking choral groups at measure 17 as the voice of a cantor.

The choral music of Webern, with its relatively straitlaced rhythms and transparent textures, makes an intriguing point of comparison.

Like *Erwartung, Die glückliche Hand* implies a continual circle of seeking and never finding. In both works we reach the end only to find ourselves where we were at the beginning. In both, the audience finds itself in a dream that seems oddly familiar, one in which the protagonist is alone, subject to phantom voices, in an unresolvable search that seems in part romantic, in part spiritual.

SILENCE, ORDER, AND TERROR

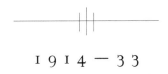

1 9 1 4 — 3 3

It was not possible, especially not for a Jew in public life, to ignore the fact that he was a Jew. . . . And even if you managed somehow to conduct yourself so that nothing showed, it was impossible to remain completely untouched; as for instance a person may not remain unconcerned whose skin has been anesthetized but who has to watch, with his eyes open, how it is scratched by an unclean knife, even cut until the blood flows.

ARTHUR SCHNITZLER, *MY YOUTH IN VIENNA*

15

INCIDENT AT MATTSEE

Between 1913 and 1917, Schoenberg completed only one new work, the Four Orchestral Songs, op. 22. His only other composing during this period consisted of the completion of *Die glückliche Hand*, begun in 1910, and the first part and a section of an interlude in his (never completed) oratorio *Die Jakobsleiter* (*Jacob's Ladder*). No further music emerged from him until he began to compose again in 1920.

This was a considerable silence, due in part to the war, in part to the creative impasse that followed, perhaps inevitably, from the outpouring of the great, new, and strange works he had composed between 1909 and 1913. In this interim time he was seeking organizational principles, those "laws not yet written," for the new nontonal music. It was during this period that he developed the "method of composing with twelve tones related only to each other."

Beginning in 1917 with work on *Die Jakobsleiter*, he began to choose sacred texts and subject matter drawn from the Old Testament to set to music, in contrast to his former penchant for romantic, poetic, and expressionistic literary material. Although officially still a convert to Protestantism, he had resumed considering himself a Jew in his work and in his thinking.

An early effect of the war on Schoenberg personally was the loss of many of his students to the army. The financial circumstances of his family were dreadful and they spent some of this period living in boardinghouses. He himself was at first rejected, then, in December 1915, accepted into the army reserves. By June 1916, however, he was released on an extended leave due to his asthma and other ailments, an aggravation of his health problems not unlike the response of his student Alban Berg to his stint in officer's training school and later on sentry duty in Vienna during the same period. Both men had frail constitutions and suffered from asthma throughout their lives. Berg wrote to his wife of the brutality of military life and later drew directly from his own experiences when composing his opera *Wozzeck*.

In October 1916, after questions had been raised about the participation of Jews in the military, an edict from the Austrian government called for a full accounting of all Jews in the armed forces at that time.

In 1917, Schoenberg returned briefly to the army, fortunately with lighter duties, but it was in the interim that he had composed the first section of *Die Jakobsleiter*. After his final release he was able to return to this work only to the extent of completing the one additional section mentioned above. The Schoenbergs moved to Mödling, a suburb of Vienna, in April 1917, and there he continued to give a composition seminar that he had started to hold in Vienna. It was this seminar that led to the creation of the Society for Private Musical Performances.

In 1921, Schoenberg and his family were forced by anti-Semitic pressures to leave the lakeside resort of Mattsee, where they had spent their holidays for five summers. An edict from local authorities required guests to present proof of their Christianity or leave town. Schoenberg was an avid swimmer and loved being near the water. This was a precious part of the family routine. Despite being in a position to show that they were in fact baptized, the Schoenbergs packed up and left, taking with them the students who had accompanied them there.

The years in which Schoenberg was musically less productive were also the years in which he came to the realization that, while he had always been a proud German in his own mind, to Aryan Germans he would always be a Jew. The eventual progression from anti-Semitic bigotry, fear, disgust, and paranoia, to a series of increasingly severe legislated restrictions on Jews, to the Nazis' Final Solution is one that Schoenberg foresaw, even in 1922.

An exchange of letters between Schoenberg and Kandinsky reveals the extent of the gap between their views of the current situation in Germany. The Russian-born, Christian Kandinsky thought that, Jewish friends and artists aside, there was indeed a "Jewish problem" but that this could never have an impact on his admiration and friendship for Schoenberg personally. Schoenberg broke off the relationship in a long letter that predicted the eventual outcome of the current campaign against the Jews:

> Have you also forgotten how much disaster can be evoked by a particular mode of feeling? Don't you know that in peace-time everyone was horrified by a railway-accident in which four people were killed, and that during the war one could hear people talking about 100,000 dead without

even trying to picture the misery, the pain, the fear, the consequences? . . . But what is anti-Semitism to lead to if not to acts of violence?

Kandinsky wrote to Schoenberg: "We—few of us—who can be inwardly free to some extent should not permit evil wedges to be driven between us. . . . Even if you disassociate yourself from me, I send you kindest regards and the expression of my highest esteem."

16

CRITICS AND DISCIPLES

The Society for Private Musical Performances was one short-lived solution to the question of how to prepare and perform new and difficult music in a setting free from the pressures caused by the marketplace and by unsympathetic listeners. Among the rules: no critics were permitted. The principal goal of the series was "to inform," not to judge, to give a sense of the principal musical idioms of the day in performances that were as rehearsed as they needed to be.

There were 320 subscribers to the "Verein für Musikalische Privataufführungen," each with a special pass that displayed his or her photo. Membership dues varied according to the financial means of the participants. (Schoenberg had handled fees for participation in his composition seminar in the same way.)

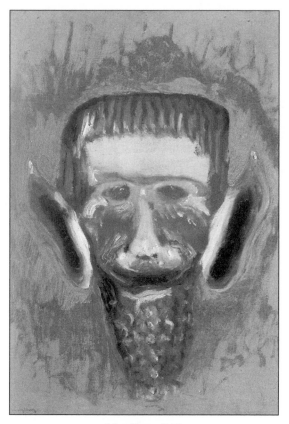

Schoenberg, *Critic*

Webern, Berg, and the pianist and composer Eduard Steuermann acted as coaches, with Schoenberg participating in the final stages of rehearsal. (One of Berg's additional duties was to arrange the audience's chairs.) Often the works, once prepared, were repeated, with several concerts framed by dual performances of the same work. No fewer than fifty-four arrangements of larger-scale works were made for the series, some for piano(s), others for chamber orchestra, and these included versions of Mahler's Fourth, Sixth, and Seventh Symphonies.

In its three years (December 29, 1918–December 5, 1921)

the society presented 113 concerts. Were the programs re-mounted today they would form a time capsule of much of the best music of the period as well as many fascinating curiosities. The range of the programming is surprising. Mahler, Reger, Busoni, and Richard Strauss are well represented, but French composers are also favored. Debussy was one of the most fre-quently performed composers, and one concert (February 21, 1921) was devoted entirely to his work. (Debussy had died on March 25, 1918.) Dukas, Satie, Ravel, and the younger Mil-haud and Poulenc were played as well. (Poulenc and Milhaud admired Schoenberg greatly and had been to visit him in Mödling.) Several of Stravinsky's chamber-sized pieces were on the programs, as was a four-hand piano arrangement of *Petrushka*. There was Mussorgsky, Zemlinsky, Karol Symanow-ski. Bela Bartók was also prominent in the concert schedule. There were first performances of works now considered land-marks of twentieth-century music by Berg and Webern. The focus on the present was relieved from time to time by per-formances of Mozart, Beethoven, and Brahms.

Schoenberg allowed his own work to be performed in the series only after a year and a half. The last concert of 1921 (there was to be only one remaining one, on October 30, 1922) was devoted to a performance of *Pierrot Lunaire*, which he conducted. Not long after this, a concert was arranged at the home of Alma Mahler in which this performance was pre-sented alongside a rendition of the same work conducted by Darius Milhaud with the text in French.

The society had a number of additional rules devised by its autocratic founder. There was to be no applause or public re-sponse of any kind and no public reporting of the concert programs ahead of time. The program was announced at the concert itself, and thus there were also no printed programs. This had the result of ensuring a kind of democracy of atten-dance. Since one had to turn up to know what was being played, one could not avoid performances of works one was predisposed against. Another stipulation was that works were not to be played from memory. In a letter written thirty years later, the composer explained that, in his opinion, "our musical notation is a puzzle picture which one cannot look at often enough in order to find the right solution."

Significantly, the society flourished during precisely the period when Schoenberg was compositionally fallow and developing the principles behind "composition using twelve tones." Might we not see this society as a kind of cocoon in which the new approach gestated, to reemerge as a butterfly in 1923?

Schoenberg's relationship with two of his students—Alban Berg and Anton Webern, who had come to study with him in 1904, his very first year of teaching—is without parallel in music history because of the stature of the students, the impact he had on their work, the intensity of their devotion to him, and the influence all three have had on subsequent music. In his role as teacher to two figures who also served as his interpreters to the rest of the world it is hard not to see a suggestion of the relationship between Moses and his brother, Aaron, that Schoenberg was later to depict in his largest opus. Friends from the period of the society describe Berg and Webern as worshipfully dependent on their teacher, yet at the same time as strong individuals, like planets in stubbornly fixed orbits around a sun. The same could be said of their work. The mentor-student relationship was never broken. In what would prove the final full year of his life (1934), Berg inscribed the score of *Lulu*, which he dedicated to his teacher on the occasion of the latter's sixtieth birthday, with the words: "Faith and hope and love for German music, with your inimitable teaching you once awakened in me. But with them there also grew in me faith, hope, and love for you, who as master and friend gave me both friendship and instruction over three decades, in which you upheld enduring values." For his part, Webern's devotion at times crossed over the line into religious adoration, as when he compared the feelings of Schoenberg's students for him to the those of Christ's disciples for their Lord or when he wrote, "Whatever I am, everything, everything is through you; I live only through you."

The three names themselves seem almost as interconnected as three row forms:

AlbAN   BERG
ArNold schoenBERG
ANtoN   weBERn

if not quite as tightly knit as the old Latin word square (a four-way palindrome) that is on Webern's tombstone:

SATOR
AREPO
TENET
OPERA
ROTAS

It means: "The Sower Arepo Keeps the Work Circling" and illustrates the principles of inversion, retrograde, and retrograde-inversion used in twelve-tone music.

Berg (who studied with Schoenberg for seven years) and We-bern (who studied with him for four) drew different kinds of musical nourishment from their teacher, and each used the twelve-tone approach in an individual way. Their docility vis-à-vis their domineering teacher coexisted fascinatingly with their greatness and separateness as individual artists. Berg, it should be noted, accomplished almost all his composing outside of Vienna and away from Schoenberg, in his country home.

When Schoenberg lived briefly in Amsterdam and later in

Berlin, Webern and Berg took over his teaching. Their philosophies and teaching techniques were congruent, even if their gifts and personalities differed. Few could match Schoenberg's legendary ability to narrate and compose various alternative approaches to a passage on the spot or even to produce whole compositions—a scherzo, a theme and variations—while his students watched. In this ability one senses a connection to his sketching and painting. Webern could not have been more different from his teacher in terms of this ease of technique. In his music each note resulted from painstaking thought and inner hearing, and the charts of rows were always near him at the piano. By contrast, after working for a while on a composition Schoenberg would know the row forms he was using by heart. When he composed examples in his classroom, according to one student, "for a moment there would be nothing. He would just sit and concentrate. And then he would write and that was it."

Nevertheless, he did not often teach his own work, the twelve-tone method, or even current music. He did sometimes teach from his own *Harmonielehre* but emphasized the study of counterpoint, using Heinrich Bellermann's textbook (based on the classic text of Johann Joseph Fux), *Der Contrapunkt*, and taught through the analysis and imitation of Bach, Beethoven, and Brahms. Reading his essays on Bach, Brahms, or Mahler one glimpses how readily he could draw on a storehouse of examples from the literature, which he knew inside and out. His analyses were a kind of retracing of the composing process; the pieces were, in effect, recomposed note by note before the class. He did not expect his students to mimic the outward characteristics of earlier idioms but wanted them to find their own creative ways. In his essay "Problems in Teaching Art" (1911), he wrote that so-called technique and invention cannot be separated:

> It is said of many an author that he may have technique,
> but no invention. That is wrong: he has no technique ei-

ther, or he has invention too. You don't have technique
when you can neatly imitate something: technique has you.

At the same time he believed that in order to develop the instincts one needs to write in a new style, one has first to become fluent in a known idiom where the elements and their
uses can be more rationally discussed and evaluated. Therefore he "never spoke about modern music to any student who
could not, let's say, write a string quartet in Brahms's style
well."

His philosophy was rooted in questioning everything and
in encouraging the student to think for himself and from
scratch. He taught from examples, not from "rules." Egon
Wellesz, a composer and one-time Schoenberg student, clari-
fies this distinction when he writes:

> How little imposing it sounds, if the teacher tells the pupil
> that one of the most advantageous means for the attain-
> ment of the effect of musical form is tonality, and how very
> different it sounds if he speaks of the *principle of tonality* as
> of a *law*. . . . According to Schoenberg's view, music be-
> longs to the explanatory sciences which teach us what a
> thing is and not how it ought to be done.

Schoenberg once claimed to be unable to write ten measures without first being inspired, and on another occasion
said he couldn't even simply improvise an effective modula-
tion. For him, composing was ultimately—to borrow from his
brief essay on Gershwin—as natural a process as it was for an
apple tree to bear apples. It was a process for which one could
be exhaustively prepared by a teacher but which in the end
could only come from within the student, from the student's
own ideas and from the course those particular ideas needed
to take. Otherwise, one would be dealing not with a piece of
real music but simply with empty mannerism. Writing of

Gershwin, he describes tellingly the unity between the artist's impulse to speak and what he in fact says. He contrasts this natural process with the mannerism of those who simply graft devices gleaned from speculation and the fashions of the day onto "a minimum of idea." "Such music," he writes, "could be taken to pieces and put together in a different way, and the result would be the same nothingness expressed by another mannerism." For many of his pupils, this integrity of process became internalized as a kind of musical conscience.

That he could be terrifying, destructive, and downright mean to some of his students is clear from a reading of Dika Newlin's accounts or those of John Cage, to whom he was musically discouraging even while considering him "an inventor of genius." (While under Schoenberg's tutelage, Cage was an unpromising student of harmony.) Yet even to Cage he gave valuable (and rather Cageian) advice:

> He said one of the ways to compose is to go over what you are doing and see if it still works as you add something else to it. Just go over it again and see how it continues, how it flows . . . so as to make something that flows.

One can also see a fascinating connection between the incipient numerology of Schoenberg and the use of numbers as the basis of Cage's "chance" music. Cage himself has called attention to this, drawing the distinction between his use of, say, the structure of DNA or the *I Ching* to generate music that is as far from conveying intentional "content" as possible and Schoenberg's or Bach's use of numerological principles to express emotions and specific ideas.

However intimidating he may have been and however intolerant of opposition (in later years the pianist and composer Oscar Levant often referred to his conversations with Schoenberg as "exchanging his ideas with him"), his focus on the masters of the past and on musical "practice" in the works of these masters, coupled with his belief in each person's creative individuality, made him exceptional among twentieth-century composers who taught: his students became his disciples, but they went their own ways creatively and were not his clones.

Among his other students from his first years of teaching were the composers Hanns Eisler, Roberto Gerhard, and Viktor Ullmann and the conductor Hermann Scherchen.

In 1923, Mathilde Schoenberg died. At the time Schoenberg drafted the text of a requiem but never set it to music. The descriptions of Mathilde in the years following the Gerstl episode ("silent," "inactive"), and even the portraits of her painted by her husband, suggest, at the very least, deep sadness. At the time of her death she had been ill for some time and living in a sanatorium outside Vienna.

After her death the composer is described as smoking and drinking heavily, taking codeine and a substance called Pantopon, an opium derivative. His daughter and son-in-law attempted to stay with him but moved out after finding him intolerably quarrelsome. He later agreed apologetically that he was impossible to live with.

On August 18, 1924, shortly before his fiftieth birthday, he married Gertrud Kolisch, the sister of his student Rudolf Kolisch, a violinist and founder of the Kolisch Quartet. Thus, for the second time in his life, he married the sister of a trusted musical colleague. He had first gotten to know Gertrud at the society, where she often attended rehearsals and performances. The composer's portraits of his new wife convey her vivacity, humor, and forthrightness and are executed with a palpable lightness of touch. Beautiful and stylish, Gertrud was to be the mother of Nuria, Ronald, and Lawrence Schoenberg. Under the assumed name "Max Blonda" she would write the libretto for the opera *Von Heute auf Morgen* (*From Today to Tomorrow*),

Schoenberg, *Portrait of Gertrud Schoenberg*

in which some of the marital and aesthetic crises of her husband's life were humorously exorcised.

Fall 1923 had also brought Hitler's unsuccessful coup d'état, followed by his jailing, during which he wrote *Mein Kampf.*

Schoenberg first expressed his support for the idea of a Jewish state in 1924. In 1925 the fourteenth Zionist Congress was held in Vienna, while outside in the streets there were attacks on Jews and on Jewish shops reminiscent of the Russian pogroms.

Fortuitously, Schoenberg was offered an important post at the Prussian Academy in Berlin at this very moment, due to the death of Busoni. Amazingly enough, and despite a barrage of published protests that were both musical and racial, it was an "appointment for life."* On his way he spent time in Venice,

---

*The worst of these protests was an October 1925 attack in the *Zeitschrift für Musik* (translated in Alexander L. Ringer, *Arnold Schoenberg: The Composer as Jew*, Oxford: Oxford University Press, 1990, p. 224).

where, on September 7, at the International Society for Contemporary Music, he conducted his important new Serenade, op. 24 (a technically hybrid work that is partly twelve-tone, partly fourteen-tone (!), and partly more "freely" atonal)* and, on September 8, Igor Stravinsky played his own new Piano Sonata.

It would appear that it was at this moment that the two composers and their "followers" became polarized, even though the record suggests that neither heard the other's work at the festival and that the two men did not meet while in Venice. They had left each other on fine terms in 1912 and Schoenberg had programmed a number of pieces by the Russian composer at his Society for Private Musical Performances, among them the *Berceuses du Chat*, *Pribaoutki*, and the Three Pieces for String Quartet. Paradoxically, the Serenade, op. 24, performed at the festival, may even show signs of a Stravin-

---

*The lively, inventive, and (in Robert Craft's phrase) instrumentally "delectable" Serenade, op. 24, was composed over a three-year period (from late July or early August 1920 to April 14, 1923) during which the composer also worked on *Die Jakobsleiter* (abandoned for good in 1922), completed the Five Piano Pieces, op. 23, and began and completed the Piano Suite, op. 25. This was the very period in which he was first discovering the possible applications of the serial principle and a way to compose as he had always done (that is, working with discrete musical themes and motifs and subjecting them to what he called "developing variation") while referring everything that happened back to one basic row (or "series"). This unfolding evolution in his compositional methods in all probability contributed to his abandonment of *Die Jakobsleiter*, begun in his previous style (that of free atonality), which interested him less and less. It also had a fascinating impact on the eventual character of the Serenade. In the summer of 1920, Schoenberg made sketches for music in five of the work's seven movements, all based on a row of fourteen notes comprising eleven different pitches. Eventually only the variations movement retained this fourteen-note row and used it consistently, but the original impulse had clearly been to have a unified source for all the movements. The row of the march remained fourteen-tone, but the pitches from the original sketch were later changed. In addition, none of the other six movements of the Serenade is as strictly serial as the variations movement; rather they are marriages of serial organization and freer atonal chromaticism, with the sonnet being based not on a fourteen-note row, as had been originally planned, but on a twelve-note one. Two additional movements that were intended to be part of the Serenade and that were also inconsistently serial were left unfinished. The penultimate movement, the hauntingly delicate "Lied (ohne Worte)," marked pianissimo throughout, was composed in a single day (March 30, 1923). Thus, while aesthetically wonderfully unified, the Serenade is a technically heterogeneous work.

skyan influence in its witty march movements. (Schoenberg was known to have liked *L'Histoire du Soldat*.) But in the partisan atmosphere of the festival, with back-to-back performances illustrating two such divergent directions for new music—this being the first public performance of a work containing twelve-tone writing as well as an early airing of Stravinsky's so-called neoclassical vein—the stage was set for rivalry. Continually stoked by feuding proponents of the two approaches and fueled by polemics, misunderstandings, and journalistic misquotes, the sense of a polarity between the two camps of contemporary music persisted until Schoenberg's death in 1951. The composers never met again and Stravinsky heard no work of Schoenberg's from the time of their powerful encounter in Berlin in 1912 until 1945.

After the festival Schoenberg was irritated by the direction taken by a number of his colleagues, including Křenek and Hindemith, who thought of themselves as pursuing a "new classicism" (a classicism that he found for the most part illusory, arbitrary, false, impoverished, and not new), but it was clearly the Russian who was the target of his verse, set to a mirror canon, used as the second of his *Three Satires for Mixed Chorus*, op. 28:

> *Why, who could be drumming away there?*
> *If it isn't little Modernsky!* [kleine Modernsky]*
> *He's had his pigtails cut.*
> *Looks pretty good!*
> *What authentic false hair!*
> *Like a wig!*
> *Quite (as little Modernsky conceives of him)*
> *Quite the Papa Bach.*

Kleine Modernsky would in turn many years later describe Schoenberg as, among other things, "small in stature." "I am five feet three inches," he said, "and weigh 120 pounds. These measurements were exactly the same fifty years ago, but Schoenberg was shorter than I am" (Stravinsky and Craft, *Dialogues*, p. 54).

To Schoenberg, Stravinsky's celebrated evolution must have seemed like so many chic, attention-grabbing shifts in direction, like the donning of successive wigs. In addition, the Russian had made some remarks to journalists about the ridiculousness of the idea of "music of the future" that the Viennese composer took personally. Later Schoenberg was to write a few more specific attacks against Stravinsky's current idiom, including a 1926 essay, "Igor Stravinsky: *Der Restaurateur*," and a 1928 assessment of *Oedipus Rex* that, in a manner similar to that of the later critiques of Theodor Adorno, accused it of containing nothing to like—only the studied absence of the usual. These are among Schoenberg's least convincing writings.

But beyond these few statements there is very little in the way of documentation of the antagonism between these supposed arch rivals, and considerable evidence of a mutual fascination. Nevertheless, after 1925, anyone who was friends with both men knew to keep this dual allegiance secret.

It goes without saying that when two artists of the stature of Schoenberg and Stravinsky deride each other's work, a selective deafness is in operation. Yet it is staggering to see how much these two brilliant musicians must have misunderstood each other. In Stravinsky's case, of course, after *Pierrot Lunaire* he simply heard nothing by Schoenberg for many years— which was a simple enough matter since one would have had to deliberately seek out performances by Schoenberg—and, until the arrival of Robert Craft on the scene, he was supported in his ignorance and biases by those around him. Schoenberg, however, had heard a certain amount of his "rival's" music and often seemed to appreciate it.

Each was struggling to bring into the world something new and perhaps could only do so with the thought that he alone was right. They were alike in their search for renewal but diverged on the nature of that renewal. Stravinsky still heard music tonally but was finding an extraordinarily original way of *being* tonal, a whole new harmonic syntax to go with his unique sense of formal and rhythmic structure. He was steeped in history, but his tonality was as if reinvented rather than postromantic. He had focused and pared down his tonal language in a way that made tonality function with a renewed and contemporary freshness. Schoenberg had meanwhile created a systematic way of working in his atonal world. And, to state the obvious and oversimplify as well, the two men came from different worlds. While Schoenberg was trying to continue the Germanic tradition of thematic development, which valued internal qualities of coherence, substance, and human expression over external charm, Stravinsky's work sprang from Russian and French roots, music of a less obviously "emotional" cast in which beauty seemed to issue more directly from sound itself than from the working out of its ideas, the tradition behind impressionism and the world of ballet: a tradition in which the composer was more inspired artisan than musical philosopher or intense visionary, a music in which, ideally, the composer practically disappeared.* Russian and French music also had roots outside the concert hall in folklore, emulating its spontaneity, the powerful simplicity of its elements, and its ability to create something arresting with limited harmonic means. Debussy, who strongly influenced Stravinsky's first works, avoided traces of motivic development that drew attention to themselves as such. (There is a story that the young Debussy, attending a symphony concert with a friend, walked out on a "Germanic" symphony with the words "Let's go, he's beginning to 'develop.'") Stravinsky considered himself a "maker" in the tradition of the medieval *homo faber*. Before the premiere of his choral work *Persephone* he said that he wanted his work to simply be, "like a nose." In this music the strivings and mystical yearnings of the individual creator were subsumed in the object

---

*This is not to minimize the appreciation of many French composers—Ravel and later Milhaud and Poulenc among them—for Schoenberg's music or to gloss over Schoenberg's deep admiration for the music of Debussy and Ravel.

that was the work itself. It is no coincidence that Nadia Boulanger, who was to be such a champion of Stravinsky's music, was of both Russian and French ancestry.

These two traditions lie behind Schoenberg's perception, on the one hand, that Stravinsky's music represented "style" over "idea" and Stravinsky's prejudice, on the other, that Schoenberg's work, while masterful, was overly complex, systematic, cerebral, and narrowly expressionistic. Both composers considered the other naive in some respects. Stravinsky's researches into the nature of music and into music history, rhythm, instrumentation, and musical construction made him run in the opposite direction from his Viennese counterpart. Even late in life, his appreciation of Hugo Wolf and Mahler was limited and his admiration for Wagner covert and overshadowed by the all-out attack he had directed against him in his lectures and his book *Poetics of Music.**

In a sense the quarrel had even to do with sound itself. The clear, bell-like sonorities at the close of *Les Noces*, the austere litanies of the Symphonies of Wind Instruments, or the serene transparency of *Apollo's* string writing contrast markedly with the densities and timbral mixtures of Five Pieces, *Moses und Aron*, or even the Serenade, one of the works of Schoenberg's that comes closest in places to sounding something like that of the Russian composer.

Yet they were not necessarily natural antagonists and the story of their first encounter suggests as much.

The problems between the two camps seem to have been exacerbated when they arrived at a seasoned middle age, at the exact point when each was pursuing a steady path that seemed to point a way forward, a path that could be articulated and fought for by adherents, as it no doubt was at the International Society for Contemporary Music festival in 1923. Both composers also made frequent use of older formal structures

---

*Though nothing Stravinsky said about Wagner quite equals his succinct dismissal of the music of Richard Strauss: "I do not like the major works, and I do not like the minor works."

during the twenties and thirties, and in a sense both were in a phase to which the term *classical* could be applied.

It was in the context of explaining his new way of working to his students that Schoenberg made the statement, which later came back to haunt him (and, after his death, to haunt his reputation), that the new "method of composing with twelve tones related only to each other" would ensure the "hegemony of German music" for the next hundred years. Not only would he soon discover that as a Jew he was not to be considered German, Austrian, or even a true Viennese, but the word *hegemony* itself would also seem to have been ill-chosen in light of Hitler's plans for Germany's role in the world. The repetition of the phrase created an unpleasant impression, too, in musical circles, including Stravinsky's, where the "hegemony" of the Austro-German tradition—even if meant only benignly as "leadership"—was not a welcome idea.

In his 1948 *Philosophy of Modern Music*, the philosopher Theodor W. Adorno (who had studied with Berg) articulates the difference between the two camps as it was perceived by Schoenberg's followers. Stravinsky's music emerges as that of a talented mimic and mannerist—a wizard at juxtaposition but essentially shallow when compared with the great composers of the past. Scorn is heaped on his supposed "objectivity" and "neoclassicism," as in fact reflecting a negativism that betrays

> the secret of a rebellion which from the very first impulse was not concerned with freedom, but with the suppression of the impulse. . . . Artists such as he . . . have the tactical advantage that they need only bring forth again, from a period of imprisonment, one single means, which they had once cast aside as hopelessly antiquated, in order to launch it as an avant-grade achievement.

And Stravinsky's method is criticized for relying on "the static juxtaposition of 'blocks' " rather than on true development, in the sense that even the development-like contrapuntal interpolations have no power over the fate of the formal course of the composition. . . . Stravinsky . . . spares himself the tormenting self-animation of the material and treats it as would a producer. . . . The decay of the subject—which the Schoenberg school bitterly defends itself against—is directly interpreted by Stravinsky's music as that higher form in which the subject is to be preserved.

By contrast, Schoenberg and his school are said to pursue a deeper and more honest path that acknowledges that "objectivity" or "greatness" or "authenticity" can't just be adopted as a stance but must be earned:

Everything depends, however, upon whether this music, by its attitude, advertises this authenticity as something which it has already attained, or whether—with closed eyes, as it were—it surrenders itself to the demands of the entire matter in the hope of mastering it. It is the willingness to do this which defines . . . the incomparable superiority of Schoenberg.

In the same year that Adorno was writing these words, however, Schoenberg wrote to a friend that he respected the dignity of Stravinsky's current behavior, and later he referred to the book's treatment of Stravinsky as "disgusting." In point of fact, Schoenberg regarded Adorno's writing as convoluted and obscure. In the end, despite Adorno's penetrating intellect and insight, his arguments are rooted only in the surface of Stravinsky's music and, even more fatally, in philosophical concepts. Some of these concepts were provided by Stravinsky himself, who spoke little and rarely of the technical aspect of his composing but whose aesthetic outlooks were well documented (even if often expressed in collaboration with others). But much of what he said acted as a shield to protect his creative process. For example, about composing *Le Sacre du*

Printemps, one of the most original and powerfully cohesive musical structures created in the twentieth century, he wrote simply that he was guided by "no theory" and that "I was a vessel through which 'Le Sacre' passed."

The entire "neoclassical" phase of Stravinsky's work has yet to be well understood technically. Certainly it has turned out to be completely inimitable, which argues against its being described as a "style" at all. Beneath the surface of what appeared to be a kind of collage technique in pieces such as the Symphonies of Wind Instruments and the Serenade for Piano, a profound continuity has been unearthed by recent studies, and what may have appeared to some in Schoenberg's circle to have been simply a compromised and corrupted tonality has emerged as a triumph of original thinking and hearing. In addition, the issue of who this composer was from a psychological point of view has yet to be dealt with. Even if there *is* no such thing as true "objectivity," who is to say that Stravinsky's unique angle of mind, which he once described as directing his attention away from himself and toward "the thing made," needs to be described by *us* as "objective"? In the end, whatever they may think they are doing, artists paint their own portraits, even as they also make things that can survive without them.

For their part, the Stravinsky crowd often seemed deaf to Schoenberg and overzealously partisan. Close associates such as Arthur Lourie, Nadia Boulanger, Ernest Ansermet, and Georges Auric, among others, reinforced Stravinsky's perception of a feud and a divide and made their views public, as if to suggest that the composer they preferred could only flourish at the expense of the Schoenberg circle. Boulanger, who had herself heard *Pierrot* in Berlin, nevertheless maintained a lifelong distance from Schoenberg's music, methods, way of hearing, and aesthetic world, insisting that "Stravinsky was right." (The Austrian composer was likewise disparaging in *his* references to the great French pedagogue, in one humorous passage referring to her as 'Budia Nalanger.') In a 1928 article,

Auric wrote that Berg's *Chamber Concerto* was a "scholastic bore masking under a lugubrious aesthetic at the furthest extreme from the strong and great art of Stravinsky."

The characteristics one notices in the work of artists on first acquaintance with them is bound to be influenced not only by what they have thought and said about themselves but by knowledge of the works by others that superficially resemble theirs. Other equally—or more—important characteristics remain buried. Regrettably, artistic alliances may be formed on grounds that in the end are superficial or even deeply false. In this way an artist can acquire "champions" whom he actually abhors. As Schoenberg himself pointed out, in his day Brahms would find himself irritatingly *praised* for upholding the "classical" tradition so uprooted by his so-called antipode Wagner, when in fact there was "as much organizational order, if not pedantry in Wagner as there was daring courage, if not even bizarre fantasy in Brahms."

In the end one can only marvel that the composer of *Erwartung*, who considered Max Reger a "genius," could so easily dismiss the music of the composer of *Le Sacre du Printemps* and the *Symphony of Psalms* and that "Kleine Modernsky," while lavishing praise on French composer Henri Sauget, would neglect to investigate the music of the composer of *Pierrot Lunaire* until that composer had died.

One anecdote from the festival of 1923 has it that when Schoenberg had overrun his rehearsal time for the Serenade, the director of the festival, Edward Dent, "asked him if he thought that he was the *only* composer in the festival. Schoenberg answered: 'Yes.' "*

*This story is confirmed—although in slightly different form—by Alma Mahler, who was present at the rehearsal (*And the Bridge*, p. 180).

17

———╫———

A CLEARING IN THE FOREST:

TWELVE-TONE MUSIC

The formulation of the twelve tone-approach, "this concoction of childish mathematics and debatable historical perception" (in the words of Glenn Gould), ushered in a new period of productivity for Schoenberg and a new kind of confidence. His love of older music expressed itself in the adoption of traditional forms and stylistic traits, while he pursued the exploration of his new melodic and harmonic language in a thoroughly modern manner. The mathematical and the deeply musical—innovation and tradition—were wedded; all of Schoenberg's tendencies—the need for order, for unity of materials combined with unceasing development, for principles that could underpin works on a large scale, for innovation and a sense that music was progressing, for a new sound world that could express inner truths free of modishness, his love of games and reverence for numbers—came together in this approach. The resulting music, when compared with the works of the expressionist period, exuded its own kind of "new classicism." In retrospect it can be seen how very close he had been to this method of writing in the works of 1908–17. But now he had a way of thinking about and planning his work that he could explain to himself.

Schoenberg was quite reluctant, however, to speak publicly about this new "twelve-tone approach." With characteristic foresight, he felt that because it constituted a new "method" it would distract people from the essence of the compositions. It wasn't until he had become aware of the experiments of Josef Hauer in what appeared to be a similar direction that he called his students together one morning in February 1923 to explain it.* He felt that Hauer's efforts were abstractions divorced from music. He emphasized that he was, in fact, composing as he always had and that his pieces in this phase were twelve-tone *compositions*, not *twelve-tone* compositions.

There is a wonderful account of the meeting at the Schoenberg home in Mödling at which the method was first explained. (During this period, Schoenberg's students were welcome at his home at almost any time, and chamber music reading sessions of Haydn, Mozart, Beethoven, and Brahms were held every Sunday. At these, Schoenberg played viola and Anton Webern the cello.) As the "master" talked and demonstrated the use of the row in a new piano piece, his friends and students struggled to follow what he was saying but showed increasing understanding and enthusiasm. The one with misgivings was Webern. He seemed to be holding his acceptance of the idea in reserve, waiting for something. Finally, when Schoenberg mentioned that

---

*Hauer, who lived from 1883 to 1959, never recovered from the sense that he, rather than Schoenberg, deserved to be considered the inventor and preeminent practitioner of twelve-tone music. He even attached this description to his name on a rubber stamp with which he signed his letters.

in a certain spot he had transposed the row up a tritone, Webern asked him why. Schoenberg answered, "I don't know." Webern was pleased. That confirmation that the ear still remained the final arbiter of the music was what Webern needed to hear.

Schoenberg's original definition of his "new procedure in musical construction" was, "Method of Composing with Twelve Tones Which Are Related Only with One Another." The operative word in his definition is the first *with*. The composer still has to *be* a composer, or the "method" *with* which he is composing will not be much help. He did not write: "A Method for Composing: Use Twelve Tones Which Are Related Only with One Another."

In fact, properly speaking, it is not a "method for composing" but a method for establishing the tonal (tonal meaning "tones") world of a specific piece out of the twelve notes of the chromatic scale. Once it is established, one must then create a piece of *music* in this tonal world. This definition makes it plain why there are twelve-tone pieces of every level of quality.

The word *related* is also crucial. What *relates* tones that succeed one another, whether or not they are in a certain scale or mode, are the intervals between them. Twelve different tones in a row create a specific tune, which is really a series of intervals, and what Schoenberg had been working with for more than a decade now was *a language of intervals not used in a tonal context*. (Think of the thirds in the *Pierrot Lunaire* tune.) To prove that a tune is not a series of specific tones but rather a series of *relationships*—or "intervals"—between tones, we need only think of singing a tune to a child and hearing the child sing the tune back in his or her own range and *own key*. Clearly the child has retained the *shape* the tune makes—the intervals—and can reproduce and recognize that shape even when it is made of different tones.

As he had worked with twelve tones in the period before developing his "method," Schoenberg had become an expert on what the ear recognizes—consciously or not—as a variation or outgrowth of what has gone before. He found that if he used a specific succession of notes as his basis for a composition, the ear would hear any other version of the same succession of the *intervals* created by these tones as belonging to the same tonal family. This was true if he turned the original "row" (or, later, "series") upside down (inverted), and it was also true even if he played the row backwards, thus reversing the order of the intervals (retrograde) or if he turned *that* form of the row upside down (retrograde inversion). So the original row carried within it three additional forms that quite naturally derived from it, in the same way that in Bach's fugues, let's say, the fugue subject gives rise to many versions of itself—twice as fast, twice as slow, upside down, in minor instead of major—that the ear easily recognizes as springing from the original tune. These are not so much four versions of the row as they are the *same* row presented in different ways. If a duck is reflected in a pond we recognize the mirror image of the duck without thinking of it as a "second duck." In the same way, the "inversion" of the basic set is simply the "reflection" of the original set, and the retrograde is simply the set played backwards, and the retrograde-inversion is simply the inversion played backwards.

Considering these four original versions of the row as a basis for the composition, Schoenberg could then transpose his row to begin on *any* pitch and produce the same four basic related row "shapes" using different notes—in a different "key," as it were. The result was a constellation of forty-eight possible twelve-tone rows, all of which were generated, like replicating cells, from the original one. Whether or not the use of these transpositions would mimic tonality to the extent of making its original row a quasi-tonal "home base" for the piece would depend on choice. There are many twelve-tone compositions in which something like this seems to be true, and many others in which the question of *which* of the twelve "prime" forms of the row is the "original" one is unclear or irrelevant. But in any case, this constellation of rows paralleled the circular, self-contained solar system of tonality, in which when one moved from one place to another in a composition—from one key area to another—one felt it to be motion because of the tonal relationships established earlier in the piece. In other words, with this "method" the composer would, as in tonality, establish at the outset of the piece, or at least in the background of it, a series of relationships between tones that would hold true for the notes in that piece—"rules," one might say—only the relationships would be purely intervalic and not "tonal" in the old sense. So this, too, would be a self-contained world.

And this is where the word *only* in his definition comes from. The twelve tones would not be tied to tonality or to what one would might have previously expected of them. They would be "related *only* with one another."

In a 1923 essay concerning twelve-tone music, he explained that at the root of the idea was "the unconscious urge to try out the new resources independently," to enjoy "whatever can *only* be attained by new resources when the old ones are excluded!" This is why octave doublings tended to be avoided in the first twelve-tone works (though this restriction became looser over time) since octave doublings create an emphasis—the momentary impression of "a root, or maybe even a tonic," the implications of which would not be pursued. And for this reason Schoenberg tended in many twelve-tone pieces to use rows that were made in such a way that the inversion a fifth below the original set produced the notes of the two halves of the row in their reverse order. This meant that when they were used in different voices at the same time, they did not repeat one another's notes. It is interesting to see that latent in this idea is a suggestion of the old contrapuntal elegance of *contrary motion*, since the line of an inversion is, by definition, the mirror image in contour of the original form. Intriguing, too, is the remnant of tonic-dominant thinking implicit in the use of the fifth for transposition, but it should be remembered that in twelve-tone music each interval is exactly what it always was, and each interval has a distinctly different sound. The tones are still tones. *They* don't know what number in the row they are! And so a fifth still retains its powers as a fifth. (It is again irresistible not to draw the connection here to the "powers" allotted to each of the chess pieces in the "coalition chess" game that the composer designed. See ch. 22.)

	I	II	III	IV	V	VI	VII	VIII	IX	X	XI	XII
1	C#	D	G#	F#	G	F	B	A	B♭	C	E♭	E
2	C	C#	G	F	F#	E	B♭	G#	A	B	D	E♭
3	F#	G	C#	B	C	B♭	E	D	E♭	F	G#	A
4	G#	A	E♭	C#	D	C	F#	E	F	G	B♭	B
5	G	G#	D	C	C#	B	F	E♭	E	F#	A	B♭
6	A	B♭	E	D	E♭	C#	G	F	F#	G#	B	C
7	E♭	E	B♭	G#	A	G	C#	B	C	D	F	F#
8	F	F#	C	B♭	B	A	E♭	C#	D	E	G	G#
9	E	F	B	A	B♭	G#	D	C	C#	E♭	F#	G
10	D	E♭	A	G	G#	F#	C	B♭	B	C#	E	F
11	B	C	F#	E	F	E♭	A	G	G#	B♭	C#	D
12	B♭	B	F	E♭	E	D	G#	F#	G	A	C	C#

Row Forms for *Moses und Aron*

Forty-eight rows, with twelve notes in each, amount to 576 notes! But a chart of all the possible row forms deriving from the original row requires writing down only 144. By writing them down in the form of a twelve-by-twelve square, as in a crossword puzzle, one has all the forms if one writes the original row across the top line and its inversion down the first column on the left and simply adds all the transposed original (also called "prime") forms of the row across each line, starting with the notes (of the inversion) given at the beginning of each line. In this way, one ends up with a magic square containing the original forms when read across, the retrograde when read across backwards, from right to left, the inversion when read down, and the retrograde of the inversion when read up.

The notion of the forty-eight possible row forms was only the beginning, of course. For one thing, the construction of the row itself was already a part of the composing. The rows often contained symmetries, striking melodic or intervalic characteristics, or, particularly in Schoenberg's case, "complementarities." Often the row would be constructed out of a preexisting melody—one could easily make a row out of the series of notes that begin *Pierrot Lunaire*, for instance—or would be extrapolated from a small intervalic motif. And often in the first twelve-tone works, very few row transpositions or even row forms were used to make pieces that sound remarkably varied. For example, Webern, composing a charming atonal minuet in 1925 (no doubt in emulation of his teacher's Piano Suite (see below) managed to take advantage of the consistency of the row—using *nothing* but the original form—while very much disguising it. The phrase lengths are varied so that they almost always start at a different point in the series. This and the wide leaps of the writing (since the notes of the row can be used in any octave) beguile the listener away from hearing that the piece is made of nineteen repetitions of twelve notes in the same order:

Webern, Minuet (op. posthumous)

The fact of the matter is that the *sound* of the piece, its materials, its aesthetic represent not a change in direction from Webern's earlier music but rather a kind of consolidation. To this day listeners and writers about music routinely refer to atonal works that preceeded twelve-tone writing, such as Berg's *Wozzeck*, as "twelve-tone," so latent was the twelve-tone principle in the works written by Schoenberg, Webern, and Berg in the years before they adopted it. At the time it must have seemed as much a "discovery" as an "invention"—an insight into how they were hearing. For many years they had been using not only the twelve tones of the chromatic scale as a basis but twelve "equal" tones, with "equal rights," to use Webern's words.

Glenn Gould again:

> . . . the odd thing about it was that with this oversimplified, exaggerated system Schoenberg began to compose again; and, not only did he compose, he embarked upon a period of about five years which contains some of the most beautiful, colorful, imaginative, fresh, inspired music which he ever wrote. . . . Of what strange alchemy was this man compounded that the sources of his inspiration flowed most freely when stemmed and checked by legislation of the most stifling kind?

Although it coincided with the rise of Nazism, this period was one of stability and much accomplishment for Schoenberg personally. If one senses less angst, regret, and world-weariness in the music written during this time, this can be attributed in part to his newfound compositional fluency and also, surely, in part to his new marriage.

It is obvious to the reader by now that Schoenberg loved to look at *everything* in as many ways as possible. One of the barriers to an immediate understanding of his music is surely both the rapidity with which he develops and transforms his ideas and also the nature of these transformations. After all, it may be relatively easy to recognize a tune when it is played twice as slowly or twice as quickly, but not necessarily when it is also in reverse or upside down. But his techniques truly reflected how his mind worked. Even in his casual doodles, he experimented with all forms of visual play: mirror writing, image reversal, and an almost hallucinatory transformation of forms.

Ex. 20

Examples of doodles by Schoenberg

We have also seen how the chromatic scale increasingly became the underlying basis for his composing and how his almost fanatical respect for tonality itself made the avoidance of tonal references essential to his new approach. In 1926 he had written: "According to my feeling for form the playing of even one tonal triad will bring its own consequences and demand a certain space, which cannot be allowed inside my form. A tonal chord arouses expectations of what is to follow, and, working backwards, of everything that has gone before it."

We have also seen him working with themes that are played backwards (in retrograde), upside down (inverted), or both at the same time (retrograde-inversion) in the course of being developed. From here it might not seem a great leap to the idea of making a single twelve-note theme, even if it is never *stated* as a theme, the underlying basis for an entire composition.

The twelve-tone row is not a scale. It is a "quarry," in the words of H. H. Stuckenschmidt, from which all the material used in a single work is derived, imparting to it an individual sound world, its own source material in the form of a particular sequence of intervals. It is like a musical DNA chain.

The row is not a scale, nor is it necessarily a theme, but since the linear aspect of a twelve-tone piece will inevitably trace the intervals of the row again and again, that row can easily be stated as a theme if the composer choses to use it that way. There are moments when Schoenberg does just this and other moments when his themes begin at different points in the row, thereby obscuring it as a melodic source. In the "Sonnet of Petrarch" movement of his Serenade, for example, the bass voice sings the same row in the same transposition thirteen times, but since each line of the poem contains eleven syllables and since the vocal setting is entirely syllabic, the melodic line always begins at a new place in the row (starting with the first note, then the twelfth note, then the eleventh note, etc.) and ends in a new place (the eleventh note, followed by the tenth, the ninth, etc.). Theorists call these changing presentations of the same series of pitches "rotated set statements."

The twelve-tone idea in no way replaces tonality. It creates an organizing principle but leaves the issues of how the piece will really "sound," how it will move from place to place, how it will be composed entirely unanswered. These matters will be influenced by the nature of the row itself, which will be the first creative and aesthetic choice of the composition.

To explain a piece in terms of its twelve-tone organization may answer questions about its underlying unity but will not tell us if the music is rewarding to listen to, beautiful, or coherent. In short, it will not tell us if the piece is worthy of being called "music."

Tonality itself is not some self-contained system that can work apart from all the aspects of music that have nothing to do with pitch. To see this demonstrated, one has only to look at compositions by music students attempting to write in the style of Haydn, which, while obeying the "rules" of correct voice leading and harmony, nevertheless are nonsense as music.

While beauty may presuppose some underlying unity and order, unity and order in no way guarantee beauty. If a twelve-tone work is beautiful, then, it is because of what the composer has done with the twelve-tone principle. The organizing principle he invented does not explain Schoenberg's ear for sound. Schoenberg found a way to organize the music he wanted to make, to organize the world of tones that appealed to him as sounds. He did not find a way to organize music and then use it to justify the resulting sounds. The miracle of his twelve-tone works, and the mystery, is that the notes are right, that he discovered new properties of sound and ways of relating tones that made them new and beautiful again. It is only when one listens to these works as music that one appreciates what he accomplished.

Schoenberg himself used the twelve-tone approach differently at different times. His first works of this type were simpler in terms of pitch than those from his "free" atonal phase, and different in their psychological effect as well. These pieces also used comparatively few of the forty-eight row forms available to him for a given piece, when compared with such later large-scale works as *Moses und Aron* or the Violin Concerto. (Webern's first twelve-tone pieces, similarly, are surprisingly simple in this respect.) Notions of play, of aristocratic refinement, of objectivity and graciousness reenter his works with the new "method."

The distinction between "play" and "work" is already hard to draw in the case of artists (as composer Louis Andriessen points out, it is no coincidence that we say that a person "plays" an instrument), but in Schoenberg's case it is especially hard to make since he brought discipline, originality, and playful inventiveness to so many of his activities. His lifelong interest in construction and handicrafts proved useful for musical as well as domestic endeavors. He handmade no fewer than twenty-two different kinds of contraptions—"charts, cylinders, booklets, slide rules"—for transposing and deriving twelve-tone rows. For *Moses und Aron* alone, he constructed five different kinds of devices for deriving rows from the original set, while also producing constructions of more general use that served him for multiple works. For the Wind Quintet, op. 26, he made a chart suggestive of a sundial with inner and outer rotating circles.

It is worth remembering here that the idea of a "series" or "row" has far-reaching connections to musical procedures in the arts of other cultures (gamelan and Ghanaian music come immediately to mind), as well as to techniques in Western music that go back to the beginnings of polyphony—for example, to the use of Gregorian chant melodies as the basis of sacred works in the late Middle Ages and the Renaissance. The "serial" principle was perhaps most conspicuously anticipated in the isorhythmic motets and masses of the fourteenth and fifteenth centuries. In these works a rigorous and unified polyphony was created by combining varied melodic lines that had common sources in a single series of notes ("color") and a fixed pattern of durations ("talea"). Even Schoenberg didn't exploit the possibilities of a rhythmical series, a notion that wasn't taken up again until the era of the post–World War II serial composers.

Inversion and retrograde have surely been around as long as music has been. One finds them in all eras. In Bach we find almost every variety of contrapuntal technique that there is in Schoenberg. In Bach's *Art of the Fugue*, for example, we find an endless storehouse of such examples:

J. S. Bach, Contrapunctus XV,
Art of the Fugue

In the finale of Beethoven's String Quartet, op. 135, an example Schoenberg himself used, we hear:

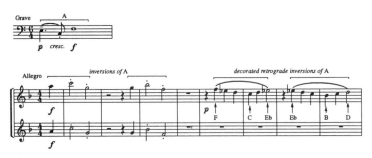

Beethoven, String Quartet, op. 135

Parallels to the twelve-tone approach can be found in the other arts. Paul Klee's suggestively titled 1936 oil *New Har-*

mony, for example, is made up of a series of colored rectangles in six horizontal and seven vertical columns. The sequence of colors is almost completely symmetrical in that, if you divide the painting vertically down the middle, the sequence on the right side is the inverted mirror image of that on the left and, if you divide the picture laterally through the middle, the bottom half is the inverted mirror image of the top half. While the edges of the canvas are perfectly straight, the rectangles themselves are roughly and approximately drawn, and the colors are complex mixtures that are not perfectly duplicated (the two gray rectangles in the center row, for example, are noticeably distinct). The overall effect of this "bilaterally inverted symmetry"—which is the equivalent of a retrograde inversion of the color sequence—is, aptly, harmonious. Interestingly, there are twelve basic color "tones" in use here, though they are individually produced and therefore far from identical. In fact, the "harmony" of the painting relies on just this tension between the mathematical nature of the design and the nuanced imperfection of the execution. The basic shades are dark gray, mud brown, standard brown, tan-brown, black-brown, orange, deep olive green, rust, pinkish red, muddy yellow, light blue-gray, and slate gray.

Klee's early work had emphasized line. He was a gifted caricaturist and illustrator who evolved only gradually into a colorist. In his middle years he went from employing a grid to structure his compositions to sometimes basing a painting on the grid itself. Perhaps this can be compared to the way in which Schoenberg developed a systematic approach to his use of the twelve tones that were already the materials of his expressionist works. Klee's use of line, now in a subservient—though crucial—role, both structures and humanizes this painting. The lines create a balanced order but are executed unevenly. Influenced by music all his life, Klee was the son of a musician and had played in the municipal orchestra of Bern before deciding to become a painter. The analogy to twelve-tone music in this work may well be intentional.

Schoenberg's Suite for Piano, op. 25, is based on a row that is in itself witty:

The first two groups of four notes (called "tetrachords") end in a tritone, and the first and last notes are a tritone apart. The last four notes of the row suggest a cadence on B-flat (perhaps over a V/V–V–I progression) and furthermore spell the name Bach backwards (H means B, and B means B-flat in German).* This four-note "Bach" motto is also given prominence in the Variations for Orchestra, op. 31. (It should be observed that the caricature of the female pianist on page 73, above, was done during the year the composer began the Suite. The name Bach is placed where the manufacturer's name usually appears on the keyboard.)

By basing all the movements of the Suite on the four forms of this row plus the transposition of the row that *begins* on B-flat, Schoenberg creates a field of possible row forms all of which begin on B-flat and end on E, or vice versa. (This bit of pitch magic occurs because the tritone is exactly half of an octave and therefore when inverted simply becomes another tritone.) This means that the end of every row can

---

*According to C. P. E. Bach, these were the very last notes J. S. Bach himself wrote in his final work, *Art of the Fugue* (see Ray Robinson and Allen Winold, *A Study of the Penderecki St. Luke Passion*, Celle: Moeck Verlag, 1983, p. 64).

also be the first note of another form of the row. One can see this principle in action in measures 3–4 of the Praeludium, the work's first movement, where the repeating B-flats that ended the first statement of the original form of the row become the first notes of the I6 form. (In the term *I6 form* of the row, *I* stands for "inversion" and *6* for the number of half steps above the original inverted form of the set. Here it means a transposition of the inversion up six half steps from E, to B-flat.)

Other surprising correspondences result from this particular transposition, allowing for variety and audible connections between different row forms. For example, in the very first two measures of the Praeludium the left hand imitates the right hand in canon at the tritone (the transposed form of the row). The left-hand tune is the same as the right-hand, but in a different rhythm. Because of the nature of this particular transposition, though, the third and fourth notes of the left hand are the *same* as the third and fourth notes in the right. If one checks this with the group of rows shown at the outset, it becomes clear that the tritones within the row, as well as those at each end, also correspond in an interesting way, and Schoenberg makes musical use of this fact. (Incidentally, the tritone of the third and fourth pitches G–D-flat is the same as the tritone in the "Pierrot tune.")

The suite contains four movements based on Baroque dance forms, and two that are freer: the stylishly Baroque

Praeludium that begins the work and the more introspective, Brahmsian Intermezzo that marks the halfway point. Interestingly, the composer worked on these two less "Baroque" pieces first, in 1921, and finished the rest of the score in 1923.* Looking at just the beginnings of the movements, one sees how the rows create ideas that connect the pieces in multiple ways, giving them the character of a series of variations on a set of twelve notes. If one plays the first measure and a half of the Praeludium, Gavotte, and Musette and the first six eighth notes of the Gigue, they give the impression of a theme and variations: after all, the melody and most of the other notes are the same. Sometimes a particular segment of the row becomes the melody. The Minuet begins with the second tetrachord of the row in the right hand. Tuneful as it is, when one rehears the piece one is likely to notice it anticipated in the left hand of the Praeludium in measure 2 (transposed up a tritone) and in the left hand of the Intermezzo (at the same pitches as in the Minuet).

The musette was a court dance form associated with the rustic bagpipe of the same name that was popular in seventeenth- and eighteenth-century France. (One can find examples in the keyboard pieces of Couperin, and there is a musette in Bach's English Suite no. 3). Schoenberg's Musette makes a quasi-cubist object out of the bagpipe drone, spreading his repeating Gs over three octaves, which if properly played set up a bell-like resonance that simulates a drone. The dainty and amusing Musette is not without its expressionistic outbursts, too:

---

*Not only was his 1921 conception of the work not "neo-Baroque," but the two movements composed at that time, as well as his original sketches, show no fixed linear ordering of the basic twelve-tone row. Several scholars have argued that the Praeludium and Intermezzo are based on the consistent use of three tetrachords that were turned into one linear series only in 1923. For a full discussion of the gestation period of Schoenberg's opuses 23, 24, and 25, see Ethan Haimo, *Schoenberg's Serial Odyssey*, Oxford: Clarendon Press, 1990.

The Gigue is ferociously difficult to play. Its manic energy evokes cubistically the multivoiced counterpoint of Bach's gigues for solo instruments, which often create the outlines of several simultaneous voices through wide-leaping melodic contours:

J. S. Bach, Gigue,
Violin Partita no. 2 in D Minor

Rhythmically, there is a playful alternation of groups of three and two that recalls similar moments in gigues from past times. In pieces with a steady rhythm in six, a simple change in articulation makes the difference between hearing the notes as two groups of three or three groups of two.

As it hurtles along, with its repeated notes recalling the opening Praeludium, the Gigue builds up a head of steam and for the only time in the piece briefly spins out an entirely new row (beginning at measure 16), deriving from passages in the Gigue itself rather than from the original row order, and created as if out of the music's own exuberance.

Because the row ends with an ascending half step—as does a major or minor scale or a full cadence—it is easy to create imitation "tonal" cadences throughout the Suite. These are, in effect, musical "puns."

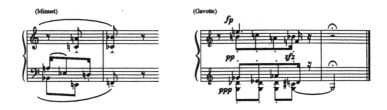

I disagree with commentators who describe the Suite as a demonstration of the twelve-tone method's ability to be in continuity with the past. I think it is something more natural than a demonstration: it is pure dance music.

18

SATIRES

You must not take it amiss that I have not written you—to make up for that, I have often thought of you, and that at least has more, and better, style than it would have in writing. And is also more legible. And I don't get writer's cramp, or you yawner's cramp from boredom. And I must not insult myself by the mere suspicion that anyone can find me boring.

—Schoenberg, in a 1909 letter to Alma Mahler

Schoenberg smiles in his Wind Quintet, op. 26. How could players in 1924, the year of its completion, play this huge, challenging work with the charm, ease, and restraint it calls for? To begin with, it is technically difficult and a test of endurance. And at first glance it would appear to combine the worst of two worlds: the academic and the (then) avant-garde. Entirely twelve-tone (and based on one row and its derivative versions throughout), it is also carefully modeled on the classical examples taught in conservatory. On paper it looks scholastic, recalling those studies in form (*Formenlehre*) that in European music education of the late nineteenth century were mandatory alongside harmony and counterpoint, as if the "forms" themselves were essentially separate from the elements of the language that gave rise to them. But Schoenberg didn't believe in forms as "molds," only as results.

The quintet medium is problematic for performer and composer alike. One reedless woodwind (the flute), one single reed (clarinet), two double reeds (oboe and bassoon), and a takeover, less than agile brass instrument (French horn) must be made to work together as a chamber ensemble. The instruments do not constitute a family, as does a string quartet; the means of sound production are varied. Dynamically, the flute is weak in its low register, the oboe is difficult to control and loud in *its* low register, the clarinet tends to stridency in its upper register, and the horn is hard to play discreetly in *its* upper register. In addition to these questions of balance there is the problem of the sameness of orchestration that results from placing the instruments too much of the time in the same general registers and relationships to one another. But how else is one to proceed when only the bassoon can easily cover the lowest register and the flute the uppermost?

Needless to say, there are many wonderful wind quintets. But in some of them this potentially ill-matched assortment of instruments seems to fuse into one rather neutral vehicle, less expressive and interesting than any one of the instruments is alone.

Opus 26 is Schoenberg's only work employing winds alone.* He approaches the ensemble as an essentially contrapuntal medium of disparate individual timbres. The agility and sparkle characteristic of the medium are there—we find the nimbleness and clarity of *Pierrot* without that work's eeriness—but the piece has a weight and substance that is rare in the literature for the ensemble. The timbres are deftly varied. Moments for trio and quartet groupings give relief, as does

---

*The 1943 Theme and Variations for Band employs string basses.

the use of piccolo in all of movement 2 and briefly in movement 4.

Years later his son-in-law described his work process:

> I saw how he worked for instance on the woodwind quintet, and it was from measure to measure. In the evening, he stopped and it continued there and he never [erased anything unless] there was a slip of the pencil. Otherwise it came out of his mind . . . when he was at the last movement, he knew the row in all its forms by heart. He didn't have to write it down again.

Early performers of the work must have been particularly conscious of its twelve-tone methodology. As with the Suite for Piano, its use of the row forms is immediately apparent to the eye:

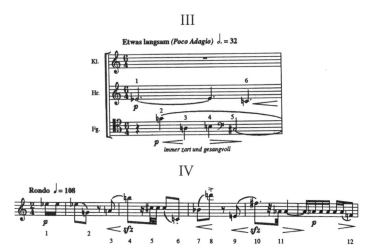

But to the ear, which can't and won't count, more apparent are
the counterpoint, the long lyrical lines, the forms (Sonata/
Scherzo and Trio/ABA Song Form/Rondo), the colors, and
the moods of the work. A wit and ebullience verging on the
ecstatic permeates movements 2 and 4, and a quality of transparency, of *serenitas* rare in this composer's output is felt in the
perfectly proportioned loveliness of the opening movement or
in a phrase such as this one from the extraordinarily beautiful
Poco Adagio (movement 3):

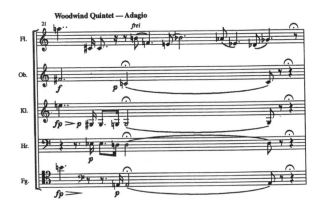

Therefore, even at forty minutes, opus 26 is not too long.

The descriptions of Schoenberg by his colleagues emphasize his magnetism, warmth, liveliness, energy, ability to inspire, and, frequently, his mischievous, "unique sense of humor," alongside the darker character traits (among them his famous need for unswerving loyalty from his students) that are perhaps better known. There may be no smiling "self-portraits" in his artistic output and relatively few smiling photographs of him, but there is considerable humor in his writings and correspondence, and there is a range of humor in the music.

The note of satire sounded subtly in the early cabaret songs comes to the fore in the twelve-tone works, particularly the Serenade, op. 24, the Suite, op. 29 for seven instruments, *Von Heute auf Morgen*, and, of course, the *Drei Satiren*. (For a brief time during the period in which he composed these works, he also grew a moustache, a personal "stylization" of a kind.) There are many gradations of humor to be found in his work overall, ranging from the ghoulish and sardonic ("Galgenlied" and "Gemeinheit" in *Pierrot*) to the satiric (*Von Heute auf Morgen*), the parodistic (Suite, op. 29), the playful (March from the Serenade), and the extremely funny ("The New Classicism" in *Drei Satiren*). In order to perceive and enjoy this humor, however, one needs to become accustomed enough to Schoenberg's language to discover that his chromaticism is not always associated with the expression of extreme seriousness and angst.

The first movement of the Serenade (for clarinet, bass clarinet, mandolin, guitar, violin, viola, and cello) seems a kind of apotheosis of the cabaret "Nachtwandler" from 1901. The march rhythm, a festival of plucked sounds, is a Keystone Kops dance of uncertainty, tripping over itself, proceeding securely for a few beats, running into its own retrograde, falling on its face. The tune, by contrast, is a comedy of three different voices in rhythmic unison, like drunken out-of-tune singers. Meanwhile there is an off-kilter oompah bass in the cello:

In the "Tanzschritte" ("Dance Steps") from the Septet Suite, op. 29 (a work dedicated to Gertrud Schoenberg that uses the pitches derived from her initials as a musical motto), the violin plays a waltz whose sweeping romantic gestures bring a smile, all the more so because on the page the waltz appears to be in two rather than three:

Change the notes, and one is in the realm of Johann Strauss. The twelve-tone tune is a humorous hybrid, like one of those George Grosz caricatures of an aristocrat wearing a top hat, shirt, and tie, and nothing else.

19

╫

CATASTROPHE

One should never forget that what one learns in school about history is the truth only insofar as it does not interfere with the political, philosophical, moral or other beliefs of those in whose interest the facts are told, colored or arranged. The same holds true for the history of music.

—"Composition with Twelve Tones" (1941)

One of Schoenberg's most immediately appealing twelve-tone works in his concise and moody Accompaniment to a Film Scene (Begleitmusik zu einer Lichtspielszene). Although the "film scene" was imaginary, Schoenberg appended a useful "synopsis" to the score:

Fear—Threatening Danger—Catastrophe

The work dates from 1929–30, years before the very real "catastrophe," but to the contemporary listener the course of events played out musically creates a mental *Lichtspielszene* that does not feel imaginary. The climactic moment of tragedy is followed by a coda that moves like a cortege—solemn rhythms in the brass under a low-lying, full-throated melody in the violins—dwindling into a restatement of the questioning, twilight sounds of the opening and a final sigh. As in all Schoenberg's large-scale works there is no grandiosity in this piece; the voice is personal, concise, almost plain. This is not suffering recollected in tranquillity; the 1930 work feels like foresight.

During the First World War, while Schoenberg and Berg were enduring their stints as soldiers, another Vienna-born soldier, Adolf Hitler, was finding military life congenial. Becoming a part of the German army in 1914, the historian Peter Neville observes, gave Hitler "the comradeship and security he craved," as well as a place to share his increasingly virulent right-wing views. Like the monstrousness of the Holocaust itself, Hitler's monstrousness progressed in stages, starting with the confusions, troubles, and anger of his childhood and early manhood. The fourth son of his father's third wife, and not entirely certain of his own ancestry, he became obsessed with the concept of lineage early on. (Like many of the other future leaders of the Nazi party and defenders of "German blood," he was not actually born in Germany.) A famously bad-tempered and arrogant young person, he attended the same secondary school in Linz as Ludwig Wittgenstein but failed to get his diploma. For a brief period he tried to become an artist, growing a beard and living as a bohemian in Vienna while he tried to peddle his paintings and roomed in boardinghouses, where he was known for his frightening outbursts of rage. It was in the army that he began to develop a clear sense of purpose, and it was the German defeat and treaty at Versailles, which many people absurdly linked to Jewish influences, that became his first springboard to political action.

The rise of the Nazi party was not entirely the result of the popularity of its anti-Semitic views. In fact, for a period between 1928 and 1932, the very period in which it accumulated the seats it needed in the parliament, Hitler and the Nazi party moderated their anti-Semitic rhetoric and directed more of their message to the unemployed, to the disillusioned military, and to bankers panicked by losses from the worldwide economic crisis. Even though their views were well known and anti-Semitism was extremely widespread (by 1933 there were over 400 anti-Semitic associations and 700 anti-Jewish periodicals published in Germany), it was possible even for Jews to fool themselves into thinking that once the party was in power it would in fact lose its need to stress this side of its program.

After the Nazis made further advances in the 1932 parliamentary elections, the Schoenbergs, then traveling in Spain, were well aware of what lay in store for them at home and were loath even to return to Germany. But in order to have access to the money in their bank account, they had to. Schoenberg wrote to Berg from Berlin on September 23 that being back made it difficult for him to take any pleasure in his work:

> For here I'm constantly obliged to consider the question whether and, if so, to what extent I am doing the right thing in regarding myself as belonging here or there, and whether it is forced upon me. . . . Of course I know perfectly well where I belong. I've had it hammered into me so loudly and so long that only by being deaf to begin with could I have failed to understand it. . . . Today I am proud to call myself a Jew; but I know the difficulties of really being one.

(As we know, as of 1930 he had been at work on the music for his opera *Moses und Aron.* He had completed a play with a Zionist theme, *Der biblische Weg,* in 1927.)

On January 30, 1933, President Paul von Hindenburg, greatly underestimating Hitler's independence, appointed him chancellor, whereupon thousands of Nazis in uniform took to the streets of Berlin and for several hours paraded in ranks carrying torches and singing the "Horst Wessel Lied" proclaiming the New Order. On May 10 came the orgy of book burning, when works of Jewish writers from Heinrich Heine to Albert Einstein were torched in huge public bonfires.

Once anti-Semitism had become official policy it penetrated into the smallest crevices of daily life. The music community was affected more and more intensely in myriad ways, some highly public, some not. It was in this atmosphere of terror— in which the precise nature of "racial impurity" could always be redefined to fit the circumstances—that, for example, the composer Paul Hindemith came under attack and the conductor Wilhelm Furtwängler ended up resigning his positions as director of the Berlin Philharmonic and of the State Opera. Neither Hindemith nor Furtwängler were Jews, but Hindemith's wife was Jewish (by 1935 such marriages were banned in Germany). In addition, Hindemith regularly performed in a trio with two colleagues who had been fired from their posts for their origins (violinist Szymon Goldberg and cellist Emanuel Feuermann), and his new opera, *Mathis der Maler*, was considered to be a condemnation of Hitler and to contain direct references to the book burnings. When Hindemith came under attack and performances of his works were banned, Furtwängler wrote an impassioned public letter in his defense. The enthusiastic support that audiences showed Furtwängler at the opera and at the Philharmonic following this protest caused Hermann Göring to report the entire matter to Hitler, and Furtwängler, who had a history of speaking out against the wave of dismissals of Jewish musicians, thought it best to step down from his conducting posts. But he decided not to leave Germany, and in 1935 he was reinstalled as conductor of the Philharmonic. In 1937 the Hindemiths fled Germany, eventually settling in the United States.

Today Hitler's views on art can be the object of amusement and mockery, but in the 1930s they were a matter of life and death. On July 18, 1937, at the opening of the Munich House of German Art, on which he himself had worked as a designer, he declared:

Works of art that cannot be understood but need a swollen set of instructions to prove their right to exist and find their way to neurotics who are receptive to such stupid or insolent nonsense will no longer openly reach the German nation. . . . From now on we will conduct a merciless war of purification against the last elements of our cultural decomposition.

The push to expunge "non-Aryan" and "degenerate" influences from the arts was expressed in protests that erupted even during concerts of composition students, such as one given in February 1933, by Professor Walter Gmeindl's class at the Prussian Academy, where Schoenberg also taught. When at this concert a vocally pro-Nazi composer (the head of the Stern Conservatory) stood and loudly denounced a student's music as an offense to German art, the director of the academy, the musicologist Georg Schünemann, a man known for his "political neutrality" and racial tolerance, felt obliged to offer up a weak defense of the young composer, calling him "a good German" whose racial background and politics were irreproachable. Although the senate of the academy originally sided with Schünemann over this incident, in the wake of it he lost his job.

By March 1, the president of the academy announced at a meeting of the senate, with Schoenberg in attendance, that the academy needed to purge itself of "Jewish influences." The newly installed minister of culture and education, Hans Hinkel, had ordered a cultural cleansing of the institution. Schoenberg did not wait to be dismissed. He left the meeting and handed in his resignation from the academy. Thus ended his "appointment for life." On March 17, taking only very few belongings, Schoenberg and his wife, Gertrud, with their one-year-old daughter, Nuria, left for Paris.

20

--------|||------

MOSES AND ARNOLD

*My immediate plan is to do a big tour of America in order to
raise help for the Jews in Germany.... For this has always happened
to me: the person who has gained an impression from what I have
said to him and has believed me is seldom in the position of handing
on the impression to a third person and moving him to believe it.*
—Schoenberg to Anton Webern, August 4, 1933

*It is my fault, for I wanted to be Moses and Aaron in one and the
same person."*
—The character Max Aruns in Schoenberg's play *Der biblische Weg*

In the introduction to this book I wondered if Schoenberg's musical "voice" has had a proper chance to be heard and appreciated
without being fed through the interpretation and mediation of
others. How appropriate, then, is his choice of the story of
Moses and Aaron for opera subject. Moses, who in the Bible
"lacks the gift of speech" and is "slow of speech and slow of
tongue" (or alternatively "heavy of mouth and heavy of tongue"),
is given a *Sprechstimme* role in the opera, singing at only one
point in the entire work, as noted below. Aron, however, is a
mellifluous tenor. Schoenberg's Moses can sing (that is, speak)

only through his brother. Moses' ideas become Aron's music.

Moses is a theatricalized meditation on spiritual matters and the difficulty of expressing them. Sixty-five years ago the critic Paul Rosenfeld identified Schoenberg as above all a creator of fragile and exquisite poetry, an "expression of the gleaming, evanescent moment of feeling." The score of *Moses* is noteworthy among operas for its delicacy of orchestration, often in moments depicting Moses' internal spiritual state, the first of which, the scene of Moses and the Burning Bush, opens the work and prepares the listener for an evening of subtle music. Although, to be sure, by evening's end some mighty sounds have issued from both chorus and orchestra, the score is predominantly a matter of chamber music and chamber singing.

The opening scene places us instantly in the mind of Moses. The mysterious "call" is rendered in the simultaneous presentation of two different types of choruses singing in counterpoint with each other—a singing choir of six soloists and a larger chorus in four- and six-part *Sprechstimme*. These give disorienting musical form to Moses' vision ("Only one, infinite, thou omnipresent one, unperceived, and inconceivable God!") and suggest the multidimensionality of the word for God in the Hebrew language, which is interpreted differently in different contexts but is ultimately untranslatable. *Was*, *is*, and *will be* are all contained in the Hebrew letters *YHWH*, which represent the unknowable God, as are the words *infinite*, *universe*, and *universal*. The music, too, seems everywhere at once, and has Moses in its grip.

When I was in my early twenties I had the pleasure of attending a screening of the Jean-Marie Straub film of *Moses und Aron* at the New York Film Festival. The pleasure was mixed with pain, however, since in my eagerness to get a better seat I had leapt over the row in front of me and broken the fourth toe of my right foot just as the film was starting. The sensation of watching this severe and illuminating version of the opera while being in intense—if strangely remote—pain has stayed with me. Somehow feelings of sacrifice, the sense that there is a cost to things, intimations that understanding and beauty do not come easily, have adhered, not inappropriately, to my feelings about this work.

As noted earlier, the opening of *Die glückliche Hand,* written twenty years previously, in which the character of the man—the isolated, embattled artist—confronts the voices in his head, parallels to an extraordinary degree, in both text and sound, the calling of Moses at the opening of this work. Perhaps *Die glückliche Hand* can be viewed as essentially a mono-drama, like its companion piece *Erwartung,* for one character and the chorus the character *imagines* hearing. Perhaps *Moses* is in some of its scenes really a monodrama, too. The dialogue between the brothers, and between Moses and God, can be seen as an internal one. The Straub film approaches the Burning Bush scene in just this way, by filming it in its entirety with a nearly motionless shot of the back of Moses' head. This not only draws the viewer's attention to the music in a magical way but also makes the head into the very theater in which the drama is occurring. Its earthbound literalism, steeped in the here and now, also seems deeply Jewish.

In this interpretation, *Moses und Aron* expresses a series of dichotomies, beginning with the duality "spoken word—song," all of which could be the expressions of one mind. In Moses' head we find:

Moses	Aron
idea	style
inexpressibility	speech
abstraction	the concrete (miracles)
concept	image
freedom	bondage
prayer	pagan rites
God	Golden Calf
faith	evidence

otherworld   world
prophet   priest

Although the composer himself discouraged this interpretation, parallels have frequently been drawn between the character of the lawgiving, severe Moses and that of the embattled
"prophet" Schoenberg. Certainly from a musical standpoint
Schoenberg brings an equally passionate commitment to the
music of Moses, Aron, and—perhaps the true "star" of the
opera—"the people," the chorus. And surely the composer
identified closely with both brothers. One need look no further
than Aron's soaring melodies; it is Aron who sings the twelve-
tone row behind the entire work note for note in his first appearance in the drama (measures 124–145). The symbolism
here is multifaceted. "O son of my fathers, are you sent by
mighty God?" questions Aron, himself a kind of mirror image
or retrograde of his brother. Likewise the forms of the row he is
singing (retrograde, inversion, and retrograde-inversion) issue
like genetic offspring from the parent row of the work with
which he has begun his speech. Having encountered Moses in
scene 1, we the spectators meet Aron for the first time as he
does Moses, and are introduced simultaneously to the original
material behind the music we have been hearing.

The opera is itself an artistic expression in music of abstract
ideas, and therefore similar to Aron's own expression; it is a
spinning out of music derived from a "sacred tablet," the
twelve tones in all their forms; it is addressed to the public—
the people. Looked at another way, the composer (Moses)
sings his song through a grid—the twelve-tone magic square
(Aron), without which he has no voice. (This perhaps parodies the point of view espoused by Leonard Bernstein in his
Norton Lectures, in which he said in effect that Schoenberg
was such a musician that he could make music *even* through
the artificial constraints of the twelve-tone system.)

It is Aron who is an artist, performer, communicator. If the opera concerns art, it concerns the dilemma of the artist who longs to communicate a vision that will be betrayed if it is made overly concrete. On the other hand, left uncommunicated, the vision itself is valueless. As we have seen, the name Aaron was shortened to Aron so that the opera would not have a title containing thirteen letters. (Also it *would* contain twelve letters.) The name Aron also makes an intriguing comparison with three other first names: Anton, Alban, and Arnold. It is closest to Arnold.

Schoenberg also identified with the other characters in the opera, which is almost Tolstoyan in its delineation of each unnamed character who emerges from the choral mass for a brief moment as a soloist—Tolstoyan in the sense of seeming to portray these moments as if from the character's own point of view. Act 2, scene 3, the scene of the erotic and destructive orgies, is particularly rich in such individualized moments. Whether it be the chorus of old men offering up their last moments in sacrifice, the invalid woman who is miraculously cured, the four naked virgins who are sacrificed, or the youth who is killed protesting the return of idolatry, the attention of the listener is drawn in a sympathetic way to each by the soloistic characterizations of the vocal writing and the aptness and individuality of what happens in the orchestra. For example, the invalid woman sings her brief aria accompanied by the unique orchestration of solo oboe and solo English horn, forming with them a beautifully contrapuntal trio. Her miraculous cure is sketched by six and a half measures of transcendently serene music by another timbral trio, consisting of flute, clarinet, and violin (act 2, measures 469–75). The death of the old men (act 2, measures 493–96) is illustrated by music that seems to hark back to the world of *Pierrot Lunaire* (in which a very different kind of "blood offering" occurs in "Rote Messe").

The scene of the Golden Calf also allows the composer to borrow tellingly from characteristics of vernacular music, as he had in so many previous works. The tribal leaders and the

Ephraimite arriving on horseback are suggested by a feverish march, (beginning at act 2, measure 502), the drunken reveling by a waltz that begins rather placidly with harmonies that echo the music of the Burning Bush (act 2, measures 611–15) but becomes frenetic. After the killing of the naked virgins and the almost jazzy primitivism (is the composer drawing on some feelings of rivalry with *The Rite of Spring* for inspiration here?) accompanying the suicides, destruction, and wild dancing that are the aftermath of the erotic orgies, the waltz spirit returns (act 2, measure 929) and accompanies the ebbing frenzy. Nothing could be more human than the music accompanying the dwindling of energies, the exhaustion, the dying down of the pyres and torches, the drift into sleep that occur at the end of this scene. The accompaniment here is identical to the ostinato in the Piano Piece, op. 11, no. 2 (act 2, measures 963–66). This scene of false idolatry is vividly alive and passionate, dramatic and exciting, and part of the story's and the opera's appeal. It, too, reflects the composer's personality.

Having said all this, I return to the notion that in the end, Moses reminds us of Schoenberg himself, an artist who hears a "call" that others do not and has the obligation to heed this call—paradoxically, for the very sake of those who mock him. The Golden Calf is the equivalent of "giving the people what they want" (a nice hummable tune, say); Moses' task, like Schoenberg's, is not to give them what they want but to give them the deepest and truest thing he has to give.

The question of why Schoenberg never managed to set his final scene of text to music has elicited much speculation and commentary. Schoenberg himself said that in order to complete the task he would have needed to set aside time that he did not have. In 1945, his application for a Guggenheim fellowship to complete *Moses und Aron* and *Die Jakobsleiter* was unsuccessful. Already in retirement from UCLA and living on a tiny pension, he was obliged to occupy most of his time and creative energy with private teaching. Nevertheless, he did produce some important works after 1945, including the the String Trio, *A Survivor from Warsaw*, and the Phantasy for Violin and Piano. And *Moses* had already remained close to completion for thirteen years, during which time he had written many times the amount of music required to complete the opera, even managing, in 1939, to bring to a wonderful conclusion one earlier work that he had abandoned in 1916, the Chamber Symphony no. 2.

When we look elsewhere for explanations of the work's incomplete state, the first that comes to mind is borne out by viewing any production of the opera: it is indeed theatrically and musically complete. It would be hard to imagine a more powerful ending than the one it already has. The wrenching confrontation of the two brothers following the bacchanalian orgy around the Golden Calf, Moses' smashing of the tablets, and his despairing cry "O word, thou word, that I lack," accompanied by a gradual thinning of the orchestral texture down to the final searing single line from the first violins, leaves one with a sense of tragic finality. The realization that the task set for Moses by the call from the Burning Bush can never be fully realized is the best and truest ending point to the story.

It is also realistic to say that Schoenberg's psychological motivation could never have remained the same in the late 1940s as it had been in 1932, when his identification with the main protagonist reflected not only his embattled artistic life but also his sense of mission as a member of a persecuted minority in need of rescue. As will be seen in the next chapter, he even viewed himself as a potential leader of his people to the "promised land" of a Jewish refuge. And discussing the opera in 1930, he did write to Alban Berg: "Everything I have written has a certain inner likeness to myself."

There is also a spiritual dimension to the lack of completion of *Moses und Aron*. In Judaism a lack of certainty, a lack of closure, is part of the tradition. While the service creates in the congregant an "awe for the mysterious," God remains abstract, without form or gender, and cannot be defined or represented. Other major sacred works that Schoenberg did not complete include *Die Jakobsleiter* and the *Modern Psalm.*

In Moses' *Sprechstimme* Schoenberg found the most poignant use for the strange technique that he had developed, the dramatically and spiritually ideal outlet for his lifelong fascination with the part of the spectrum of vocalization between speech and song.* In the context of this biblical opera, *Sprechstimme*, a kind of modern "recitative" style, is the perfect vocal symbol for the humbleness of man, who aspires to understand but can't, and to something higher—to be able to sing. How apt, then, that for the opera's final scene the composer himself "lacked the gift of speech." The incomplete state of the opera fuses in the listener's mind with Moses' final outcry ("O word, thou word, that I lack"). The truncation of the work seems to express the limits of our reach.

Oliver Neighbour beautifully summarizes *Moses und Aron* as concerning "the simultaneous duty and impossibility of giving expression to inexpressible truths."

At the core of Judaism is the idea of the oneness of God and of the unknowability and unrepresentability of that oneness. It

---

*Schoenberg notated *Sprechstimme* (also called *Sprechgesang*) differently in different works. The notation he used in *Pierrot Lunaire* and *Die glückliche Hand* is the closest in appearance to normal song, and some current performers of *Pierrot*, particularly, come quite close to singing the role. The *Sprechstimme* of the *Gurre-Lieder* is notated with an open diamond notation in the manner of a harmonic. *Moses und Aron* notates the pitches of Moses and of the chorus with an X when they are to perform *Sprechstimme*, but there are several passages for the chorus where the absence of any accidentals would seem to suggest something still closer to speech. In all these cases, the pitches and rhythms are given exactly as if the part were to be sung in a conventional manner, and in these works a large vocal range is indicated. In his last pieces that use *Sprechstimme*, *Ode to Napoleon*, *A Survivor from Warsaw*, and *Modern Psalm*, a smaller range is suggested by the use of only one staff line, around which the vocal line is placed (in conventional notation). Although the intervals are written exactly, the neutral-looking one-line staff, which resembles that of an unpitched percussion part, would seem to discourage true "singing." In *Kol Nidre* the speaking part of the rabbi is written without a clef on a normal staff, with conventional rhythmic notation but with only four different pitches used, indicated by an X, the highest of which is only used once, on the word "light" in "Let there be light!"

seems to me that a part of the meaning of Judaism is this abstraction, this deep sense that we do not know. The not knowing is itself sacred. So in order to communicate the sacred, Schoenberg's challenge was to find a concrete form of expressing not the inexpressible but "inexpressibility" itself. Not to be able to fully form an opera on this very theme is to make the opera itself an expression of the powerlessness of man in the face of ultimate truths.

Paradoxically, another aspect of the practice of Judaism is a very real dialogue with this abstraction, the addressing of God in a very personal way. There is no "Son" to act as intermediary, since there is no "Father." And there is no human intermediary in the sense that a Catholic priest or Protestant minister is speaking as God's interpreter. The rabbi interprets and discusses the Torah, but it is God who is the direct object of protest and complaint, praise, thanks and atonement. One even creates a specific empty, silent space for God in the Sabbath. It is not surprising, given the meaning of that space, that in the Hebrew language silence itself—the absence of a Hebrew letter—has a specific meaning.

This somewhat tortured, harsh, unresolvable, indefinable relationship with the Supreme Being sets the tone for Schoenberg's sacred works from *Die Jakobsleiter* to *Kol Nidre* to *Modern Psalm*, a tone in which praise, protest, fear, awe, and humility are commingled. As simplistic as this reminder to the reader is, a listening to the first sixty seconds of *Modern Psalm* or *Moses und Aron* will bear me out: if one is expecting the unalloyed glory or comforting communality of a Bach cantata, this sacred music will come as a bit of a shock. Played in a synagogue, however, it is deeply of a piece with the tradition.

Like the woman in *Die glückliche Hand* who turns cold and indifferent when her worshipful admirer—the man—drinks from the goblet she has seemed to proffer, God is only near when he is not defined.

AMERICA

1933 — 51

21

———— ||| ————

EXODUS

It was no coincidence that the Schoenberg family fled to Paris, and from there to the United States, in 1933. Within that year came the quota on Jewish children in schools; the establishment of the Reich Chamber of Culture by Joseph Goebbels, which effectively put an end to Jewish participation in the theater, film, and music professions; and the dismissals of many Jewish lawyers and professors from their posts. If Schoenberg had not left of his own volition at the time of the fateful academy senate meeting, he would no doubt have been dismissed within a very few weeks. And if the Schoenberg family had not left Germany and Austria, it is highly unlikely that any of them would have survived.

In Paris, Schoenberg made his return to Judaism official.

One of the witnesses at his reconversion ceremony on July 24, 1933, was the painter Marc Chagall.

Schoenberg's experience was echoed a thousand times over in the experiences of other persecuted Austrians and Germans. Many in the same position as he was were artists known to him, but of course not all were Jews. The Swiss-born (non-Jew) Paul Klee, for example, lost his professorship at Düsseldorf Academy in 1933 during the drive to restore "the indigenous character of German art," after which he returned to Bern. Later his art was banned as "degenerate." (He died in 1940.)

In August 1933, Webern, already deeply shaken by Schoenberg's persecution and flight as well as by what he saw as the destruction of the cultural and spiritual life of Germany, received a letter from Schoenberg that stunned him further. The nervous, idealistic, introverted, unworldly, and politically naive Webern (whose son Peter von Webern would later prove a frail but enthusiastic soldier for the homeland and would be killed at the front), had written his teacher and friend that in such times it was best to keep "as busy as possible."* Schoenberg replied that he had cut himself off from all that connected him "with the Occident" and was prepared to devote all his energies to helping the Jews in Germany and working for the Jewish national cause, calling this "more important than my art."

Schoenberg's propensity for suspiciousness was fueled by the real-life betrayals occurring daily among those he had considered friends and artistic allies in Germany and Austria, and

---

*Kathryn Bailey devotes considerable attention to the complex subject of Webern's politics in her short biography *The Life of Webern*. While his circle of friends and associates were almost entirely socialists and Jews, many of whom he hid and helped during the war, he remained, even after his own music had been banned and the entire fabric of his working world torn apart, a staunch German nationalist who supported Germany in the war. Three of his four children supported the Nazis; his wife did not.

when, following his August 1933 letter to Webern, he did not hear from either Berg or Webern for several months, he feared that they had "gone over to the other side." His relief and his despair overflowed in a letter to Webern written January 1, 1934, after Webern had finally been in touch and it was clear that all was as it had been between them. Expressing his amazement that people he had respected could approve of the program outlined by the National Socialists and in Hitler's *Mein Kampf,* Schoenberg wrote: "And this program intends no more and no less than the *extermination* of all Jews!"

Starting immediately upon his arrival in France and continuing after he and his family reached America in October, Schoenberg worked on proposals of all kinds for the rescue of those Jews remaining in Germany and Austria. As Hitler's sphere of control grew to include Czechoslovakia, Hungary, and Italy and threatened Poland, Rumania, Bulgaria, Greece, Lithuania, and Latvia, Schoenberg widened the scope of his proposals accordingly. Already in 1933 he had drafted a four- to five-year plan that he sent to potential donors proposing himself as the initial leader of an organization to negotitate the release of Jews from Germany on terms that would benefit Germany financially. He also proposed founding a daily paper for Jews that would appear in Yiddish, German, and Hebrew and perhaps in English, French, and Russian, since one of his principal points was that Jewish information and thinking needed to be unified and focused. He was particularly concerned that Jewish leaders were distracted by organizing debilitating and ultimately useless forms of protest, such as the boycott of 1933, instead of pursuing global, practical solutions to the major disaster that was impending. Acknowledging that anti-Semitism was deeply rooted and resulted partly from misunderstandings of the Jews' own ideas of themselves, he favored facing the inevitability of persecution and forming an independent Jewish state rather than wasting precious energies combating prejudice. Seeing no point in fighting back piecemeal against the overwhelming machinery of oppression, he advocated a consolidated, creative, realistic effort on behalf of those being oppressed. All of these and other ideas eventually coalesced in a document entitled "A Four-Point Program for Jewry."

The images of the concentration camps are so vivid in our minds today that it is often forgotten how many small steps led to that stage. Some of the restrictions on Jews created the kind of segregation familiar to Americans from our own history. For example, Stefan Zweig in his memoir *The World of Yesterday* mentions the impact on his eighty-year-old mother of one of the relatively minor Viennese ordinances that took effect upon the occupation of Austria in March 1938: "At her advanced age she was a little shaky on her legs and was accustomed, when on her daily laborious walk, to rest on a bench in the Ringstrasse or in the park, every five or ten minutes. Hitler had not been master of the city for a week when the bestial order forbidding Jews to sit on public benches was issued—one of those orders obviously thought up only for the sadistic purpose of malicious torture . . . to deny an aged woman or an exhausted old man a few minutes on a park bench to catch his breath."

From the United States Schoenberg watched as those Jews who remained in Germany, Austria, and Poland suffered from increasing privations and were sent to the camps in staggering numbers. As the possible escape routes were cut off one by one, Schoenberg worked on a vast number of articles, speeches, memoranda, and proposals designed to persuade the international Jewish community to act in concert. He also worked on behalf of a great number of individuals who were in need.

By October 1938 all Jewish passports were marked with a large red *J*. On Kristallnacht, the night of November 9–10, Jewish businesses were destroyed, synagogues were burned down, and thirty thousand people from throughout Germany were arrested and sent to Dachau, Buchenwald, and Sachsen-hausen. State schools expelled their remaining Jewish children. All Jewish assets were appropriated. The invasion of Poland on September 1, 1939, meant that, for the persecuted, escape was becoming increasingly difficult if not impossible.

Anton Webern, 1933

22

———|||———

1940: STRAVINSKY

AND SCHOENBERG

Upon his arrival in the United States in 1933, Schoenberg spent an arduous year traveling between New York and Boston (where he taught at the Malkin Conservatory), during which his health deteriorated. In 1934, after a restorative summer spent in Chatauqua, New York, the family moved to Los Angeles. After two years of teaching privately and lecturing at the University of California at Los Angeles, he became a professor there in 1936, and the Schoenbergs settled in Brentwood Park.

Stravinsky's move to Los Angeles in 1940 put the two composers within only a few miles of each other. But such was the habit of their mutual antipathy that, although they had a number of acquaintances in common and on several occasions were even in the same room, not once during the next eleven years did they speak to each other. This becomes all the more poignant in view of their potential for mutual understanding and when one remembers that as of 1945 Webern and Berg were both dead. (As of 1945, Bela Bartók, whom Schoenberg had apparently considered the "second-greatest living composer," was also dead.)

In addition to the poignancy there is the irony that comes from knowing that these were not true "antipodes," that their paths would indeed converge in a remarkable way in Stravinsky's last works. Like two trains running parallel to each other on different tracks, at slightly different speeds and with different itineraries, the two composers had actually been alongside each other during their periods of experiment and innovation, as well as during their moments of greatest rationality and "classicism."

To be sure, one can easily create the impression of a clear opposition between the two with a list of facile dualisms:

AS—expressionism
IS—neoclassicism
AS—revered teacher
IS—not a teacher
AS—wrote *Harmonielehre* and *Models for Beginners in Composition*, invented the twelve-tone method
IS—No theoretical works of any kind and very little technical talk
AS—had "disciples," a "school"
IS—Boulanger aside, founded no "school"; was a loner
AS—predilection for strings
IS—predilection for winds
AS—melody, developing variation; psychological; through-composed opera; no ballets
IS—rhythm; visceral; numbers opera; best known for ballets

AS—childhood heros Wagner and Brahms
IS—childhood hero Tchaikovsky
AS—struggled financially; known primarily to cognoscenti
IS—a celebrity; wrote autobiography; was much photo-
    graphed; almost a dandy

But many parallels can be found between the two composers:

Both were highly superstitious.
Both had big egos and were colossally self-absorbed.
Both were small, dynamic men (with large ears).
Both were athletic yet physically frail in later life.
Both were disinclined to psychological self-analysis.
Both were irascible. "Slight of frame, pale, . . . with an
air both worldly and abstracted and a little angry," was how
Osbert Sitwell described Stravinsky. "Angry, tortured, burning" was how Stravinsky described Schoenberg's face when
he saw the composer for the first time in thirty-three years
on the occasion of Franz Werfel's funeral.
Both were highly opinionated, forthright in expression,
and masters of the ironic critique, of which Schoenberg's
verse "Kleine Modernsky" is an example. A parallel drawn
from the many in Stravinsky's writings would be his riposte
to an article by the composer Vernon Duke that he entitled
"Some Observations on V.D." (see *Themes and Episodes*,
p. 89).
Both could instantly drop a friend if they felt betrayed.
Both were supreme craftsmen, masters of great range
(Schoenberg's emotional variety certainly outstrips that of
Berg and Webern), and, in the end, composers of difficult
music that is resistant to analysis and resistant to summary,
music that is almost militantly unsentimental and for
which Kandinsky's remarkable description of what he called

the coming romanticism—"a piece of ice in which a flame burns"—could apply. (Indeed, if one looks at Kandinsky's late paintings one could imagine him a staunch ally of Igor Stravinsky's.)

Both have been represented in concert halls principally by a very few, primarily early works.

Both were steeped in the music of the past (although Stravinsky's interests stretched much farther back than Schoenberg's) and described themselves as evolutionaries rather than revolutionaries.

Both made many arrangements and transformations of older music—although in very different ways (or were they?)—and both revered and orchestrated works by J. S. Bach.

Both had handicraft abilities, although Schoenberg's were far more developed. Both men, for instance, devised mechanisms for drawing musical staves on blank paper. Arnold's was a five-pen holder; Igor's a staff roller that was inked like a library date stamp (he had it patented). During the Second World War Stravinsky followed the progress of the Allies' attack on a map in which he placed little flags that he made himself. The visual impulse was also not foreign to Stravinsky, whose musical calligraphy was often done in multiple colors and whose manuscript scores are works of art. Although his drawing was of a casual, occasional nature, those drawings that have been reproduced show the same artistic eye and talent as his scores.

Both were deeply religious, produced major sacred works, but were lax and ambivalent in terms of personal religious practice.

In *Dialogues and a Diary*, Stravinsky himself wrote out similar lists of comparisons with Schoenberg.

The general shapes of their lives make for an interesting comparison: Stravinsky's musical aesthetic remained essentially unaltered from his early years on. In Schoenberg's case one could argue that an evolution took place from the period of his letters to Kandinsky in 1912, when he believed particularly in the power of the unconscious, to the works of 1923 onward. But in the outputs of both composers an explosion of innovation was followed by a period of a kind of stability, sanity, and classicizing.

In terms of their work, they were of unshakable integrity and would have been sympathetic to each other's deepest convictions had they been in a position to know them firsthand. Although there are probably no passages—no measures—of music in the works of either man that could truly be mistaken for the work of the other, many of their written and spoken words could speak for both of them. It was Stravinsky, not Schoenberg, who said:

> It is the individual that matters, never the mass. . . . The numbers of people who consume music is of interest to people like Mr. Hurok [the impresario], but it is of no interest to me. The mass adds nothing to art. It cannot raise the level, and the artist who aims consciously at mass-appeal can do so only by lowering his own level. The soul of each individual who listens to my music is important to me, not the mass feeling of the group. Music cannot be helped by an increase in the quantity of listeners . . . [but] only through an increase in the quality of listening, the quality of the individual soul.

23

GAMES

Like Mozart and Stravinsky, Schoenberg had a lifelong interest in games and sports. He loved swimming and rowing, played tennis avidly, and was a fierce opponent in Ping-Pong. His passion for rules, order, and numbers made him approach these activities with inventiveness. From a "normal" perspective, he brought more analysis to bear than is customary in amateur games. When he lost a shot in tennis, he would explain what he had done wrong. He originated his own strokes. He developed a notational system for recording and reviewing his son Ronald's tennis matches. This amounted to a kind of labanotation for the sport.

He created his own chess game, Coalition Chess (*Koalitionsschach*), a contest between the armies of four countries arrayed on the four sides of the board, for which he designed and constructed the pieces himself. The board is similar to a chessboard, except that instead of comprising eight rows of eight squares, it contains ten rows of ten. The pieces represent machine guns, artillery, airplanes, submarines, tanks, and other instruments of war (also cyclists) and are painted gold, black, green, and red. There are six pieces arrayed on two sides of the board, and twelve pieces facing one another across the other two sides. The rules for the game, which require that the four players form alliances at the outset, are clearly typed in a booklet, with the capabilities of each piece and analyses of play procedure carefully explained.

In earlier years he had created two beautiful and humorous sets of playing cards. One set seems an offshoot of his caricatures and doodles in their grotesque imagery and use of visual puns. In these the hearts, spades, clubs, and diamonds do double duty as hats, shields, and body parts:

Playing cards by Schoenberg, 1909

The other set is more severe and geometric and revels in the mirror images that are a familiar feature of most playing cards.

In his California years he produced all manner of constructions, including toys and a cardboard violin, and small household inventions such as tape dispensers, Rolodex-style address books, and skirt hangers. He did his own bookbinding. In his papers is an architectural-style sketch for a bathroom shelf with perfume and cosmetic dispensers. In the yard stood his original wood-and-cardboard traffic signal, complete with three electric colored lights, for his children's tricycle and bicycle riding.

He also worked on the design of a musical typewriter, anticipating by half a century the development of musical computer software.

Along with the celebrity status accorded Stravinsky, Picasso, and other major artists of the time came a public awareness of their personal style and habits and a sense of their domestic life. This helped offset the impression created by the difficulty and severity of their work and, by reminding audiences of the respects in which their lives were completely ordinary, gave a feeling of intimacy with—and an illusion of accessibility to—them. Schoenberg did not benefit from this gap-bridging mechanism, and it wasn't until after his death that a more rounded portrait of him began to emerge. At first it was startling to find out, for example, that the composer of such learned and at times forbidding music might teach a class, as he did on April 13, 1939, wearing "a peach-colored shirt, a green tie with white polka-dots, a knit belt of the most vivid purple with a large and ostentatious gold buckle, and an unbelievably loud gray suit with lots of black and brown stripes."

24

ON BEING SHORT

There is something to be said for being short.

By being short one is closer to the ground, closer to the world of slithering worms, crawling bugs, and the minute organisms that flit through ponds, to the velvety coats of moss growing on dead, softening tree limbs in the woods, and to the busy colonies of ants doggedly at work in their tunnels hauling bits of bark, leaves, and dry seeds. One is closer to the earth itself.

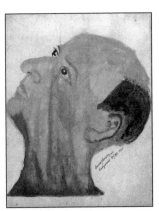

Self-Portrait, 1935

Webern, who was about Schoenberg's height, was particularly fond of the lichen and mushrooms and exquisite wildflowers he found growing in the rarefied climes of the Carinthian mountains he loved, from whose heights he could hear the distant church bells that he mimicked with glockenspiel and celeste in his orchestral pieces.

The short person gets used to looking up, aspiring upward generally. And this angle from which one views most of one's fellowmen and women actually conforms better to the effort required to understand them than looking straight across or downward does. The gaze of saints and of those patrons depicted in prayer at the lower right-hand corner of Renaissance altarpieces is generally upward, too. Etymologically, the concepts of *low, ground,* and *humility* are related. The word *humble* derives from the Latin *humilis* (meaning low, lowly), which comes from *humus* (ground, earth)—which relates in turn to *homo* (*man*). The short person knows in a physical way that things on the top shelf are not within easy reach.

The short person knows economy and compactness from the inside, knows the sturdiness of a frame well supported by its foundation. (It is a fact that King Kong could not actually exist, since on the scale he is envisioned he could not possibly support his own weight.)

Among composers, Berg, Britten, and Tippett were tall. Schubert, Mahler, Stravinsky, Webern, and Schoenberg were all under five foot four.*

The diminutive Schoenberg, who was occasionally described as "Napoleonic" himself, found in Byron's "Ode to Napoleon Buonaparte" the ideal text with which to attack a tyrant. At five feet, six and a half inches, Napoleon had been much taller than Schoenberg. Adolf Hitler stood five foot nine.

---

*Chopin, who is also frequently described as small, was of average height for his day (five foot seven) but so slight of build that he never weighed more than a hundred pounds.

If one is short relative to one's peers* one is more likely to have been beaten up and generally trodden upon as a child, which can inspire certain personality traits—for example, a "philosophical attitude"; the ability to accomplish with force of personality and ingenuity what one cannot accomplish with brute strength; moral courage; resiliency; the development of whatever physical prowess might offset one's diminutive stature (both Stravinsky and Schoenberg were agile and athletic and had healthy exercise regimes); a tendency to paranoia; a nagging (though perhaps buried) sense of insecurity and need to compensate; an ingrained hatred of bullies and tyrants. Oscar Levant wrote, "Schoenberg, it is well known, is quick to defend himself even when he is not attacked."

Compactness is not exactly idealized in human beings. Our expressions of hierarchy suggest that we value height—*superior* comes from *super* (above), *inferior* from *inferus* (low)—and the experience of being diminutive, by raising questions of scale early on (average-sized children don't hear the expression "Good things come in small packages"), can lead to questioning hierarchies generally. Not surprisingly, the shorter person, viewing things from a devalued angle, may be a particularly shrewd judge of proportions and measurements, sympathetic to a philosophy of values over appearances (idea over style), and inclined to revere the accomplishments of the mind.

A paradox of being small is that it can lead to the development of an inflamed, oversized ego. Such is the flexibility of the mind that being small can make one feel large.

Schoenberg's essay "Heart and Brain in Music" from 1946 begins with a quotation from Balzac's novel *Seraphita*, a description of the character Wilfrid: "Though strongly built, his proportions did not lack harmony. He was of medium height as is the case with almost all men who tower above the rest."

---

*As in fact I am, as well, at five foot two.

25

——— ||| ———

PIANO CONCERTO

For all that, and the manifest sincerity and craftsmanship dis-
played, the ideas appear to have little to do with beauty or real
musicianship.

—Olin Downes reviewing the Piano Concerto, op. 42,
The New York Times, February 7, 1944

Although he never did write the third act of *Moses und Aron* or
complete his oratorio *Die Jakobsleiter,* Schoenberg produced a
series of works in his American years that show how well the
twelve-tone approach suited him. Having written the two
hours of music in *Moses und Aron* all based on one row, he was
now a master of this method. The years from 1936 to 1941
saw little in the way of new music from Schoenberg, who was
no doubt profoundly shattered by all that he had gone
through and all that the world was going through. The Violin
Concerto (dedicated "To my dear friend Anton von Webern
in cordial gratitude for his unsurpassable loyalty") and the
Fourth String Quartet were completed in 1936, after which,
apart from the beautiful *Kol Nidre* for speaker, chorus, and or-

chestra of 1938, he composed nothing until 1942. This second hiatus in his output, while less dramatic than that of 1913 to 1923, nevertheless also roughly coincided with a world war.

The composer of the Violin Concerto was not the same man as the composer of *Pierrot Lunaire*. A quarter of a century had passed; he was sixty-two years old. He had been forced from his homeland, and he was living in the United States, uncertain of his and his family's future. He must have been able to forsee, it is fair to speculate, that the rejections he had faced from the *Gurre-Lieder* on had set a pattern that was unlikely to suddenly ameliorate and that, while he would be performed sporadically and esteemed by cognoscenti in the field, he would never be able to seriously cut back on his teaching and devote the bulk of his time to composing.

His students in Los Angeles included the young John Cage (whom at first he taught for free), Leon Kirchner, Earl Kim, Dika Newlin, Oscar Levant, and several film composers, who, one assumes, had an easier style of life than their teacher and probably more time to compose. Levant tells of a film composer who asked for Schoenberg's advice about a scene showing airplanes. The teacher replied, perhaps sarcastically, that the music should be just like music for big bees, "only louder." The dramatically hilarious Levant was a devoted student and a very serious composer. Schoenberg once in fact commented to him about his music: "It could use a little of your humor." Levant called the Kolisch Quartet's 1937 performances of the complete Schoenberg string quartets alongside Beethoven's late quartets one of the high points of his musical life. (He attended the performances with George and Ira Gershwin.)

To his friend philosopher Jakob Klatzkin, Schoenberg wrote that he was not accomplishing much in his own music but was working on a "practical" handbook of composition "in so far as I'm not occupied with answering letters from unfortunate people in Germany and Austria, and in so far as I don't give way to unbearable depression."

If one were to generalize about this phase of his life's work, one would have to say that it was a period of maximum unpredictability. If in the first phase he had rapidly assimilated the language of his predecessors and created great works in the late romantic tradition, in the second he had created an entirely new (and uncharted) musical world with his "expressionist" works. In his third phase he had responded to an inner need for what he later termed greater "perceptible formal logic," creating a way of organizing his hitherto unsytematized nontonal language so as to build large-scale forms in a consistent manner.

In this last phase each piece was extraordinarily different from the one before. Starting with the Suite for String Orchestra of 1934 he even wrote a series of works that are largely tonal (albeit in a strange way) and were intended to be useful for particular purposes. *Kol Nidre* (1938) was for use in synagogue, the Suite for Strings (his third suite) was written for youth orchestra, and the Theme and Variations in G Minor (1943) was composed for band. He had continued to produce tonal pieces from time to time, particularly for private occasions (the exquisite *Weihnachtsmusik* [*Christmas Music*] of 1921 is a wonderful example). In 1929, he had made some rapturously beautiful tonal arrangements of folk songs for chorus, and he wrote another group of three in a similar vein in 1948. Such works seem like anchors to a more solid past to which he remained actively connected in a way that Webern and even Berg and succeeding generations did not. This is to say that these works are not merely exercises or demonstrations of skill: they are full-fledged compositions. In a sense they represent a "secret" Schoenberg. The composer of *Verklärte Nacht*, *Gurre-Lieder*, and the little folk song setting "Schein uns, du liebe Sonne" ("Shine on us, dear sun") wrote some of the most beautiful *tonal* music of the twentieth century.

And this reconceived tonality, like Stravinsky's in, for example, *Le Baiser de la Fée* (a ballet score based on themes of Tchaikovsky), was of its time. One cannot agree with the opinion expressed by one of the composer's students that the Suite for String Orchestra could be mistaken for an unknown piece by Brahms. Even in the first measures, where, according to objective criteria the harmonies are completely within G major, one senses in their odd presentation—both as sonorities and rhythmically—that one has passed 1900, and by measure 8, when one seems momentarily to have modulated to B minor, the listener knows that the composer has bypassed common practice and is in an original tonal world. Throughout, the unexpected progress of motion—with its irregularity of phrase lengths and sudden shifts in gait—causes continual surprise, as do the weird but somehow logical harmonic relationships. If any ghost haunts this work, which in the original manuscript was called "Suite in Olden Style," it is the ghost of *Verklärte Nacht*, for example in this measure from the Adagio:

No, it isn't Brahms (unless it were perhaps a Brahms who had not slept for a full week), and in fact no other twentieth-century composer besides Stravinsky could have written a piece "in olden style" as consistently involving and intriguing as this one. It is fascinating to see the composer grappling with the Baroque forms to which he had also turned in his Piano

Suite, op. 25. As someone who viewed the traditional structures as shapes *formed by* ideas rather than as shapes *to be filled* by ideas, he can almost be heard testing each convention of the old dance structures along the way for its necessity. There are no more *literal* repeats than the ideas themselves warrant.

The Theme and Variations in G Minor for Band, op. 43a, which also exists in an orchestral version, is another curiosity. What fun it would be to hear it alongside *its* twelve-tone counterpart, the Variations for Orchestra, op. 31, which in some way it resembles structurally. Here one *could* invoke the name of Brahms, at least in the handling of the theme and variations idea, which, as in the Brahms Variations on a Theme by J. Haydn, op. 56 (the "theme" of which, incidentally, is probably not by Haydn), has a sense of continuity and an architecture that overide the segmentation that is a pitfall of the form. Like the twelve-tone method itself, the theme and variations tool kit provides one only with the wherewithal for making each part but tells nothing of how to conceive the whole, which is the real trick. Here the G-minor theme itself seems to *want* to be varied, and the variations dovetail and present an ongoing, developing line of argument. The wonderfully triumphant G-major ending to this work in minor mode has an almost nose-thumbing blatancy: "And you thought I only wrote *atonal* music!" it seems to say. It also rather unmistakably—intentionally or not—evokes Gershwin, friend, tennis partner, fellow painter, who had died unexpectedly on July 11, 1937. Describing the piece to conductor Fritz Reiner as not one of his "chief works," Schoenberg nevertheless modestly called it "a technical masterpiece."

During his American period he kept exploring new ways to use the twelve-tone idea, including employing rows that had some properties of tonality. One can't resist interpreting the startling appearance of tonal elements in the twelve-tone pieces as a kind of reverse image of the process at work years before in the Second Quartet. It is as if he were now seeing tonality from the "other side." Composers of Schoenberg's generation were the only ones for whom tonality and youth were indissolubly linked and for whom the loss of tonality coincided with growing up. Schoenberg could recall tonality with a nostalgia that was both personal and universal. He had already discovered and demonstrated that one could write whole majestic works without ever suggesting that one was in a key. The older composer could now write a twelve-tone piece like the *Ode to Napoleon* and, because of the row employed, contrive to end on a blazing E-flat major chord. In the context of this bitter piece, which uses the Byron text to rage against Hitler, the major triad at the end has all the nicety of a clenched fist. In relation to the language of the rest of the piece, its effect is dissonant. The older Schoenberg could also afford to write in his own former style and to be, for moments within a twelve-tone piece, wistful about the roots of the modern idiom.

So it isn't just chance that, as Robert Craft points out, the Violin Concerto contains several instances where tonal gravity seems to suddenly be in operation. This is also a work that occupies its space with an unhurried mastery—secure in its large-scale form and in its every detail—that perhaps only an older composer could achieve.

The 1930s were a great decade for violin concertos: Stravinsky's dates from 1931; Berg's, his final work, from 1935; Bartók's Second Violin Concerto from 1938. Schoenberg's deserves to be seen in the context of these—a violin concerto as passionately emotional and hauntingly beautiful as any of them. Nevertheless, its formidable technical difficulties for the soloist, coupled with its autumnal, Brahmsian gravity, have made it seem remote and formal to some listeners, more a picture of a great piece than a great piece. Its technical consistency—the entire piece is built seemingly effortlessly from one row—has almost seemed to act against it, inviting the criticism of "academicism." The strain and inevitable rough edges in performances up until now have choked its song and made it seem severe, tarnishing its natural radiance. Recent performances have begun to catch up with the glory of the music itself.

Whereas in earlier twelve-tone pieces like the (now classic) Variations for Orchestra of 1928 one is led by the music away from perceiving the various transformations of the row, now, while drawing on the wealth of derived forms of the row available to him, he sometimes used row forms almost like tonal areas and sometimes as the primary melodic material of the music.* For example, in the Piano Concerto, op. 42 (written in 1942 and intended for Oscar Levant), many of the melodies come in groups of twelve notes, meaning that the row actually *is* the tune. You hear the opening twelve-pitch melody in the piano starting on E-flat (measures 1–8)

and the second phrase of twelve pitches, an RI form (measures 8–16),

and then you hear all that again in the violins (measures 46–53 and 54–62), starting on B-flat (the "dominant"),

---

*Some scholars see in his sketches for his first twelve-tone pieces indications that he conceived some relationships between row forms as quasitonic-dominant ones.

and at the recapitulation of this first section (measure 134), again in the violins, on the original E-flat.

Furthermore, the intervals of this tune row are so memorable that all the other melodies emerging from it (such as measures 17–28 in the piano, a plain old retrograde of the E-flat form,

or measures 28–39, in the piano and clarinet, an I form),

when presented in similar rhythms, as they are, clearly sound as if they are all from the same family. Coupled with its Brahmsian phrasings, its relatively traditional—that is, string-based—orchestration, the way the soloist is used with and pitted against the orchestra, the kind of piano writing, and the relatively clear-cut overall form, this makes the concerto almost as worthy of being described as "neoclassical" (or "neo-romantic") as Stravinsky's works of this same period, when the two composers were living only ten miles apart. While the pitches used in the piece are twelve-tone, from other points of view—rhythm, phrasing, character, texture (melody and accompaniment, etc.)—this is not all that far from a late-nineteenth-century work. Shortly after Leopold Stokowski premiered the piece in his radio broadcast with the NBC Symphony Orchestra (with Eduard Steuermann at the piano), his contract was discontinued by the sponsor, General Motors. Observers attributed this to his advocacy of contemporary works, and some to his advocacy of the Schoenberg concerto.

In New York, Virgil Thomson gave the Piano Concerto an understanding, enthusiastic review, which moved Schoenberg very much. Thomson characterized the orchestration as varied and delicate, "chamber music for a hundred players" that avoided all "massing of instruments." The music, he wrote, "builds up its moments of emphasis" like Bach's, "by rhythmic device and contrapuntal complication." Never "grandiloquent" or theatrical, it was rather a "poetical and reflective" work combining "lyrical freedom and figurational fancy with the strictest tonal logic." Ranking it "high among the musical achievements of our century," Thomson also usefully described the twelve-tone method as one in which "the employment of dissonance is integral rather than ornamental." Schoenberg's original emotional outline of the piece, found among his papers, reads: "Life was so easy. Suddenly hatred broke out (Presto). A grave situation was created (Adagio). But life goes on." This corresponds to the four sections: Andante, Molto Allegro (measure 176), Adagio with a piano cadenza (measure 264), Rondo giocoso (measure 329). Like the *Ode to Napoleon* and several other pieces from his American years, this one ends with a (row-derived) tonal-sounding cadence.

...

In his work habits Schoenberg was a romantic. He wrote when inspired. His muse spoke to him as powerfully as it ever had in *A Survivor from Warsaw,* which was composed in two weeks in August 1947. In seven minutes of music—ninety-nine measures—he paints a dramatic scene of the utmost immediacy and directness that is utterly human, unpretentious, and riveting. It is universal and alive and contains nothing of a "memorial" character. In this cinema verité creation one is instantly brought into the reality of the horrifying situation as a participant, not as an observer, and each detail is conveyed in a flash, without preparation or transition. It is as if the fluid imaginary world of *Erwartung* has been fused with the brilliant architecture of Schoenberg's more recent music. The tiny bugle calls ("The day began as usual. Reveille when it was still dark . . .") and scraps of the concluding prayer (in original and inverted form) permeate the music, building toward the tremendous entrance of the voices at the eightieth bar. Listening, one forgets the twelve-tone technique, one forgets that Hebrew chant does not usually sound this way, one forgets that this is a work of musical "fiction." One experiences only a straight line through the story as narrated by the invented protagonist, the survivor of a massacre who has heard the victims spontaneously raise their voices in the prayer "Shema Yisrael" before being shot. The sound of the male chorus as it cries out in its twenty bars of Hebrew stays in the mind long after the devastating final chord.

Some "American" Works:

Suite in G Major for String Orchestra (1934)
Violin Concerto, op. 36 (1936)
String Quartet no. 4 (1936)
Kol Nidre (1938)
Ode to Napoleon (1942)
Piano Concerto (1942)

String Trio, op. 45 (1946)
A Survivor from Warsaw (1947)
Phantasy for Violin with Piano Accompaniment (1949)
De Profundis (1950)
Modern Psalm, no. 1 (1950; unfinished)

Lawrence, Arnold, Ronald, Gertrud,
and Nuria Schoenberg in Los Angeles

26

——|||——

DEATH AND REBIRTH

Although the last decade of Schoenberg's life was a period of increasingly poor health (he suffered from poor eyesight, dizziness, and asthma in addition to heart trouble), it was also one in which he took great pleasure in his family. Nuria had been born in Barcelona in 1932 before the family took flight; Rodolf Ronald (later called "Ronnie") and Lawrence were both born in the United States, in 1937 and 1941, respectively. For some reason it is a bit difficult to picture the composer of *Moses und Aron* and the *Gurre-Lieder* making up his children's box lunches, as he did, in the mornings. One friend from that time remembers him cutting peanut butter and jelly sandwiches into the shapes of musical instruments. The family always had a dog, as well as other pets, including roosters and rabbits. The composer played tennis with the Marx Brothers, with George Gershwin, and with many other acquaintances with less familiar names, and became friends with Charlie Chaplin. Gershwin, who shared his talent for painting, painted Schoenberg's portrait in 1936. Schoenberg corresponded with progressive fellow composers, including Edgard Varèse and Charles Ives. As of 1945, Berg and Webern were both dead.

On August 2, 1946, Schoenberg, then seventy-two, suffered an acute asthmatic attack during which his heart stopped beating. After a significant interval, he was resuscitated by an injection directly into the heart. During his recovery he experienced a day or two of delirium. Within three weeks of this event, which he characterized somewhat humorously as "my fatality," although very frail and still on his sickbed, he began working on his String Trio. To the composer Hanns Eisler he explained that the piece was intended as a depiction of his illness—heart injection included—and Schoenberg's friends and family later referred to the work informally as his "delirium trio." Somehow it seems apt that all of this would occur to the composer of *Pierrot Lunaire*; the story reminds us of "Rote Messe," in which Pierrot offers his own heart in Holy Communion.

The String Trio, which was composed in just five weeks, is one of the few great works for the medium and seems a kind of synthesis of Schoenberg's entire musical development, as if in his delirium he had reviewed his life. Wildly evocative, "expressionistic," and instrumentally at the far-flung reaches of virtuosity, it is also a work exhibiting some of the "new classicism" of his early twelve-tone pieces, including as it does some near-exact sectional repeats. And there are also some of the reemerging tonal reference points characteristic of his late style. His son Lawrence also hears fragments of purely familial tunes as well. (There is a precedent for these kinds of quotations in the second movement of the Second String Quartet, written thirty-eight years earlier.)

Hearing this work now, more than fifty years after its writing, one is reminded of so many pieces that have been written by others in succeeding years; the piece almost seems to be in dialogue with its own legacy. Some of the string effects Schoenberg employed have become standard in contemporary string music. These techniques include playing near the bridge (sul ponticello), on the bridge (ponticello), with the wood of the bow on the bridge (col legno tratto—ponticello); tapping with the wood of the bow (col legno battuto); frequent use of harmonics and double harmonics, often interspersed with notes played normally; glissandi; pizzicato used in a combined texture with arco playing; bouncing bow (saltando); tremolos; and tremolos on the bridge. Although Webern, Berg, and many other composers also used these techniques, the rapidity with which they alternate in this piece, combined with the frequent radical contrasts in dynamics, is very original. Sometimes many of these ways of playing are combined in a single phrase. For instance, at measures 101–03 the first violin plays a double stop with a glissando upward to another double stop, followed by two pizzicato notes, a sixteenth rest, and another double stop; there follow a high harmonic and a double harmonic, and another pair of pizzicato notes. Yet one is struck by how integral these techniques—these flutings, flutterings, and scrapings—are to the "story" being told by this particular piece. Indeed, the form and content of the music and the way the sounds are produced are inseparable. The character of these varied ways of "talking," like the erratic leaps and hesitations of the more hysterical moments of the vocal line in *Erwartung*, written thirty-seven years earlier, has a specific expressive impact and, also as in *Erwartung*, is balanced and answered by moments of extraordinarily touching lyricism and more conventional string writing. In short, there is no sense of

mannerism about the piece. It is downright orchestral in the
varieties of timbre it employs, but one's attention is not drawn
to the "effects." Rather it is the effects that draw one's attention to the ideas and to the form, and every note "sounds."

The trio lasts approximately seventeen minutes and is in a
single movement. The overall structure of the piece is marked
in the score: part 1—first episode, part 2—second episode,
part 3.

In discussing the work with Eisler, Schoenberg indicated
that certain chords represented the injection into his heart. It
is not clear to which chords he was referring, but there is no
doubt that the opening itself gives the sense of a febrile springing to life. As Stuckenschmidt puts it, "the shock effect of the
first minutes is inescapable." One has the feeling that the
composing process itself has been galvanized into action by
the nearness of death. The opening presents a number of ideas
in succession, starting with the first bar of trills in the violin
and viola with the cello alternating low notes and high harmonics. Only after several hearings does one get to know the
various motifs that follow each other in a chain of associations
in the first forty-four measures, creating an impression of intense anguish and strangeness, but also of a kind of light-
headed buoyancy. There is an exhilaration in hearing such a
wild imagination brought to bear on such a reduced and
transparent ensemble of instruments. The ideas that at first
seem numerous and disjunct eventually clarify themselves as
belonging to a few families of motives. But as Stuckenschmidt
remarks, "each repetition is widely removed . . . and becomes
so unlike the form in which it first appeared that it can be regarded more as a surrealistic event produced by psychical au-
tomatism and not as an 'act of convention.' "

One needs no score to hear what follows the first forty-four
measures: a strange, very quiet transition consisting of five
events, each separated by silence. A high tremolo chord is followed by a low fourth chord played on the bridge; another

high tremolo chord is followed by another low fourth chord; then the first violin plays a forte triple stop, pizzicato. One feels at the doorway of something.

That something turns out to be a brief moment in what is very close to A major, a sustained A–C-sharp in viola and cello with an ascending violin line above. (The violin pizzicato chord that precedes it contains the essential elements of the dominant of A.) This ushers in the first episode, in which a sustained and almost Mahlerian expressive lyricism is continually interrupted by disjunct fragments related to the feverish opening. An interesting impression of time is created by this episode. Not only do the ideas themselves suggest memories and "surreal" impressions, but some of the principal figures in this episode would appear to be the themes from which the fragments of the opening part derived, as if the opening were a group of flashbacks to materials presented here. One example is the beautiful oscillating idea in the first violin at measure 79–80, which returns later in different guises at measures 151–53, 186–88, and elsewhere. This now seems the "source" of the cello figure (oscillating between low register and high harmonic) of bar 1.

The vocabulary of agitated fragments is expanded to include a recitative-like moment containing a glissando in the violin. The songful music that follows the "A major" moment (measure 57)—not far in language from the Berg of the Lyric Suite or the Quartet, op. 3—returns periodically (at measure 71 in inversion in the cello, and then in violin harmonics and viola harmonics, and at measure 111 in the violin), and a haunting waltzlike 6/8 music is introduced at measure 85. This passage of completely traditional counterpoint, with its unmistakably Viennese overtones, played without "modernistic" techniques, gives off a deep wistfulness. It becomes the principal material of part 2, which can be heard as three variations on this passage interrupted by intrusions (repeated notes, tremolos, the oscillating figure, harmonics) from part 1.

The second episode, at measure 180, opens with a series of sardonic double-stop fanfares in cello, viola, and violin, which are then swallowed by ponticello trills. The 6/8 waltz returns (as always with a high degree of variation from previous times), followed by an extended variant of the oscillating idea, expansions of the glissando idea, and the "fanfares." Two moments stand out audibly: a climactic instance of unison playing (the only one in the whole work) at measure 199 and a hint of the "A major" moment at measures 201–02, now a whole step down on G (G–B–D–E). In a piece full of apparitions, this gentle echo is a magical sleight of hand. The second episode dwindles down to a muttering of repeated notes. Then something extraordinary happens.

The repeated notes end in a sustained G that becomes the first note of an exact repetition of the opening of the piece—part 3. Unlike *Erwartung*, which Schoenberg once referred to as an "*Angsttraum*" (a nightmare), this delirium starts to remember itself. The effect of this last part is hard to describe, since it creates new layers of memory in what is already a veritable onion of layers. The first memory rekindled by part 3 is, of course, of sonata form itself, of the recapitulation that returns us to all the themes of the exposition in the tonic key. Part 3 does repeat the opening exactly at pitch, but in artfully compressed form, so that it seems to be more of a recollection than a formal repeat. With slight changes and elisions, part 3 begins with exactly the music of measures 1, 2, 4, 5, 8, and 9, and then transposes and paraphrases sections of the music from measures 12–44. At this point there is a duplication of the transition (that is, "bridge passage") leading to the first episode, missing two of its chords but including the pizzicato "dominant" and, astonishingly, an exact return of the quasi-A-major music and the Mahlerian songful passage that followed it. Schoenberg then skips to a repeat of the important oscillating figure as it was introduced at measure 79 with its implications of E-flat minor, and it is followed, as it was then, by a version of the "recitative" idea with glissando, now in a new form, and then by an active passage featuring the repeated-note motif used throughout the work in so many ways.

From the beginning of part 3 to this point, then, the succession of ideas follows the plan of the opening of the piece and—notwithstanding the compressed presentation—in an uninterrupted fashion. At measure 248 we have a mostly literal—if transposed and instrumentally reassigned—repetition of a recitative and scherzando passage from the first episode. At this point the 6/8 waltzlike music and other moments from part 2 succeed each other in a more dreamlike manner, as if only recalled as fragments. The trills and disembodied harmonics of the opening return, sometimes as accompaniment to the 6/8 material, an unearthly version of which is given at measure 282 in the highest registers of all three instruments. This quasi-inverted form of the music from 159–62 is followed by a more literal recall of it (at measure 286), with the melody in the viola. Against this the cello plays the oscillating idea in stepwise chromaticism. The music's references narrow to a few simple figures linked to the 6/8 music, ever so faintly grazioso, and the violin is left as the final quiet, plaintive melodic voice against steady rhythmically unison steps in the viola and cello.

In part 3, then, the progress of the previous two parts and episodes pass in review, more or less in order, as if in memory. And how amazing it is that the glaring tonal reference point of the beginning of part 2 reappears in the "recapitulation" in the same "key" as it had previously. In a standard sonata form the material from the "secondary key group" of the exposition in the dominant would return in the recapitulation in the tonic. But this is not really a sonata form, and it is not a tonal work. It is entirely twelve-tone, based, quite unexpectedly, on a row and a half, which of course not only helps unify all these seemingly disparate ideas but also creates a deep network of relationships and similarities beyond the motivic ones I have been referring to. When "A major" returns in exactly the same form, it seems a memory of tonality itself, a serene chimera of hope and nostalgia. (Hans Keller makes the marvelous point that in Schoenberg's later music tonal references intrude just as atonal ones did in his early work.) In his String Trio Schoenberg produced an utterly personal piece full of fantasy, freedom, flexibility, and a new kind of beauty, one that seems effortlessly to place the listener in the theater of the mind.

27

---|||---

SEVENTY-FIFTH

BIRTHDAY

During this time Schoenberg was not unrecognized by people interested in music. He heard of many performances of his work in Europe, and in his adopted homeland there were concerts of great significance. As of September 13, 1944, he had reached the age of seventy—mandatory retirement age of the University of California. He was living on a pension of thirty-eight dollars a month from the university, plus whatever he could still earn from private teaching. He was exhausted and applied for help from the Guggenheim Foundation in early 1945 so that he could finally complete *Moses und Aron* and *Die Jakobsleiter*. His application was turned down. In April of 1947 he received an award of a thousand dollars from the American Academy of Arts and Letters. In his letter of thanks to the academy (written in May) he expresses gratitude that his work is "now evaluated as an achievement" but gives the credit for his accomplishment to his "opponents." He summarizes his entire life in one image: that of a man wriggling desperately in "an ocean of boiling water." While acknowledging that he may somehow have inadvertently caused the aggressiveness and maliciousness of those who would have "liked to see me succumb" ("maybe I myself had failed to understand their viewpoints, was not considerate enough"), he returns to his essential predicament:

> But I have one excuse: I had fallen into an ocean . . . and it burned not only my skin, it burned also internally. And I could not swim. At least I could not swim with the tide. All I could do was swim against the tide—whether it saved me or not! . . . And when you call this an achievement, so—forgive me—I do not understand of what it might consist. That I never gave up? I could not—I would have liked to.

In 1949 the Austrian Society of Dramatists and Composers, which had turned down his application to be a member in 1935 because he was a Jew, made him an honorary member. His seventy-fifth birthday later that year saw the publication of two international musical magazines devoted to tributes and brought him many performances and honors. The city of Vienna feted him with letters of citizenship. On October fifth he delivered a speech thanking the city. Igor Stravinsky was in the audience. Schoenberg's eyesight was so poor that he had to read from a series of pages on each of which he had written only a few large words.

The composer's last years were physically draining and painful. In addition to his poor eyesight he was particularly plagued by the asthma that had forced an interruption in his service as a soldier long ago. This necessitated his sleeping in a chair. He awoke with a start in the middle of every night and sometimes coughed for three to four hours. He had erratic blood pressure, experienced nervous agitation, depression, and extreme weakness and was "treated for diabetes, pneumonia, kidney disease, hernia, and dropsy."

In 1950 the Juilliard String Quartet performed all four of his string quartets in a cycle at Times Hall in New York City, and in Pittsburgh Eduard Steuermann performed the entire piano works in one evening.

The young conductor Robert Craft visited him on July 5, 1950, finding him slow of step, thin, "stooped and wizened," and looking older than his years, but still able to be cheered and energized by news of upcoming performances of his music. On a visit one year later, on July 7, 1951, only a week before Schoenberg's death, he only heard his voice; the composer was too unwell to come downstairs.

In Schoenberg's last two or three weeks of life, by his wife's account, his dread of death turned to resignation. But he still remained apprehensive of Friday the thirteenth and did die on that day, close to midnight, July 13, 1951.

On his death certificate, under "Usual Occupation," is written: "Composer of Modern Music."

Gertrud Schoenberg lived another sixteen years, until February 1967.

AFTERLIFE

28

DEATH AND REBIRTH II

On July 14, 1951, the telephone rang in the Stravinsky household, bringing news of the death of Schoenberg. After drafting a telegram of condolence (which turned out to be the first one received by Mrs. Schoenberg), Stravinsky, according to Robert Craft, "was silent all day." Five days later he was at the home of Alma Mahler-Werfel and by chance was the first person to see Schoenberg's death mask, still not dry, which had been made by Mahler's daughter, the sculptor Anna Mahler. He was "visibly moved" by the face of the composer to whom he had not spoken since 1912.

That September *The Rake's Progress*, the longest and culminating work of Stravinsky's so-called neoclassical phase, premiered in Venice. A few months later, Stravinsky confessed to his wife and to Craft that, for only the second time in his life, he was at a creative impasse. The crisis was internal—he needed new sources of nourishment for his musical growth— and external, too: he was well aware that *The Rake's Progress* and the works that had led to it were of no interest to young composers and that he had become cut off from what was exciting in new music. So isolated had he been from his "rival's" circle of influence that until meeting Craft in 1948 he did not even know what a tone row was. He had been deeply struck by the music he had recently heard of Webern and Schoenberg.

With what seems in retrospect an uncanny instinct, Stravinsky had welcomed Craft into his family circle the year in which he began *The Rake*. Craft was no ordinary conductor. He was a brilliant young man in the process of performing and recording for the first time much of the music of the Second Viennese School (as Schoenberg, Berg, and Webern were now called), along with other major twentieth-century music and a wonderful range of as yet unheard "early" music by Monteverdi, Gesualdo, and Schutz; amazingly enough, he had even known Schoenberg personally. He was phenomenally erudite in a variety of fields, up-to-date in his knowledge of current music, and a formidable writer. His ability to explain, and introduce Stravinsky to, music outside of his experience and to collaborate on a series of books with him transformed the composer's last years.

Within a year of Schoenberg's death, the sixty-nine-year-old Russian composer, score in hand, was attending rehearsals of such pieces as Schoenberg's Septet Suite and Wind Quintet and Webern's Quartet, op. 22. From Craft he was able to learn what he needed to begin to apply serial principles to his own writing. Starting with the tenor aria ("Tomorrow shall be my dancing day") in the Cantata of 1952, Stravinsky began to adapt serialism to his own purposes. Such is the mystery of how personality and artwork intersect that his music still sounded "Stravinskyan" even though many of the characteristics people had given that label were either gone or radically transformed. In works such as the Cantata and *Agon*, serial writing sits alongside remnants of tonality, and in other completely serialized pieces such as *Threni, A Sermon, a Narrative and a Prayer*, Movements for Piano and Orchestra, and his last major work, the extraordinarily compressed *Requiem Canticles*, the methods of the "three Viennese" are made to serve in an entirely changed emotional climate and sound world. In the small cantata *Abraham and Isaac* (1963), Stravinsky composed a work to a Hebrew text and dedicated it to the people of the state of Israel, where it was first performed.

Yet even as an adherent Stravinsky kept his distance from the father of twelve-tone music, finding greater kinship and stimulus in the work of the "son," Webern (whose framed picture can be seen in photographs of his study during this period), and limiting his endorsement of Schoenberg to a short list of what he termed the "perfect" works, a list that pointedly leaves out *Erwartung*, among other pieces. There is, of course, plenty of evidence in his music that he was influenced by pieces other than the "perfect" works he lists (for example, the Gigue in Schoenberg's Suite, op. 29, for seven instruments surely served as a stimulus for the Gigue in Stravinsky's own Septet), and some passages in his serial works, while "Webernian" in their sparse clarity, can perhaps be seen as freeze-dried memories of passages in Schoenberg:

Stravinsky, "Bransle Gay" from *Agon*

Schoenberg, Five Pieces, no. 2

His "conversion" to Schoenberg's method was an expression of his own needs as a composer, and its limits were an expression of his musical beliefs and aesthetic views at the time, but the impact that his adoption of serial principles had on his colleagues—four generations of them—was global. For fellow composers it was as if two independently winding roads to the future had suddenly fused into one. Significantly, Stravinsky even saw himself (in the dichotomous terms mentioned in ch. 21) as Aaron to Schoenberg's Moses, which, as far as twelve-tone music is concerned, he surely was, arguably having more influence on its worldwide recognition than any other single person, through his writings and interviews; the use of such scores as his Movements for Piano and Orchestra, *Agon, Requiem Canticles,* and *Variations* in the New York City Ballet repertoire; and the highly public presentation of such serial works as *The Flood* (composed for television) and *Canticum Sacrum* (composed for performance in St. Mark's in Venice). Stravinsky's last original composition, the song "The Owl and the Pussycat," is dodecaphony raised to the height of childlike sophistication. It is composed entirely of the four basic row forms (prime, retrograde, inversion, retrograde inversion) and in its simplicity and charm would be musically comprehensible to a five-year-old. Perhaps one can also perceive an echo of *Moses und Aron* in the "Libera Me" movement of the *Requiem Canticles* of 1966, in which, as in the Burning Bush scene and the entr'acte of that biblical opera, the chorus is divided into two groups and speaking and singing are combined. Unable to compose in his final years, Stravinsky produced a few orchestrations, among them, rather startlingly, two songs of Hugo Wolf. He had become the most documented and well-known composer of the century even as, paradoxically, his work entered its least popular phase. But the power and freshness of his new works galvanized the academic and musical communities and added to the sense that the momentum and excitement of the day seemed to lie with those composers tracing their lineage back to the Second Viennese School.

In the world's academies and conservatories, twelve-tone music and its derivatives were taught alongside harmony and counterpoint, and some brand of serialism seemed for a brief moment de rigueur among young composers. (Schoenberg himself had, as we know, declined to teach his method, preferring to teach composition through the study of eighteenth- and nineteenth-century works and holding to the belief that his techniques wouldn't suit everybody.) This meant that the world suddenly heard an enormous amount of music that it attributed, for better or worse, to Schoenberg's influence.

A number of other distinguished composers were, simultaneously with Stravinsky, availing themselves of elements of serialism in their work, and "serialism" was belatedly detected in the technical arsenals of early-twentieth-century masters such as Bartók and Ives. Aaron Copland, whose early Piano Variations (1930) could already be described as having been composed with a quasi-serial approach, was a full fledged twelve-toner in works such as the lovely Piano Quartet of 1950 and his *Connotations* for orchestra (1962). In his thirty-minute Piano Fantasy (1952–57), Copland employed a row that with its fourths and seconds easily creates his characteristic sound world:

Aaron Copland: Piano Fantasy

Yet Copland found that the method also took his ear in new directions, helping him refresh his language with "new chords." At the same time, he confessed to a complete lack of interest in some of the more mathematical explorations of his younger colleagues, explaining that "the new terminology is Greek to me. . . . I don't have that kind of brain. . . . No, I am interested in the simple outlines of the theory, and in adapting them to my own purposes." Copland's Piano Quartet is based on a row that is primarily stepwise, with three expressive leaps. While not exactly tonal it has as strong a melodic shape as a Gregorian chant, with its last note a leading tone back to its first note.

But in fact, almost all exponents of the approach had amended, extended, limited, and applied it to their own purposes, starting with Berg and Webern themselves. In most cases the very rows employed reflect the melodic and harmonic predilections of their composers. For example, Webern's tend to be angular and architectonic. Some are constructed out of cells of three pitches that "generate" three more related cells, creating a highly symmetrical sound world already suggestive of small musical motives. Berg's are sensuous, often emphasizing tonal areas; they already sound "like Berg." The well-known row for his Violin Concerto is like an outline for the piece itself, beginning with its ascending chain of thirds and ending with the four whole steps that begin the Bach chorale ("Es ist genug") quoted near the work's end. The row is constructed so that the first, third, fifth, and seventh notes are those of the violin's open strings and so that the opening pitches outline major, minor, diminished, and augmented triads and several types of seventh and ninth chords. In *Lulu*, Berg created an entire family of rows associated with the different characters in the opera that nevertheless maintain a connection to the basic set of the work.

Stravinsky himself used serial procedures to form melodies and chords that had a consistent hidden source. But by tending to use only smaller groups of notes that were then "rotated" to form what theorists call "arrays," he created music that often had a strong sense of tonal gravity and was very far in its sound from that of serial pieces that continually recycled the entire twelve tones of the chromatic scale. Pianist, composer, lover of the vertical, maker of unique chorales, and genius of the individual sonority, Stravinsky used his arrays to create Stravinskyan harmonies that seem to occupy—in one writer's words—"a tonality beyond tonality."

The young generation of the fifties took serialism in a number of directions outside the scope of this book. Of particular importance were the ideas of Milton Babbitt, who alongside his composing became a leading theoretical explicator of dodecaphony, and Pierre Boulez, whose encounter with twelve-tone music in the late 1940s came as a revelation to him and led to his expansion of the serial principle into the domains of rhythm, dynamics, timbres, and even articulations. At the same time, a number of composers whose music contained twelve-tone procedures resisted the notion of a serial approach to other parameters besides pitch. Roger Sessions, for example, characterized music as a "chemical reaction" and cautioned that, since only the simultaneous relationship between the various elements of music gives them their meaning, a musical entity could not be assembled by giving each element an independent trajectory. In the postwar craving to start music with a clean slate it was Webern, who already foreshadowed a serial approach to timbre and rhythm in his music and

Igor Stravinsky,
photographed by Henri Cartier-Bresson, June 1966

whose later works have an atonal purity seemingly "uncon-
taminated" by tonal longings, who was viewed as the father
figure by many. Stravinsky dubbed him "Saint Anton." The
fiercely unsentimental Boulez, only twenty-seven and still
years away from his conducting career, argued for the centrality of Webern in a 1952 article charmingly entitled "Schoen-

berg Is DEAD!" that appeared in the English music magazine *The Score*. The new composers called themselves "Post-Webernists." Schoenberg, who had still believed in the development and metamorphosis of recognizable musical motives and who, his own expressionistic works notwithstanding, considered "athematic" music to be unintelligible, suddenly looked like a transitional figure.

In the sixties many former Schoenberg students became important voices in the world of new music. In addition, there began to be many composers, such as Charles Wuorinen, who had come to twelve-tone writing by way of late Stravinsky and of Milton Babbitt. When the highly influential Boulez declared that "after the discoveries of the Viennese" nonserial music was "useless," the statement therefore carried a great deal of weight. Even as many other currents of musical thinking were gaining adherents, for a brief moment the impact of Schoenberg's techniques seemed almost worldwide. Yet there was no parallel increase in performances of his music.

29

$$|\!|\!|$$

WRITINGS ABOUT

SCHOENBERG

Do not call it twelve-tone Theory, call it Composition with twelve Tones. Personally it is on the word composition that I place the emphasis. Unfortunately most would-be followers of this method do something removed from the idea of writing music.
—Schoenberg in a 1949 letter to Joseph Rufer,
who was planning a book on twelve-tone composition

When I compose, I try to forget all theories and I continue composing only after having freed my mind of them.
—"My Evolution," 1949

It would take many pages to properly summarize the history of writings about Schoenberg. But judging from any random sampling of reviews and criticism from any period, it would seem that a great deal of uneasiness surrounded his music from its inception. Even Alban Berg's early and brilliant analytically based article "Why Is Schoenberg's Music So Difficult to Understand?" embraces the music from a posture of defense. Many reviews over the decades are expressions of outright disgust, others of rejection on a variety of grounds.

Among the early critics who not only loved his work but were able to express their sense of it in general and human terms, Paul Rosenfeld stands out both for the undoctrinaire nature of his enthusiasm (after all, he championed composers of many different stripes) and for the quality of his insight. Though critical of what he perceived as a "tendency to go wandering in the waste lands of abstraction" and of "some over-theorizing habit of mind in the man" that can turn some of his work to mere "paper music," he returns again and again to the word *exquisite* in his descriptions, as in this passage about *Pierrot Lunaire*:

> And still, it is as one of the exquisites among the musicians that he comes to us. Since Debussy, no one had written daintier, frailer, more diaphanous music. The solo cello in "Serenade" is beautiful as scarcely anything in the new music is beautiful.

About *Das Buch der Hängenden Gärten, Erwartung,* and *Die glückliche Hand,* Rosenfeld wrote:

> More consistently and continually than any other contemporary composer of worth, Schoenberg is the musician of the exquisite, the deep, and also the bitter and painful erotic experience.

And in 1923 he described Schoenberg this way:

> This mind has the tempo of the modern world. . . . It has the power of exceedingly rapid experience. . . . In what appears to be a succession of dissonances, he hears a common pitch. . . . The voices of his music have almost anarchistic independence. They seem to lie far out from the common center, on the edge of things. They are always like overtones of an implicit and unmentioned tone. But the links which connect, though they are fine almost to the

point of invisibility, are formed of coldest durable steel.
Great bales of substance, far lying, have been condensed.

Today Schoenberg is considered a master but, fascinatingly,
the tone of unease in critical responses has persisted. There
have been many notable performances of Schoenberg in recent years, and his work has been played with the fluidity, naturalness, and understanding that he hoped for in his lifetime.
Unrestrained expressions of enthusiasm for this music do surface in the widely read media from time to time. For example,
writing of *Moses und Aron* in the *New York Times* in 1999,
Paul Griffiths didn't hesitate to call the opera a "great work"
and to describe the production as "glorious" and "overwhelming," encouraging listeners to "forget to expect major chords"
and to "listen to what wonderful and meaningful sounds music can make without them." But more common, even in relatively positive reviews, are reactions that mingle respect or
pleasure with nagging doubts. A casual reader of the *New York
Times* in the last months of the twentieth century and the first
few of the twenty-first could have read a considerable amount
about Schoenberg, but most of it suggests that in some ways
his music remains a problem. For example, Bernard Holland
seems to want to respond wholeheartedly to Schoenberg's
work but can't quite do so:

> It was possible to come away from this performance
> with deep suspicions of "Gurrelieder" and everything it
> stands for, and yet with an impression of an evening mem-
> orably spent.

> One hears everywhere a composer's craft and energy, but
> no amount of listening and experience with the Schoen-
> berg Serenade seems to calm the queasiness it causes me.
> The gestures belong to a music rooted in tonal centers. The
> language expounds constant change and variation.

Holland's words ("queasiness," "suspicions") are not precisely musical. They seem to verge on the personal. He acknowledges something that may help explain why many composers who are arguably more distant from their historical predecessors than was Schoenberg are paradoxically less discomfiting to some listeners: the tension in his work between the traditions and features of the language that remain recognizable and those that are radically transformed. Music *more* alien in instrumentation, phrasing, rhythm, and spirit to nineteenth-century models might actually be less disturbing. Virgil Thomson anticipated this point back in 1944 when he offered his view that twelve-tone music, which he described as tonally "the most exciting, the most original, the most modern-sounding music there is," would be more intelligible when a "rhythmic syntax comparable to [its] tonal one" was developed.

Composer-critic David Schiff has also struggled in print with much of Schoenberg's music and, noting that many of his colleagues accord *Moses und Aron* only grudging praise at best, has accounted for his own wildly divergent responses with the assessment that Schoenberg's best music came from white-hot inspiration but that, failing that, it was guilty of a kind of "hollow technical bravura": "Schoenberg's music is really tolerable only when it is extraordinary. . . . He was a volcano that erupted erratically and incandescently." In common with the novels of D. H. Lawrence, his work is, according to Schiff, "pedantic and preachy when uninspired but unmatchable when the lightning actually struck."

Among writers about music read by the general public there have been few passionate advocates. Disastrously, given his vast influence and gifts of persuasion, Leonard Bernstein in his Norton Lectures at Harvard in 1973 (later released on video and as a book under the title *The Unanswered Question*) expressed admiration for Schoenberg the musician while questioning the music itself, leaving his large audience with an ambiguous impression, all the more injurious because so insightfully and sympathetically expressed:

> The trouble is that the new musical "rules" of Schoenberg are not apparently based on innate awareness, on the intuition of tonal relationships. They are like rules of an artificial language, and therefore must be learned. This would seem to lead to what used to be called "form without content." . . . We know that Schoenberg never meant anything of the kind. He was just too musical to hold such an attitude, too much of a music lover. . . .
>
> It seems inevitable that the sense of tonality haunts his most beautiful works; even when it's not demonstrably present, it still haunts those works by its conspicuous absence.

Despite his high regard for the music, Bernstein seems to be hunting in it for something that he more fully locates in the music of Alban Berg, a fragment of whose Violin Concerto he plays, contrasting it with a Schoenberg example with the words

> Isn't that delicious? . . . It is twelve-tone writing; only it exists somehow in a tonal universe where it's accessible to us in all its warmth and charm.

Apparently the absence in Schoenberg's music of something that—to him—implies a "tonal universe" is perceived by Bernstein as an absence in the music itself, the absence of "color," "charm," or, one might guess, an essential aspect of what makes music music.

In his lecture, Bernstein supports his tastes and views with an analysis of the origins of tonality in the overtone series. What he doesn't convince this reader of, though, is that this does any more than account for the powerful acoustical resonance of certain harmonies and sounds over others. Instinctively we might even go along with him—in an unscientific way—in acknowledging that the *order* in which certain sounds were admitted into the language of Western tonality might have a basis in this series. But to conclude that we know how so-called tonal relationships function or to give them a primacy over less "tonal" relationships seems false. The truth is that, despite the development of a theoretical vocabulary and system of numerical symbols to describe and discuss tonal music, we have learned only to assign verbal labels to its functioning elements, not to actually understand them. We are like herbal doctors who know that certain herbs cure certain ills, without knowing why. We know something about scales and intervals and harmonies, and we know how these were used by composers, and we know that certain things happen less commonly and other things tend to sound "good," and so on, but why all this truly works and why it affects us through our auditory and nervous systems so powerfully that as humans we consider music one of life's great experiences ("Music is a power that justifies things," says Stravinsky): this we do not know. And therefore to conclude that we "understand" the pitch relationships in tonal music but not in "atonal" music is not true. The very *same* relationships may in fact apply to both kinds of music.

In a brilliantly written (though far less widely disseminated) article on Schoenberg, composer George Rochberg, making a point related to Bernstein's, describes Schoenberg in works such as *Erwartung* and Five Pieces for Orchestra as the "consummate musical expressionist of the period who acted out with terrible personal intensity the dilemma of a world gone haywire." He speaks of Schoenberg's

> terrifying intuition of the state of the cultural chaos of the early decades of the twentieth century. . . . Schoenberg attempted to reformulate the language of music in an effort to regain faith in existence—his own and the world's. His mistake, as I see it, was to seek salvation in methodology

and the rational controls methodology demands . . . separated from and kept apart from the very works based on it, which can then only be explained or justified by reference to the operations of that system.

Despite his admiration and love for many of Schoenberg's works, he, like Bernstein, concludes that twelve-tone music is rooted in a fallacy:

> The ear remains the best judge of music, however composed, but this intuitive perceiver of sound is not susceptible to outside numerical or verbal logic. That is what serial harmony rests on, theoretically speaking: verbal and/or numerical logic rather than aural perception.

He also finds in the 1911 *Harmonielehre* a demonstration of a horror vacui, a kind of harmonic breathlessness, that in his view characterizes Schoenberg's music in all his phases. "No rhythmic spaces," he says, "are left unfilled."

In contrast to these critiques, attacks, questions, and underminings there exists a huge body of work in which Schoenberg is minutely dissected from a theoretical point of view by passionate admirers, many of whom have a depth of understanding and knowledge far surpassing that of those "reviewing" the composer on a more daily level but who also, unfortunately from the point of view of any public influence, often speak in a mathematical shorthand and technical jargon created specifically to describe serial music. The result is often writing that consists primarily of numbers and mathematical terms, is needlessly obscure and close to ungrammatical, and uses terms that Schoenberg himself would not have used or known.* Although this does not invalidate the writers' insights, it does limit their readership to the chosen few who are

---

*A notable exception to this tendency is the graceful and straightforward theoretical writing of Kathryn Bailey on the work of Webern (see "Suggested Readings, p. 309).

pursuing similar studies and almost guarantees that any others happening upon their "explanations"—even when these are important and well-written—will feel further estranged from the music in question, not attracted to it. Surely anyone who suspects that this music is intended only for those who can read a score will be disheartened to discover that, in addition, its appreciation presupposes a knowledge of higher mathematics.

Many of the more philosophically oriented writings dealing with Schoenberg also have had the effect of alienating potential listeners, either by emphasizing his historical and theoretical importance, thereby presenting him more as the exponent of an approach to composing than as a composer, or by adopting a rigid and doctrinaire view of his superiority to his more popular contemporaries.

Among those who have tried to humanize him and write insightfully about his music in plain English are Charles Rosen, Robert Craft, Dika Newlin, Glenn Gould, the contributors to the *Journal of the Arnold Schoenberg Institute*, Joan Allen Smith (whose *Schoenberg and His Circle* contains valuable oral history) the composer's own children, and his biographers Egon Wellesz (whose early study traces his development up to 1923) and H. H. Stuckenschmidt (whose minutely detailed work chronicles the life in 550 pages). Schoenberg himself had a deep suspicion of those who considered themselves experts and made it clear that he wished his music to communicate directly to listeners. In a memo found in his papers after his death, he acknowledged that the closed "clique" surrounding him needed to be broken. His brief essay ironically titled "My Public" describes various encounters with people who had enjoyed his music, including one in a hotel where the elevator man

> asked me whether it was I who had written *Pierrot Lunaire*. For he had heard it before the war (about 1912) at the first performance, and still had the sound of it in his ears, par-

ticularly of one piece where red jewels were mentioned ("Rote fürstliche Rubine"). And he had heard at the time that the musicians had no idea what to make of the piece . . .

Characteristically, Craft, the inaugural American conductor of so many of Schoenberg's works, is also an astute observer of his character. While he doesn't flinch from noting the less attractive qualities, among which he includes Schoenberg's legendary suspiciousness ("most of the letters center on real or imagined slights"), belligerence, overbearing censoriousness, egocentricism, and, at least by implication, competitiveness, he also takes the measure of some of the enduring virtues, including the rock-solid integrity, the uncommon honesty ("Schoenberg, the same man to everybody, never diplomatic or political"), and, ultimately, the psychological fortitude of the man: "so far from being a 'misfit,' Schoenberg was an eminently sane, well-integrated, and socially responsible citizen, fully able to 'function' and to 'cope.' " He also suggests that the composer carried the seeds of public rejection within him: "Schoenberg believed that . . . an encroaching malignant force foredoomed him." In an early liner note, he delivers a penetrating rejoinder to those among the post-Webernists who criticized what they viewed as the composer's anachronistic application of his serial technique to eighteenth- and nineteenth-century forms that were the "products of tonality":

> . . . though this criticism is instructive, its main point ignores the great truth of Schoenberg's whole art: that the presence of form in music does not depend upon tonality. The question about a serial form is nonsensical. The listener's awareness of form is his memory of notes. A work such as Boulez' Polyphony X is a piece with rhythmic and mood and tempo changes alternating in significant contrast. But the actual pitches of notes seem in no way to compel the listener's sense of form.

Boulez himself, who has also recorded much of Schoenberg's work, sees in his character an irritating "messianic" streak. Like Stravinsky, Boulez is selective in his praise, singling out the "visionary" period (of *Pierrot, Erwartung,* etc.) as the one in which Schoenberg "played a unique role as a composer" and claiming that the fascination of the more codified works of the twelve-tone era has faded. The cause of this, in Boulez's view, is that during the twelve-tone period the artist sought reassurance from uncertainty in the delusion of historical clairvoyance: "Finding himself the object of hostility and attack, he took refuge in assuming the attitude of a prophet." Reminding us that "the future never turns out as expected, still less as imagined," Boulez asserts that it was not the music that Schoenberg saw as paving the way for future generations of composers that was his most significant; rather it was the music written "when he was most acutely aware of the transitory."

Until the twentieth century the purpose of music was probably only discussed, when it was, by philosophers and clerics, and the methods used to create it were in the background of the minds of its hearers. There was a minimum of conceptual or analytical self-consciousness to the act of listening. Music made the eardrums vibrate and entered the mind, and the psyche/body/spirit responded according to its mysterious laws.

Any art presupposes a dialogue between what we perceive with our organs and consciousness and what we sense of a work that we do not consciously grasp. Part of the joy of hearing a work of Beethoven's or of looking at a medieval altarpiece is the experience of being in the presence of something undergirded by designs and inventions that we aren't told about. Their purpose is to strengthen the meaning and force and even mystery of what we *do* experience. Artists, with varying degrees of self-awareness, develop the techniques and technical strategies that suit their aims and materials. If the undergirding structure is in contradiction to the surface, if it does not come from the same creative spirit as what is readily apparent, we experience the discontinuity as a falseness, pretentiousness, or failure in the work itself. Even if the structure is artificial as opposed to artful for one moment, as in an "establishing scene" in a drama where a character summarizes his situation in a manner that is too evidently for the benefit of the audience, we, the intended audience, disengage from the work at that moment, becoming conscious of the contrivance and conscious—instead of forgetful—of ourselves. When technique is noticed at the expense of the vision it serves, it eclipses the vision.

In François Truffaut's 1968 film *Baisers Volés* (*Stolen Kisses*), Antoine Doinel's future wife, Christine, demonstrates to him that to butter a piece of melba toast without breaking it one must put an additional piece of toast underneath it for support. Truffaut—a master of symbolism drawn from the everyday—has given us a metaphor for the role of structure in the making of art. Without the foundation, the art would break into pieces; the foundation, however, is not the "point" of the whole experience: it is still the buttered toast that gets eaten. No, the underlying structure of a work, which is often of an astonishing complexity and the result of considerable contrivance, is not its ultimate meaning. The meaning is in the experience you have when you listen to the work. If you believe in the purpose to which the contrivance is put, you experience it not as an impediment to feeling but as the structure that creates the feeling.

Yet so much current technical writing about music continuously and almost casually implies that the very purpose of the "foreground" music, the purpose of what you hear, is actually to express the "background"—that what you hear is "about" the underlying structure, not the other way around. To take a sentence almost at random from *Perspectives on Schoenberg and Stravinsky*:

The rhythmic character of this presentation most strikingly
articulates—by a rest—the set into two halves, two disjunct
hexachords, and immediately suggests the fundamental role
of hexachords in the set, and so in the work . . .

The subtle change in emphasis in the following, similar description makes a world of difference:

The group of sixes also *govern melodic and harmonic patterns as well as larger phrasings and articulations.* The six-
note segments are often presented harmonically by twos,
giving the thirds and sixths that *provide the characteristic
sound of the work* [italics mine].

The beautiful Masses of Guillaume Dufay, a composer who
lived in France, Italy, and the Netherlands five hundred years
before Schoenberg, tended to be based on a *cantus firmus*,
which was a Gregorian chant or in some cases a popular song,
but I doubt that his listeners were made aware of his compositional ingeniousness before hearing the music. (No program
notes or preconcert lectures for them.) To be sure, they knew
the text. But more to the point, they could hear that the piece
was beautifully written, could feel the awe created by its architecture, and could sense that it was made not to "exemplify
good composing" but for the glory of God.

It does not necessarily bring artists closer to us if we make
their acquaintance through a study of their methods of work.
Even the greatest and most "musical" of analyses, say those of
Charles Rosen in his *The Classical Style*, might not be a prof-
itable way to *begin* to know Haydn, Mozart, and Beethoven.

In the correspondence and writings of most pre-twentieth-
century composers one looks in vain for detailed musical
analysis. In the case of Mozart, for example, even his more
technical music criticisms are put in terms any layman would
employ to say the same thing:

After many compliments he performed a concerto for two flutes. I had to play first violin part. This is what I think of it. It is not at all pleasing to the ear, not a bit natural. He often plunges into a new key far too brusquely and it is all quite devoid of charm. When it was over, I praised him very highly, for he really deserves it. The poor fellow must have taken a great deal of trouble over it and he must have studied hard.

With Schoenberg, as with any other composer, one might hope that the question of what we hear might precede that of how it is done. After all, only if we are moved, excited, or amazed by a piece does it matter to us enough for us to study it closely. I remember the reaction of a student of mine, a beautiful young English woman who was studying composition and musicology, after hearing a performance of *Pierrot Lunaire* for the first time. I had conducted the concert myself and she came running up to me afterwards: "Amazing! Just amazing!" she exclaimed in her English accent. She was back the next night to hear it again. "Amazing!" she said again. The next year she took a course on the composer. That seems a logical order of events.

Two additional points. All artists are limited, or, as Stravinsky put it, all artists do harm to something. So no artist provides everything, and to place on any one artist the burden of creating the norms and standards by which all future art will be judged is to deny his or her art the benefit of comparison, contrast, distance, context—oxygen, really. Without these an artwork cannot be judged, understood—or perhaps even tolerated. Even the artist needs to be able to escape from his or herself; surely we, the audience do. The epic poem is epic only in contrast to the haiku. Beethoven needs Mozart and Haydn; indeed, he cannot survive or be fully enjoyed without them. In order to look, to see, one has to have the ability to look away.

Artists find their voice at the point at which what they cannot do, or don't do, ceases to matter. Up until that point their art is either overly derivative or not developed enough. But if one places too great a burden on them—historical, philosophical, religious—what they are not or cannot be can engulf them. Schoenberg has been asked to be something that we have not asked of van Gogh, or Giacometti, or Jackson Pollock, or James Joyce, or Vladimir Nabokov. He has been described as "The Way." For this reason the passage of time may help Schoenberg. As his works are played more frequently, his historical position will perhaps come to seem far less important than the actual pieces of music he brought into being.

The writings about him in our time have been formed in a context in which familiarity with his "meaning" has outdistanced familarity with his work. And the "meaning" of Schoenberg to those who have sided with him or against him has always seemed to center on his historical influence. In listening to him one seems to be always asking oneself "What if *all* music from now on were like this?" One is face-to-face with all the "harm" this music has done, with all that it is *not.* I believe that this is one of the reasons it is difficult to hear it. To be sure, this tendency has its origin in Schoenberg himself (much as he also resisted it) as well as in the circle of admirers who surrounded him during his lifetime and advocated for him after his death. Moreover, the history of this period in music would have been different if, instead of emphasizing the differences in their musical philosophies, Stravinsky and Schoenberg had become allies. But those who have written about him—Bernstein, Rochberg, Babbitt, Boulez, as well as Berg and Webern—were also grappling with their own futures, their own immediate needs.

We are too close to the twentieth century to see what is universal in it. We focus too closely on what gave rise to this music. Perhaps it is only of incidental importance that Schoenberg was a twentieth-century figure and it is ultimately truer to say that music itself had to produce a Schoenberg, not in order to convey the spirit of the twentieth century but simply to convey an aspect of the human heart and mind. Webern was fond of paraphrasing Goethe's notion that "man is only the vessel into which is poured what 'nature in general' wants to express." He recalled that when Schoenberg was called up into the army, an officer asked him if by any chance he was the composer. Schoenberg answered: "Yes—nobody else wanted to be, so I had to volunteer for it."

Bernstein's discussion seemed to presuppose that Schoenberg took a wrong turn somewhere and ended up too far from where he should have been. Bernstein talked about the music in terms of what it harked back to or reminded him of. This is what we do with the music and art of cultures foreign to our own when we first encounter them. But the interesting issue—and one future listeners may find easier to face—is what this music *is*: not "Where did he take a wrong turn in the path?" but "Where did his journey take him?" What do we perceive—and where are we—when we truly hear his "wrong" notes as exactly the right ones?

30

———— ‖‖ ————

LAST NOTES:

PORTRAIT IN RETROGRADE

In the Mishnah one reads: "It is not incumbent on you to complete the work, but neither are you free to abstain from it."

Schoenberg pursued his vision with a sense of adventure, joy, urgency, and also obligation. In his work he went beyond what had previously been understood to be music, while still remaining within music's traditions. His life was a search, and although he often reached destinations of staggering freshness and beauty, some of his works, by remaining only partially completed, became metaphors for the searching itself, even as they accomplished much as pieces of music. In this way a man of great ego and stubbornness also exhibited a deeper humility before the infinite mystery of things.

Soon after turning seventy-six, Schoenberg began writing the texts of his own psalms. He completed fifteen psalm texts and wrote the beginning of a sixteenth on July 3, 1951, only ten days before he died. His last piece of music was a setting of the first of these "Modern Psalms," as he called them, for speaker, chorus, and orchestra. Listening to its strange atonal lyricism and fragile orchestration, expressive at one and the same time of anxiety, yearning, awe, and community, one is reminded of his letter to Richard Dehmel from 1912 about the "residue of ancient faith" in "modern man" and the search for reconciliation with God. The music in this last work is not an attempt to create a comforting echo of past religious expressions but is a celebration of its own time, including the ambiguities of that time. It is a modern sacred music that perfectly matches the deep honesty and contemporaneity of the prayer that is its text.

But like his two most ambitious works on sacred themes, *Die Jakobsleiter* and *Moses und Aron, Modern Psalm*, no. 1, was not to be completed. In the work, speaker and chorus alternate, the one speaking and the other singing the psalm text. The speaker reaches the words "verlustig werden" ("to lose"), after which there is a powerful orchestral interlude and the chorus enters, singing the same words he has spoken. They too get only as far as the words "verlustig werden" and then retrace that portion of the text again. The music breaks off after the words "und trotzdem bete ich" ("and yet I pray").

O Thou my God, all people praise Thee
And assure Thee of their devotion.
But what does it mean to Thee
Whether I do this or not?
Who am I, that I should believe my prayers are necessary?
When I say "God," I know that I speak of the Only, Eternal,
    Omnipotent, All-Knowing, and Inconceivable One,
Of Whom I neither can nor should make for myself an image;

On Whom I neither may nor can make any demand;
Who will fulfill my most fervent prayer, or ignore it;
And yet I pray
                    as every living creature
Prays: yet I ask for mercy and miracles;
Fulfillment.
Yet I pray because I do not want to lose
The sublime feeling of unity,
Of union with you.
O you, my Lord, your mercy has granted us
Our prayer, as a bond,
A sublime bond between us. As a
Bliss that gives us more than any fulfillment.*

As we close this book, recognizing that it is a mere hand-shake with its subject—an introduction, at best—let us imagine the last century without Schoenberg: without the String Trio, *A Survivor from Warsaw*, the Violin Concerto, the Variations for Orchestra, *Moses und Aron*, *Pierrot Lunaire*, the Five Pieces for Orchestra, *Erwartung*, the opus 11 Piano Pieces, the

---

*O du mein Gott: alle Völker preisen dich
Und versichern dich ihrer Ergebenheit.
Was aber kann es dir bedeuten,
Ob ich das auch tue oder nicht?
Wer bin ich, daß ich glauben soll, mein
Gebet sei eine Notwendigkeit?
Wenn ich Gott sage, weiß ich, daß ich damit von dem Einzigen, Ewigen, Allmächtigen,
    Allwissenden und Unvorstellbaren spreche,
Von dem ich mir ein Bild weder machen kann noch soll.
An den ich keinen Anspruch erheben darf oder kann,
Der mein heißestes Gebet erfüllen oder nicht beachten wird.
Und trotzdem bete ich, wie alles Lebende betet; trotzdem erbitte ich Gnaden und
    Wunder; Erfüllungen.
Trotzdem bete ich dennich will nicht des beseligenden Gefühls der Einigkeit, der
    Vereinigung mit dir, verlustig werden.
O du mein Gott, deine Gnade hat uns
Das Gebet gelassen, als eine Verbindung,
Eine Seligkeit, die uns mehr gibt, als jede Erfüllung.

Book of the Hanging Gardens, the *Gurre-Lieder, Verklärte Nacht,* . . . without film music as it has been, or Carter or Boulez as they have been, or Stravinsky's works after 1951, or Webern or Berg as they were. Doing this one begins to see in this difficult life something indispensable. Without Schoenberg, the music of an astonishing number of other composers would have been much the poorer and the time in which we live would have lacked one of its most eloquent and characteristic musical voices. Without him, our era would have made a different sound.

Louis Andriessen has said that Stravinsky's real influence is "only just beginning." Perhaps the era of the performance of Schoenberg's work is only just beginning. Only with the superb and natural performances of recent years—I am thinking here of the Boulez recordings of the choral music and *Moses und Aron,* the Rolf Schulte/Robert Craft performance of the Violin Concerto, Maurizio Pollini's performances of the piano music, the Arditti String Quartet playing the String Quartets and the String Trio, the Michael Gielen performance of *Von Heute auf Morgen,* among others—only with these performances can we begin to hear through the difficulties straight to the heart of Schoenberg's music. So how to know if his true influence—its second wave—may not lie further ahead still?

There are certainly "many peaks on Parnassus." Why climb only those most readily accessible? Why not at least take a walk, even one that isn't easy (as there are thorny brambles and obstructions on the path)? The view can't be seen from down here. You sweat a bit, you even lose your way from time to time, but when you arrive you know at once that you would never otherwise have seen this magnificent view! And there you are—atop the beautiful (Schoen) mountain (berg).

Schoenberg, *Self-Portrait,* 1911

SUGGESTED READINGS

By or about Arnold Schoenberg

Boehmer, Konrad, ed. *Schoenberg and Kandinsky: An Historic Encounter.* Amsterdam: Hardwood Academic, 1997.

Boretz, Benjamin, and Edward T. Cone, eds. *Perspectives on Schoenberg and Stravinsky.* Princeton: Princeton University Press, 1968.

Brand, Juliane, and Christopher Hailey, eds. *Constructive Dissonance: Arnold Schoenberg and the Transformations of Twentieth-Century Culture.* Los Angeles: University of California Press, 1997.

Brand, Juliane, Christopher Hailey, and Donald Harris, eds. *The Berg-Schoenberg Correspondence: Selected Letters.* New York: Norton, 1987.

Dunsby, Jonathan. *Schoenberg: Pierrot Lunaire.* Cambridge: Cambridge University Press, 1992.

Frisch, Walter. *The Early Works of Arnold Schoenberg, 1893–1908.* Los Angeles: University of California Press, 1993.

Frisch, Walter, ed. *Schoenberg and His World.* Princeton: Princeton University Press, 1999.

Gould, Glenn. *Arnold Schoenberg: A Perspective.* Cincinnati: University of Cincinnati Press, 1964.

Griffiths, Paul, Oliver Neighbour, and George Perle. *The New Grove Second Viennese School.* New York: Norton, 1983.

Haimo, Ethan. *Schoenberg's Serial Odyssey.* Oxford: Clarendon Press, 1990.

Hahl-Koch, Jelena, ed. *Arnold Schoenberg, Wassily Kandinsky: Letters, Pictures, and Documents.* London: Faber and Faber, 1984.

Journal of the Arnold Schönberg Center. Vienna: Arnold Schönberg Center, 2000–.

Journal of the Arnold Schoenberg Institute [*JASI*], vols. 1–19. Los Angeles: Arnold Schoenberg Institute of USC School of Music, 1976–95.

Kallir, Jane. *Arnold Schoenberg's Vienna.* New York: Galerie St. Etienne and Rizzoli, 1984.

Leibowitz, René. *Schoenberg and His School.* New York: Philosophical Library of New York, 1949.

Newlin, Dika. *Bruckner, Mahler, Schoenberg.* New York: King's Crown Press, 1947.

———. *Schoenberg Remembered: Diaries and Recollections, 1938–1976.* New York: Pendragon, 1980.

Ringer, Alexander L. *Arnold Schoenberg: The Composer as Jew.* Oxford: Oxford University Press, 1990.

Rosen, Charles. *Arnold Schoenberg.* New York: Viking, 1975.

Schoenberg, Arnold. *Arnold Schoenberg Letters.* Ed. Erwin Stein. Trans. Eithne Wilkins and Ernst Kaiser. New York: St. Martin's Press, 1965.

———. *Structural Functions of Harmony.* New York: Norton, 1969.

———. *Theory of Harmony.* Trans. Roy E. Carter. Berkeley: University of California Press, 1978.

———. *Style and Idea.* Ed. Leonard Stein. Trans. Leo Black. Berkeley: University of California Press, 1975.

Schoenberg-Nono, Nuria, ed. *Arnold Schoenberg, 1874–1951: Lebensgeschichte in Begegnungen.* Klagenfurt: Ritter Klagenfurt, 1998.

———. ed. *Arnold Schoenberg Self-Portrait.* Pacific Palisades: Belmont Music Publishers, 1988.

Smith, Joan Allen. *Schoenberg and His Circle.* New York: Schirmer Books, 1986.

Stuckenschmidt, H. H. *Arnold Schoenberg.* New York: Schirmer Books, 1977.

Thomson, William. *Schoenberg's Error.* Philadelphia: University of Pennsylvania Press, 1991.

Wellesz, Egon. *Arnold Schoenberg.* J. M. Dent, 1925.

Zaunschirm, Thomas, ed. *Arnold Schoenberg: Paintings and Drawings.* Klagenfurt: Ritter Verlag, 1991.

Additional sources

Adorno, Theodor W. *Philosophy of Modern Music.* Trans. Anne G. Mitchell and Wesley V. Blomster. New York: Seabury Press, 1973.

———. *Quasi una fantasia: Essays on Modern Music.* Trans. Rodney Livingstone. New York: Verso, 1994.

Bailey, Kathryn. *The Life of Webern.* Cambridge: Cambridge University Press, 1998.

———. *The Twelve-Note Music of Anton Webern.* Cambridge: Cambridge University Press, 1991.

Barnett, Vivian Endicott. *Kandinsky at the Guggenheim.* Abbeville Press,

Bernstein, Leonard. *The Unanswered Question: Six Talks at Harvard.* Cambridge: Harvard University Press, 1976.

Bettelheim, Bruno. *Freud's Vienna and Other Essays.* New York: Knopf, 1990.

Boulez, Pierre. *Orientations.* Trans. Martin Cooper. Cambridge: Harvard University Press, 1986.

Cone, Edward T., ed. *Roger Sessions on Music: Collected Essays.* Princeton: Princeton University Press, 1979.

Craft, Robert. *Current Convictions.* New York: Knopf, 1977.

———. *Present Perspectives.* New York: Knopf, 1984.

———. *Small Craft Advisories.* New York: Thames and Hudson, 1989.

———. *Stravinsky: Glimpses of a Life.* New York: St. Martin's, 1992.

Dennison, Lisa, and Andrew Kagan. *Paul Klee at the Guggenheim Museum.* New York: Solomon R. Guggenheim Foundation, 1993.

Klee, Paul. *Diaries, 1898–1918*. Ed. Felix Klee. Los Angeles: University of California Press, 1964.

Levant, Oscar. *The Memoirs of an Amnesiac*. New York: G. P. Putnam's Sons, 1965.

———. *A Smattering of Ignorance*. New York: Doubleday, 1940.

———. *The Unimportance of Being Oscar*. New York: G.P. Putnam's Sons, 1968.

Lindsay, Kenneth C., and Peter Vergo, eds. *Kandinsky: Complete Writings on Art*. New York: Da Capo, 1994.

Mahler-Werfel, Alma. *And the Bridge Is Love*. New York: Harcourt, Brace, 1958.

———. *Diaries, 1898–1902*. Sel. and trans. Anthony Beaumont. Ithaca: Cornell University Press, 1999.

———. *Gustav Mahler: Memories and Letters*. New York: Viking, 1969.

Moldenhauer, Hans. *Anton Webern: A Chronicle of His Life and Work*. London: Victor Gollancz, 1978.

Neville, Peter. *The Holocaust*. Cambridge: Cambridge University Press, 1999.

Page, Tim, ed. *The Glenn Gould Reader*. New York: Knopf, 1984.

Perle, George. *The Operas of Alban Berg*. 2 vols. Berkeley: University of California Press, 1980–85.

———. *Serial Composition and Atonality*. Berkeley: University of California Press, 1962.

Peyser, Joan. *Boulez*. Schirmer Books, 1971.

Retallack, Joan, ed. *Musicage: John Cage in Conversation with Joan Retallack*. Hanover: Wesleyan University Press, 1996.

Rochberg, George. *The Aesthetics of Survival*. Ann Arbor: University of Michigan Press, 1984.

Roethel, Hans K. *The Blue Rider*. Ann Arbor: Praeger, 1971.

Rosenfeld, Paul. *Discoveries of a Music Critic*. New York: Harcourt, Brace, 1936.

———. *Musical Chronicle (1917–1923)*. New York: Harcourt, Brace, 1923.

———. *Musical Impressions*. Hill and Wang, 1969.

Straus, Joseph. *Introduction to Post-Tonal Theory*. 2nd ed. Upper Saddle River: Prentice-Hall, 2000.

Stravinsky, Igor. *Stravinsky in Conversation with Robert Craft*. Harmondsworth: Penguin, 1962.

Stravinsky, Igor, and Robert Craft. *Dialogues and a Diary.* London: Faber, 1968.

——. *Expositions and Developments.* Berkeley: University of California Press, 1962.

——. *Memories and Commentaries.* New York: Doubleday, 1960.

——. *Retrospectives and Conclusions.* New York: Knopf, 1969.

——. *Themes and Episodes.* New York: Knopf, 1966.

Stravinsky, Vera, and Robert Craft. *Stravinsky in Pictures and Documents.* New York: Simon and Schuster, 1978.

Thomson, Virgil. *Music Reviewed, 1940–1954.* New York: Vintage, 1967.

Vergo, Peter. *The Blue Rider.* Oxford: Phaidon, 1977.

Vezin, Annette, and Luc Vezin. *Kandinsky and Der blaue Reiter.* Paris: Editions Pierre Terrail, 1992.

Webern, Anton. *The Path to the New Music.* Theodore Presser, 1960.

Wulf, Joseph. *Musik im Dritten Reich.* Gütersloh: Sigbert Mohn, 1963.

Zweig, Stefan. *The World of Yesterday.* Lincoln: University of Nebraska Press, 1964.

NOTES

vii   "For I know very well": Alban Berg, "Gurrelieder Guide," trans. Mark De Voto, *Journal of the Arnold Schoenberg Institute* [hereafter *JASI*], vol. 16, nos. 1 and 2 (1993), p. 125.

vii   "And finally I want to mention": Andrea Olmstead, "The Correspondence between Arnold Schoenberg and Roger Sessions," *JASI*, vol. 13, no. 1 (1990), p. 49.

1   "Personally I had the feeling": H. H. Stuckenschmidt, *Arnold Schoenberg*, New York: Schirmer Books, 1977, pp. 545–46.

7   "Everyone of a Jewish mother": Arthur Schnitzler, *My Youth in Vienna*, trans. Catherine Hutter, New York: Holt, Rinehart, and Winston, 1970, p. 128.

11   "His sheer zest": Paul Griffiths, Oliver Neighbour, and George Perle, *The New Grove Second Viennese School*, New York: Norton, 1983, p. 29.

14   "I believe that anyone": Quoted in Walter Frisch, *The Early Works of Arnold Schoenberg, 1893–1908*, Los Angeles: University of California Press, 1993, p. 81.

16   "Everything glowed": Frisch, *Early Works*, p. 112.

18   Schoenberg's colleague: Egon Wellesz, *Arnold Schoenberg*, J. M. Dent, 1925, p. 20.

20   In some analytic notes: Frisch, *Early Works*, p. 126.

25   "My senses strive": Translation from CD booklet, Arnold Schoenberg, *Gurre-Lieder*, Sony Classical SM2K 48459, p. 50.

31   "Skeleton key": Louis Andriessen and Elmer Schönberger, *The Apollonian Clockwork*, New York: Oxford University Press, 1989, p. 73.

37   During this period: Stuckenschmidt, *Arnold Schoenberg*, pp. 51–52.

44   Whatever the truth: Ibid., p. 94.

45   Some writers describe: Albrecht Dümling, in Konrad Boehmer, ed., *Schoenberg and Kandinsky: An Historic Encounter*. Amsterdam: Hardwood Academic, 1997, p. 111.

45   "Please forgive me": Quoted in Stuckenschmidt, *Arnold Schoenberg*, p. 103.

46   "How can Mahler": Ibid., p. 102.

47   "Narrow-chested energy": Alma Mahler-Werfel, *And the Bridge Is Love*, New York: Harcourt, Brace, 1958, p. 104.

48   The middle two movements: Frisch, *Early Works*, p. 266.

49   An "essential tonal-atonal conflict": Ibid., p. 269.

49   "My Evolution": Arnold Schoenberg, *Style and Idea*, ed. Leonard Stein, trans. Leo Black, Berkeley: University of California Press, 1975, p. 86.

50   Likening the disappearance: Anton Webern, *The Path to the New Music*, Theodore Presser, 1960, p. 44.

55   Mahler had turned to: Joan Allen Smith, *Schoenberg and His Circle*, New York: Schirmer Books, 1986, pp. 70–71. Alma Mahler gives an alternative account of this incident.

55   Alban Berg wrote: Ibid., p. 37.

59   "I must believe": Quoted in Jane Kallir, *Arnold Schoenberg's Vienna*, New York: Galerie St. Etienne and Rizzoli, 1984, p. 44.

60   "the facial expression": Eberhard Freitag, "German Expressionism and Schoenberg's Self-Portraits," *JASI*, vol. 2, no. 3 (1978), p. 170.

61   In her memoirs: Mahler-Werfel, *And the Bridge*, p. 147.

63   "according to their inner sound": Kenneth C. Lindsay and Peter Vergo, eds., *Kandinsky: Complete Writings on Art*, New York: Da Capo, 1994, pp. 139–95.

63   He had been spending: Cornelius Doleman, *Wassily Kandinsky*, New York: Barnes and Noble, 1964, p. 14.

66   "Composition IV, 1911": Quoted in Jelena Hahl-Koch, ed., *Arnold Schoenberg, Wassily Kandinsky: Letters, Pictures, and Documents*, London: Faber and Faber, 1984, pp. 206–08. An alternative translation can be found in Lindsay and Vergo, *Kandinsky*, pp. 383–91.

68   "What we are striving for": Hahl-Koch, *Arnold Schoenberg*, p. 21.

68   "You are such a full man": Ibid., p. 48.

72   It is the contrapuntal music: "Bach," in Schoenberg, *Style and Idea*, pp. 393–97.

79   "[The artist] does not attach": Paul Klee, *On Modern Art*, trans. Paul Findlay, London: Faber and Faber, p. 45.

79   "We want to see": Quoted in Freitag, "German Expressionism."

81   "one of the great self-portraits": *Arnold Schoenberg: Paintings and Drawings*, ed. Thomas Zaunschirm, Klagenfurt: Ritter Verlag, 1991, p. 123.

83   "If we ourselves see": Paul Rosenfeld, *Musical Chronicle (1917–1923)*, New York: Harcourt, Brace, 1923, p. 211.

84   In fact, one: New York: Igor Stravinsky and Robert Craft, *Retrospectives and Conclusions*, New York: Knopf, 1969, p. 97.

94   According to Schoenberg: Bryan R. Simms, in *Constructive Dissonance: Arnold Schoenberg and the Transformations of Twentieth-Century Culture*, eds. Juliane Brand and Christopher Hailey, Los Angeles: University of California Press, 1997.

94   "I wrote lying": Quoted in Therese Muxeneder, *Journal of the Arnold Schönberg Center*, vol. 1 (2000). No source given.

96   "traditional practice": Griffiths, Neighbour, and Perle, *New Grove*, pp. 40–41.

103   Charles Rosen refers: Charles Rosen, *Arnold Schoenberg*, New York: Viking, 1975, p. 43.

105   In their wonderful book: Andriessen and Schönberger, *Apollonian Clockwork*, p. 170.

114   "That which is new": Arnold Schoenberg, *Theory of Harmony*, trans. Roy E. Carter, Berkeley: University of California Press, 1978, page 400.

130   "The young artist": Ibid.

130   "The uproar continued": Igor Stravinsky and Robert Craft, *Expositions and Developments*, Berkeley: University of California Press, 1962, p. 143.

132   He demonstrates, for example: Schoenberg, *Theory of Harmony*, pp. 391–93.

132   In his discussion: Ibid., p. 403.

132   "The theory of dissonance": Glenn Gould, *Arnold Schoenberg: A Perspective*. Cincinnati: University of Cincinnati Press, 1964, p. 7.

133   "That it is correct": Schoenberg, *Theory of Harmony*, pp. 420–21.

134   "We are turning": Ibid., pp. 387–89.

134   "The ceremonious way": Ibid., p. 128.

135   "The evolution of no other art": Ibid., p. 7.

135   "To hell with all these theories": Ibid., p. 9.

135   "The laws of art": Ibid., p. 10.

135   "Let him know": Ibid., p. 29.

136   "Let the pupil learn": Ibid.

136   "Beauty exists only": Ibid., p. 325.

137   "Later the pupil": Ibid., p. 258.

138   "Schoenberg and the Origins": Brand and Hailey, *Constructive Dissonance*, pp. 71–84.

140   "*schwebende Tonalität*": Schoenberg, *Theory of Harmony*, p. 383.

140   "An organic disorder": Gould, *Arnold Schoenberg*, p. 5.

140   "the more remote": Schoenberg, *Theory of Harmony*, p. 21.

141   "It has never been": Ibid., p. 401.

142   "Schoenberg said that music": *Musicage: John Cage in Conversation with Joan Retallack*, ed. Joan Retallack, Hanover: Wesleyan University Press, 1996, p. 65.

147   On the train: Igor Stravinsky and Robert Craft, *Dialogues and a Diary*, New York: Doubleday, 1963, p. 53.

147   "one of the greatest": Vera Stravinsky and Robert Craft, *Stravinsky in Pictures and Documents*, New York: Simon and Schuster, 1978, p. 95.

147–48 "the solar plexus": Stravinsky and Craft, *Dialogues*, pp. 53–55.

148   An instance he cited: Dika Newlin, "Self-Revelation and the Law: Arnold Schoenberg and His Religious Works," *YUVAL: Studies of the Jewish Music Research Centre* (Jerusalem) 1 (1968): 204–20.

154   "Experience almost too bewildering": Anthony Payne, quoted in Jonathan Dunsby, *Schoenberg: Pierrot Lunaire*. Cambridge: Cambridge University Press, 1992, p. 57.

156   "For a long time": Arnold Schoenberg, *Arnold Schoenberg Letters*, ed. Erwin Stein, trans. Eithne Wilkins and Ernst Kaiser, New York: St. Martin's Press, 1965, p. 35.

157   As Joseph Auner points out: Brand and Hailey, *Constructive Dissonance*, pp. 112–30.

161   The first performance: Hahl-Koch, *Arnold Schoenberg*, p. 154.

161   Some of the reviews: Ibid., pp. 154–56.

168   "a genius will compose": Schoenberg, *Style and Idea*, p. 181.

169   "The leader of the prayer": Chemjo Vinaver, on the chant sung during the morning service of Rosh Hashanah. Quoted in Newlin, "Self-Revelation," pp. 219–20.

171   "It was not possible": Schnitzler, *My Youth*, pp. 6–7.

175   "Have you also": Hahl-Koch, *Arnold Schoenberg*, pp. 78–80.

180   "Our musical notation": Stuckenschmidt, *Arnold Schoenberg*, p. 515.

180   "Faith and hope": *Arnold Schoenberg, 1874–1951: Lebensgeschichte in Begegnungen*, ed. Nuria Schoenberg-Nono, Klagenfurt: Ritter Klagenfurt, 1998, p. 324.

180–81 For his part: Kathryn Bailey, *The Life of Webern*. Cambridge: Cambridge University Press, 1998, p. 53.

181   Berg, it should be noted: Smith, *Schoenberg and His Circle*, p. 210.

182   "for a moment": Ibid., p. 144.

182–83 "It is said": Schoenberg, *Style and Idea*, p. 366.

183   "never spoke about modern music": E. Ratz, in Smith, *Schoenberg and His Circle*, p. 145.

183   "How little imposing": Wellesz, *Arnold Schoenberg*, p. 49.

184   "He said one of the ways": Retallack, *Musicage*, p. 61.

191   "I do not like": Stravinsky and Craft, *Retrospectives and Conclusions*, p. 225.

193   In the same year: Stravinsky and Craft, *Stravinsky in Pictures and Documents*, p. 633.

194   The Austrian composer: Stuckenschmidt, *Arnold Schoenberg*, p. 548.

195   As Schoenberg himself: "Brahms the Progressive," in *Style and Idea*, p. 401.

195   "asked him if he thought": Stuckenschmidt, *Arnold Schoenberg*, p. 309.

198   Schoenberg's original definition: Schoenberg, *Style and Idea*, p. 218.

200   "the unconscious urge": Ibid., p. 207.

203   "equal rights": Webern, *Path to the New Music*, p. 47.

203   "the odd thing": Gould, *Arnold Schoenberg*, p. 14.

204–5   "According to my feeling": Stuckenschmidt, *Arnold Schoenberg*, p. 315.

207   He handmade no fewer: Susan L. Sloan, "Archival Exhibit: Schoenberg's Dodecaphonic Devices," *JASI*, vol. 12, no. 2 (1989), p. 202.

208–9   Paul Klee's suggestively titled: Andrew Kagan, *Paul Klee at the Guggenheim Museum*, New York: Solomon R. Guggenheim Foundation, 1993, pp. 29–33.

214   deriving from passages: Ethan Haimo, *Schoenberg's Serial Odyssey*, Oxford: Clarendon Press, 1940, p. 103.

215   "You must not take it": Alma Mahler-Werfel, *Gustav Mahler: Memories and Letters*, New York: Viking, 1969, p. 327.

215   On paper: Kathryn Bailey, *The Twelve-Note Music of Anton Webern*, Cambridge: Cambridge University Press, 1991, p. 147.

217   "I saw how he worked": Smith, *Schoenberg and His Circle*, p. 214.

221   "One should never forget": "Composition with Twelve Tones," *Style and Idea*, p. 239.

222   Becoming a part: Peter Neville, *The Holocaust*, Cambridge: Cambridge University Press, 1999, p. 12.

223   Even though their views: Ibid., p. 15.

223   "For here I'm constantly obliged": Schoenberg, *Letters*, p. 167.

224   Once anti-Semitism: Alexander L. Ringer, *Arnold Schoenberg: The Composer as Jew*, Oxford: Oxford University Press, 1990.

225 "Works of art": Hans Moldenhauer, *Anton Webern: A Chronicle of His Life and Work*, London: Victor Gollancz, 1978, p. 475.

226 "My immediate plan": Schoenberg to Anton Webern, Aug. 4, 1933.

226 "It is my fault": The text of *Die biblische Weg* is printed in full in *JASI*, vol. 17 (1994).

227 "expression of the gleaming": Paul Rosenfeld, *Discoveries of a Music Critic*. New York: Harcourt, Brace, 1936.

232 "Everything I have written": Schoenberg, *Letters*, p. 143.

238 In August 1933: Webern; *Path to the New Music*, p. 19.

238 The nervous, idealistic: Moldenhauer, *Anton Webern*, p. 598.

240 "At her advanced age": Stefan Zweig, *The World of Yesterday*. Lincoln: University of Nebraska Press, 1964, p. 407.

244 "slight of frame": Quoted in Stravinsky and Craft, *Stravinsky in Pictures and Documents*, p. 120.

244 "angry, tortured, burning": Stravinsky and Craft, *Expositions and Developments*, p. 78.

245 "a piece of ice": Quoted in Hahl-Koch, *Arnold Schoenberg*, p. 208.

246 "It is the individual": *Musical Digest*, Sept. 1946; quoted in Stravinsky and Craft, *Stravinsky in Pictures and Documents*, p. 358.

248 In his California years: Schoenberg-Nono, *Lebensgeschichte*, p. 377.

249 In the yard: This fact and many additional ones in this chapter are from Nuria Schoenberg-Nono, "The Role of Extra-Musical Pursuits in Arnold Schoenberg's Creative Life," *JASI*, vol. 5, no. 1 (1981), pp. 45–62.

249 "a peach-colored shirt": Dika Newlin, *Schoenberg Remembered: Diaries and Recollections, 1938–1976*, New York: Pendragon, 1980, p. 58.

252 "Schoenberg, it is well known": Oscar Levant, *A Smattering of Ignorance*, New York: Doubleday, 1940, p. 236.

254–55 "in so far as I'm not occupied": Schoenberg, *Letters*, p. 205.

255 "perceptible formal logic": 1939 letter to Fritz Stiedry quoted in CD booklet, *Schoenberg in Hollywood*, London 448 619-2, p. 10.

267   "the shock effect": Stuckenschmidt, *Arnold Schoenberg*, p. 300.

273   "But I have one excuse": Ibid., 545–46.

274   The young conductor: Igor Stravinsky and Robert Craft, *Themes and Episodes*, New York: Knopf, 1966, pp. 166–67, 176.

282   At the same time: Benjamin Boretz and Edward T. Cone, eds., *Perspectives on American Composers*, New York: Norton, 1971, p. 142.

283   "a tonality beyond tonality": Leonard Stein, in *Confronting Stravinsky*, ed. Jann Pasler, Berkeley: University of California Press, 1986, p. 318.

286   "Do not call it": Stuckenschmidt, *Arnold Schoenberg*, p. 503.

286   "When I compose": Schoenberg, *Style and Idea*, pp. 90–91.

287   "tendency to go wandering": Rosenfeld, *Musical Chronicle*, p. 313.

287   "More consistently and continually": Paul Rosenfeld, *Discoveries of a Music Critic*, New York: Harcourt, Brace, 1936, p. 208.

288   a "great work": *New York Times*, Sept. 30, 1999.

288   "It was possible": Ibid., Jan. 26, 2000.

288   "One hears everywhere": Ibid., Apr. 4, 2000.

289   "the most exciting": Virgil Thomson, *Music Reviewed, 1940–1954*, New York: Vintage, 1967, pp. 125–26.

289   "hollow technical bravura": *New York Times*, February 28, 1999.

290   "The trouble is": Leonard Bernstein, *The Unanswered Question: Six Talks at Harvard*, Cambridge: Harvard University Press, 1976, p. 283.

291–92   "terrifying intuition": George Rochberg, *The Aesthetics of Survival*, Ann Arbor: University of Michigan Press, 1984, p. 51.

292   "The ear remains": Ibid., p. 60.

293–94   "asked me whether": Schoenberg, *Style and Idea*, pp. 98–99.

294   "Schoenberg, the same man": Robert Craft, *Small Craft Advisories*, New York: Thames and Hudson, 1989, p. 29.

294   "so far from being": Ibid., p. 33.

294   "Schoenberg believed": Ibid.

294   "though this criticism": Arnold Schoenberg, Suite, op. 29, cond. Robert Craft, Columbia, ML 5099.

295   "Finding himself the object": Pierre Boulez, *Orientations*,

trans. Martin Cooper, Cambridge: Harvard University Press, 1986, pp. 325–29.

297   "The rhythmic character": Milton Babbitt, "Three Essays on Schoenberg," in Benjamin Boretz and Edward T. Cone, eds., *Perspectives on Schoenberg and Stravinsky*, Princeton: Princeton University Press, 1968, p. 48.

297   "The group of sixes": Robert Craft, note on Prelude to "Genesis," *The Music of Arnold Schoenberg*, vol. 2, Columbia, M2L 294.

298   "After many compliments": *Mozart's Letters*, ed. Eric Blom, Harmondsworth: Penguin, 1956, p. 49.

300   "man is only the vessel": Webern, *Path to the New Music*, p. 11.

300   He recalled: Ibid., p. 15.

ACKNOWLEDGMENTS

Helene Aylon, Rabbi Howard Cohen, Alva and Robert Craft, Claudia Friedlander, Suzanne Jones, Bun Ching Lam, Nicholas Lasoff, Gunnar A. Kaldewey, Rebekah Pym, David Raffeld, Susan Reis, Lawrence Schoenberg, Frederick Seidel, Yung Wha Son.

Musical examples copied by Christopher Molina.

INDEX

Italicized page numbers refer to illustrations.